APPROACHES TO ENTERPRISE RISK MANAGEMENT

APPROACHES TO
ENTERPRISE RISK MANAGEMENT

BLOOMSBURY

Copyright © Bloomsbury Information Ltd, 2010

First published in 2010 by
Bloomsbury Information Ltd
36 Soho Square
London
W1D 3QY
United Kingdom

All rights reserved; no part of this publication may be reproduced, stored in a retrieval system, or transmitted by any means, electronic, mechanical, photocopying, or otherwise, without the prior written permission of the publisher.

The information contained in this book is for general information purposes only. It does not constitute investment, financial, legal, or other advice, and should not be relied upon as such. No representation or warranty, express or implied, is made as to the accuracy or completeness of the contents. The publisher and the authors disclaim any warranty or liability for actions taken (or not taken) on the basis of information contained herein.

The views and opinions of the publisher may not necessarily coincide with some of the views and opinions expressed in this book, which are entirely those of the authors. No endorsement of them by the publisher should be inferred.

Every reasonable effort has been made to trace copyright holders of material reproduced in this book, but if any have been inadvertently overlooked then the publisher would be glad to hear from them.

A CIP record for this book is available from the British Library.

Standard edition
ISBN-10: 1-84930-003-8
ISBN-13: 978-1-84930-003-2

Middle East edition
ISBN-10: 1-84930-004-6
ISBN-13: 978-1-84930-004-9

FSC Mixed Sources
Product group from well-managed forests and recycled wood or fiber
www.fsc.org Cert no. TT-COC-002231
© 1996 Forest Stewardship Council

Project Director: Conrad Gardner
Project Manager: Ben Hickling
Assistant Project Manager: Sarah Latham

Cover design by Suna Cristall
Page design by Fiona Pike, Pike Design, Winchester, UK
Typeset by Special Edition Prepress Services, London
Printed in the UK by CPI William Clowes, Beccles, NR34 7TL

Contents

Contributors ix

Best Practice—Policies and Processes 1
Risk Management: Beyond Compliance Bill Sharon 3
A Holistic Approach to Business Risk Management Terry Carroll 9
Risk—Perspectives and Common Sense Rules for Survival John C. Groth 13
Integrated Corporate Financial Risk Policy David C. Shimko 19
Internal Auditors and Enterprise Risk Management Ian Fraser 23
Best Practices in Risk-Based Internal Auditing Sheryl Vacca 27
Implementing an Effective Internal Controls System Andrew Chambers 33
The Effect of SOX on Internal Control, Risk Management, and Corporate Governance Best Practice David A. Doney 39
Enterprise Risk Management and Solvency II Andy Davies 45
Cultural Alignment and Risk Management: Developing the Right Culture R. Brayton Bowen 51
Building Potential Catastrophe Management into a Strategic Risk Framework Duncan Martin 55
Real Options: Opportunity from Risk David C. Shimko 61
Understanding Reputation Risk and Its Importance Jenny Rayner 65
ERM, Best's Ratings, and the Financial Crisis Gene C. Lai 71
Human Risk: How Effective Strategic Risk Management Can Identify Rogues Thomas McKaig 75

Best Practice—Risk Measurement and Management 79
Managing Operational Risks Using an All-Hazards Approach Mark Abkowitz 81
Business Continuity Management: How to Prepare for the Worst Andrew Hiles 85
Countering Supply Chain Risk Vinod Lall 91
A Total Balance Sheet Approach to Financial Risk Terry Carroll 95
Quantifying Corporate Financial Risk David C. Shimko 99
To Hedge or Not to Hedge Steve Robinson 105
Minimizing Credit Risk Frank J. Fabozzi 111
Managing Interest Rate Risk Will Spinney 115
Managing Counterparty Credit Risk David C. Shimko 121
Measuring Country Risk Aswath Damodaran 125
Measuring Company Exposure to Country Risk Aswath Damodaran 129
Pension Schemes: A Unique and Unintended Basket of Risks on the Balance Sheet Amarendra Swarup 133
Essentials for Export Success: Understanding How Risks and Relationships Lead to Rewards Paul Beretz 139
How to Manage Emerging Market Risks with Third Party Insurance Rod Morris 143
Political Risk: Countering the Impact on Your Business Ian Bremmer 149
Identifying and Minimizing the Strategic Risks from M&A Peter Howson 153
Due Diligence Requirements in Financial Transactions Scott Moeller 157

Checklists—Policies and Processes 163
Balancing Hedging Objectives with Accounting Rules (FAS 133) 165
The Chief Audit Executive's (CAE) Roles and Responsibilities 167
Creating a Risk Register 169
Establishing a Framework for Assessing Risk 171
Key Components of a Corporate Risk Register 173
Managing and Auditing the Risk of Business Interruption 175
Managing Your Credit Risk 177
Setting Up a Key Risk Indicator (KRI) System 179
What Is Forensic Auditing? 181

Approaches to Enterprise Risk Management

Checklists—Risk Measurement and Management	183
Applying Stress-Testing to Business Continuity Management	185
Applying Stress-Testing to Operational Risk Exposure	187
Assessing Cash Flow and Bank Lending Requirements	189
Building a Forex Plan	191
Calculating Your Total Economic Capital	193
Captive Insurance Companies: How to Reduce Your Costs	195
Catastrophe Bonds: What They Are and How They Function	197
Directors' and Officers' (D&O) Liability Insurance	199
Hedging Credit Risk—Case Study and Strategies	201
Hedging Foreign Exchange Risk—Case Studies and Strategies	203
Hedging Interest Rate Risk—Case Study and Strategies	205
Hedging Liquidity Risk—Case Study and Strategies	207
Identifying and Managing Exposure to Interest and Exchange Rate Risks	209
Identifying Weak Points in Your Liquidity	211
Insuring Against Financial Loss	213
Methods for Dealing with Inflation Risk	215
Stress-Testing to Evaluate Insurance Cover	217
Understanding and Calculating the Total Cost of Risk	219
Understanding and Using Leverage Ratios	221
Index	223

Contributors

Mark Abkowitz is professor of civil and environmental engineering at Vanderbilt University and specializes in managing the risks associated with accidents, intentional acts, and natural disasters. He has a specific interest in the safety and security of hazardous materials and in risk mitigation using advanced information technologies. Dr Abkowitz has appeared on National Public Radio, Fox National News, and CNBC, discussing various risk management topics. Since June 2002, he has been a member of the US Nuclear Waste Technical Review Board.

Paul Beretz, CICE (Certified International Credit Executive), is managing director of Pacific Business Solutions, Clayton, CA, a company he created in 1999. In addition, he is a partner of Q2C (Quote to Cash) Solutions. He brings over 30 years of global management experience in telecommunications, semiconductors, forest products, and chemicals. His faculty postings include St Mary's College, California (MA in leadership), University of California, Berkeley, Michigan State University, and Dartmouth College. He has designed and facilitates online courses in international credit and general business. He currently serves on the advisory committee of the Export–Import Bank of the United States.

R. Brayton Bowen is author of *Recognizing and Rewarding Employees* (McGraw-Hill) and leads the Howland Group, a strategy consulting and change management firm committed to "building better worlds of work." His documentary series *Anger in the Workplace*, distributed to public radio nationally in the United States, continues to be regarded as a benchmark study on the subject of workplace issues and change. A *Best Practice* editor and contributing author to the hallmark work *Business: The Ultimate Resource* (Bloomsbury Publishing and Perseus Books), he has written for *MWorld*, the online magazine of the American Management Association. He currently serves as executive adviser for the Center for Business Excellence at McKendree University.

Ian Bremmer's career spans academic, investment, and policymaking communities. His research focuses on states in transition, global political risk, and US foreign policy. Dr Bremmer founded the research and consulting firm Eurasia Group, which today is the preeminent global political risk consultancy. In 2001, he authored Wall Street's first global political risk index, now the Global Political Risk Index (GPRI). Throughout his career, Dr Bremmer has spent much of his time advising world leaders on US foreign policy, including US presidential candidates from both Democratic and Republican parties, Russian Prime Minister Sergei Kiriyenko, and Japanese Prime Minister Shinzo Abe.

Terry Carroll heads up corporate finance and advisory services for Broadhead Peel Rhodes, following a highly successful career as finance director and CEO of a range of businesses. He was also for some years a business and financial consultant, working especially with SMEs and growing businesses. A qualified banker, corporate treasurer, and chartered accountant who trained with KPMG, Carroll has experience of many different corporate finance projects, including banking, financing, business restructuring, mergers and acquisitions, MBO/MBI, and venture and private capital. With five books and scores of published articles, he is also an established business author.

Andrew Chambers works for Management Audit LLP advising on corporate governance and internal auditing, and is also a professor at London South Bank and Birmingham City universities. Described in an editorial in *The Times* (September 15, 2006) as "a worldwide authority on corporate governance," until 2010 he chaired the Corporate Governance and Risk Management Committee of the Association of Chartered Certified Accountants. Professor Chambers was dean of what is now the Cass Business School, London, where he is professor emeritus. He is a member of the Institute of Internal Auditors' international Internal Audit Standards Board.

Aswath Damodaran is a professor of finance at the Stern School of Business at New York University, where he teaches corporate finance and equity valuation. He also teaches on the TRIUM Global Executive MBA program, an alliance of NYU Stern, the London School of Economics, and HEC School of Management. Professor Damodaran is best known as the author of several widely used academic and practitioner texts on valuation, corporate finance, and investment management. He is also widely published in leading journals of finance, including the *Journal of Financial and Quantitative Analysis*, *Journal of Finance*, *Journal of Financial Economics*, and the *Review of Financial Studies*.

vii

Approaches to Enterprise Risk Management

Andy Davies joined Terra Nova in 1994 as group financial controller of Terra Nova Bermuda Holdings. In 2000 he became finance director at Markel International, with responsibility for reporting into Markel Corporation and overseeing the operations of the finance and RAO departments.

David A. Doney is vice-president of internal audit for SIRVA, Inc., a global moving and relocation services company, where he oversees the audit team and is the coordinator for the company's Sarbanes–Oxley (SOX) compliance efforts. Prior to SIRVA, Doney led the SOX assessment efforts for Bally Total Fitness from 2004 to 2007. He has also worked for Sears, Roebuck & Company in the internal audit and financial planning areas, and for Ingersoll-Rand Company as a financial management trainee. He is a frequent speaker at the MIS Training Institute on internal audit and SOX and gave presentations at the Institute of Internal Auditors' international conferences in 2002 and 2008. Doney is a registered Certified Public Accountant (CPA) and a Certified Internal Auditor (CIA).

Frank J. Fabozzi is professor in the practice of finance at Yale School of Management and specializes in investment management and structured finance. He is editor of the *Journal of Portfolio Management* and has authored and edited many acclaimed books, three of which were coauthored with the late Franco Modigliani and one coedited with Harry Markowitz. Professor Fabozzi is a consultant to several financial institutions, is on the board of directors of the BlackRock complex of closed-end funds, and is on the advisory council for the Department of Operations Research and Financial Engineering at Princeton University. He was inducted into the Fixed Income Analysts Society Hall of Fame in November 2002 and is the 2007 recipient of the C. Stewart Sheppard Award given by the CFA Institute.

Ian Fraser is professor of accounting at the University of Stirling, Scotland, and he has previously held academic posts at the University of Strathclyde and Glasgow Caledonian University. He trained for membership of the Institute of Chartered Accountants of Scotland (ICAS) with Thomson Mclintock & Co. (one of the predecessor firms of KPMG). Professor Fraser has wide-ranging research interests in the fields of auditing, financial reporting, and corporate governance, and he has published on these areas in many academic journals. He has a particular interest in the interfaces between auditing, risk, and risk management. He is currently carrying out a major funded research project on the audit of narrative corporate reporting.

John C. Groth is professor of finance in the Department of Finance, Mays Business School, at Texas A&M University. He has received many teaching awards, authored numerous publications, and been cited as a major contributor to the finance literature. Dr Groth received his PhD from the Krannert School, Purdue University. He also holds degrees in physics and in industrial administration. He serves as a consultant in the areas of corporate finance and management education and conducts executive development programs. In addition to his work in finance, he researches and speaks on human capital and creativity. In 2006 he was designated a Mays Faculty Fellow in Teaching Innovation.

Andrew Hiles was founding director and is a fellow of the Business Continuity Institute. He was chairman of the European Information Market (EURIM) group, which supports the UK Parliament's all-party EURIM group in handling European legislation that impacts IT. He is a director of Kingswell International, an international consultancy specializing in managing business risk. Hiles is a published writer and international speaker on business continuity and risk management. He has presented at numerous conferences in Europe, the United States, Africa, the Middle East, the Pacific Rim, Australia, and New Zealand and has broadcast on IT topics on radio and television. He is a member of the British Computer Society.

Peter Howson is a director of AMR International, a London-based strategic consultancy that specializes in commercial due diligence. His particular focus is on manufacturing, building, and construction. He has over 20 years of M&A experience, gained both in industry and as an adviser. Previously he worked in corporate finance at Barings, where he focused on domestic and cross-border deals in manufacturing industries. He has also worked for TI Group plc, transforming the company from a UK supplier of mainly commodity engineering products into a global specialist engineering company through a series of acquisitions and disposals. He has also held senior finance and M&A roles with British Steel and T&N.

Gene C. Lai is Safeco distinguished professor of insurance and chairperson of the Department of Finance, Insurance, and Real Estate at

viii

Contributors

Washington State University. His publications have appeared in many journals, including the *Journal of Risk and Insurance*. Professor Lai has won numerous best paper awards, including one from the Casualty Actuarial Society. He serves as a coeditor for the *Journal of Insurance Issues* and as associate editor for many other journals, including the *Journal of Risk and Insurance*. He is vice president of the American Risk and Insurance Association (ARIA).

Vinod Lall is a professor in the School of Business at Minnesota State University Moorhead, with teaching responsibilities in supply chain management, operations management, management science, project management, and management information systems. Lall has developed and taught online and face-to-face graduate courses in his area of expertise at a number of business schools in Bulgaria, Ecuador, India, Thailand, and the United States. He is active in research and publication, has published numerous papers in peer-reviewed journals, and has presented papers at national and international conferences. He is a certified supply chain professional (CSCP) by APICS, the American Association for Operations Management. Lall is the vice president of education for the Red River Valley chapter of APICS, where he leads APICS certification training classes for a number of regional manufacturing and service organizations.

Duncan Martin is a partner and managing director in the risk management practice at the Boston Consulting Group (BCG), based in London. Prior to joining BCG, he was the head of Wholesale Credit Risk Analytics at the Royal Bank of Scotland in London, the director of Strategic Risk Management at Dresdner Kleinwort, and a senior manager at Oliver Wyman & Company. Martin was educated at Cambridge University and the Wharton School of the University of Pennsylvania. He is the author of *Managing Risk in Extreme Environments* (Kogan Page, 2008).

Thomas McKaig is a widely recognized Canadian author with 30 years of international business experience in more than 40 countries. He delivers quality business solutions to clients in five languages. He owns Thomas McKaig International Inc., found at www.tm-int.com. He speaks internationally on quality management and international trade and is an adjunct professor, teaching Global Business Today in the Executive MBA program at the University of Guelph. His most recent book is entitled *Global Business Today* (McGraw Hill-Ryerson), with his next international business book due in stores in November, 2011. He has served as executive in residence at the University of Tennessee and Universidad de Montevideo and was worldwide strategic marketing adviser to the US Treasury Department Bureau of the US Mint's Gold Eagle Bullion coin program.

Scott Moeller is the director of the M&A Research Centre at Cass Business School, London, and a former senior executive at Deutsche Bank and Morgan Stanley. While at Deutsche Bank, Professor Moeller held roles as global head of the corporate venture capital unit, managing director of the Global eBusiness division, and managing director responsible for worldwide strategy and new business acquisitions. Prior to his career in investment banking he was a management consultant with Booz, Allen & Hamilton (now Booz & Co). He is a nonexecutive director of several nonprofit and financial services companies in the United States, the United Kingdom, and Continental Europe.

Rod Morris is vice president in charge of the political risk insurance program for the Overseas Private Investment Corporation. He first came to OPIC in 2000 after serving as a senior vice president at CNA Insurance Company, where he was in charge of a number of products and divisions as well as the branch offices in Omaha and Phoenix. He has also served as the chief regulator for the captive insurance program in Arizona and has authored a number of articles and training texts on underwriting and captives. Morris has been a member of the United Nation's Expert Group on Public–Private Risk Sharing.

Jenny Rayner is director and principal consultant at Abbey Consulting, which she established in 1999 to provide consultancy and training on the positive management of risk to improve business performance and protect and enhance reputation. Prior to this, her wide-ranging career spanned more than 20 years with ICI and Zeneca in a variety of sales, marketing, purchasing, logistics, supply chain, and general business management roles, and latterly she was a chief internal auditor with ICI. Rayner also writes and lectures on risk management, corporate governance, corporate social responsibility, and reputation.

Steve Robinson was director of open executive programs at Henley Business School until the end of 2007. Previously he was with Ashridge Business School for 14 years, latterly as director of executive MBA programs. Robinson has

Approaches to Enterprise Risk Management

Contributors

designed and taught on a variety of management development and qualification programs in the United States, Europe, Asia, and Australia. He is the author of the *Financial Times Handbook of Financial Management* and is an external examiner at the Cass Business School, City University, London. He is now an independent educator, writer, and consultant working closely with Duke Corporate Education and with the Henley, Warwick, and Kingston Business Schools.

Bill Sharon has been conducting seminars, workshops, and consulting assignments in the area of risk management for the past 12 years. He has 30 years' experience in the financial services and marketing/communications industry in a variety of C-level positions and consultancies. He has been featured in numerous industry magazines (*CIO Magazine*, *Business Finance*, *Business Credit Magazine*) and has authored numerous articles as well as a blog (www.sorms.blogspot.com) that is read in more than 80 countries. Sharon holds a clinical degree, and for the first 10 years of his professional life he worked with adolescents—an experience that taught him the very difficult skill of how to listen. His website, Strategic Operational Risk Management Solutions can be found at www.sorms.com.

David C. Shimko holds a PhD in finance from Northwestern University. He has taught finance at the Kellogg Graduate School of Management at Northwestern University, the Marshall School of Business at the University of Southern California, the Harvard Business School, and the Courant Institute at New York University. His professional career included positions at JP Morgan, Bankers Trust, and Risk Capital, an independent risk advisory firm that was sold to Towers Perrin in 2006. Currently, Shimko sits on the board of trustees of the Global Association of Risk Professionals (GARP). He acts as an independent financial consultant and continues to teach part-time at the Kellogg School.

Will Spinney joined the treasury department at Johnson Matthey plc after a brief career in the Royal Navy, and took the first ever Association of Corporate Treasurers (ACT) corporate treasury exams in 1985. He has been a practicing treasurer now for 25 years, working for several companies that have included most recently Eaton Corporation and Invensys plc, where his experience ranged from risk management, cash management, and extensive refinancings to pension investment strategies. He has been a speaker at several ACT conferences and has been involved in education and training programs with the ACT for several years, both writing resources and as a member of the MCT examination board.

Amarendra Swarup is a partner at Pension Corporation, a United Kingdom-based pension buyout firm, where he oversees alternatives and the thought leadership program. Previously he was at an AAA-rated hedge fund of funds based in London. He is closely involved in both the alternatives community and the wider financial industry. Swarup is a CAIA (Chartered Alternative Investment Analyst) charter-holder and sits on the CAIA examinations council, the editorial board of AllAboutAlpha.com, and the CRO committee of the ABI (Association of British Insurers). He holds a PhD in cosmology from Imperial College, London, and MA (Hons) in Natural Sciences from the University of Cambridge. He has written extensively for a range of media and academic publications on diverse topics including alternatives, cosmology, macroeconomic issues, pensions, asset–liability management, and risk management. He is currently a visiting fellow at the London School of Economics, where he is working with the Department of Management on Pensions Tomorrow, a research initiative looking into the economic, sociopolitical, and financial aspects of pensions and longevity.

Sheryl Vacca is the senior vice president/chief compliance and audit officer at the University of California (UC). Previous to UC, she served as the West Coast practice leader and national lead for internal audit, life sciences, and healthcare. She was also the vice president of internal audit and corporate compliance officer for a large healthcare system in northern California. Vacca has published and presented nationally in the fields of healthcare compliance and internal audit to professional organizations such as the Institute of Internal Auditors, Health Care Compliance Association, Healthcare Financial Management Association, and the Practising Law Institute.

Best Practice
Policies and Processes

Risk Management: Beyond Compliance
by Bill Sharon

EXECUTIVE SUMMARY
- The boundaries between risk management and compliance have eroded over the past decade, to the detriment of both functions.
- The definition of risk should be expanded to include opportunities and uncertainties, not just hazards.
- The context for assessing operational risk is business strategy.
- The role of risk managers needs to expand so that they become coordinators of the risk information that is readily available in operational and business units.
- The perception of risk is dependent on one's organizational responsibilities, and the convergence of those perceptions is the central focus of the management of risk.

INTRODUCTION
Over the past decade the line between risk management and compliance has been blurred to the point where, in many organizations, it is impossible to determine if they are not one and the same. In part, this confusion between the two functions was initiated and then exacerbated by the passage of the Sarbanes–Oxley Act of 2002 and the implementation of Basel II. Both of these events consumed a great deal of resources, and many consulting firms labeled these efforts "risk management." They are, in fact, compliance requirements designed to protect stakeholders and, in the latter case, ensure the viability of the financial system. They are not designed for, and nor can their implementation achieve, the management of risk in individual companies or financial institutions.

This confusion between compliance and risk management has led to a defensive posture in dealing with the uncertainties of the competitive business environment. Risk has been confined to the analysis of what could go wrong rather than what needs to go right. Risk management organizations have become the arbiters of what constitutes risk and have assumed an adversarial relationship with business managers, particularly in capital allocation exercises. Failures and scandals are met with calls for more regulation, the implementation of regulations becomes the province of risk management organizations, and the execution of strategy (arguably the area in most need of risk management) becomes further separated from any kind of disciplined analysis.

AN EXPANDED DEFINITION OF RISK
As Peter Bernstein tells us in his book *Against the Gods: The Remarkable Story of Risk*, the word risk comes from the old Italian *risicare*, which means "to dare." Daring is the driving idea behind business, the idea that a product or a service can achieve excellence and value in the marketplace. Strategy necessarily incorporates risk from the perspective of those actions which are required for its success.

In 1996 Robert G. Eccles, a former Harvard Business School professor, and Lee Puschaver, a partner at Price Waterhouse (now PricewaterhouseCoopers), developed the concept of the "business risk continuum." They argued that organizations that were successful in managing risk were those that focused on uncertainties and opportunities as much as they did on hazards. The context for evaluating risk in this manner is business strategy. This idea—that the definition of risk should be expanded to include those actions that an organization needed to embrace to achieve its goals—was revolutionary and codified what some companies were already beginning to initiate. Unfortunately, the narrow view of risk has prevailed for the past decade, and Eccles' and Puschaver's work has essentially been ignored.

The overwhelming emphasis of most risk organizations today is on the hazard end of the scale. Dot.com, Enron, and now subprime, along with the increased focus on terrorism, cataclysmic natural disasters, and the potential for pandemic diseases, have placed most complex organizations in a defensive posture. The problem with this approach is that risk driven from the hazard perspective is experienced as overhead in the operational disciplines and business units; it's a cost of business, not an activity that enhances value or improves the possibility of success.

By expanding the definition of risk (or returning to its original meaning) companies can harness the inherent risk management abilities and

Approaches to Enterprise Risk Management

information available throughout their organization and develop a predictive process to address mission-critical tasks. Understanding how risk is perceived and how people react to those perceptions is an essential step in managing the opportunities and uncertainties inherent in implementing a business strategy.

ORGANIZATIONAL ROLES AND THE PERCEPTION OF RISK

Daniel Kahneman and Amos Tversky, the authors of "Prospect Theory," conducted a variety of experiments on the perception of risk and the responses that people had to identical information presented in different contexts. Among their conclusions they determined that:
1 emotion always overrides logic in the decision-making process,
2 people suffer from cognitive dysfunction in making decisions because they never have enough information,
3 people are not risk-averse, they are loss-averse.

While these conclusions may be unsettling to those involved in quantitative risk analysis, all three are useful assumptions around which to build a proactive risk management process. Emotion is at the core of any business—the desire to produce the best product, offer the best service, and compete in the marketplace comes from passion, not analytics. Managing risk is about managing emotion, not eliminating it.

From an organizational perspective, the perception of risk is colored by one's responsibilities. In the operational environment, technologists see opportunities in deploying software and hardware. HR professionals define success as the attraction and retention of high-performance employees. In business units, opportunities require risks to be taken in order to capture market share or evolve a product line to the next level. Often these business leaders are unaware of the operational capabilities and capacities on which they must rely to achieve their goals. Operational managers often lack clarity on the business models they support. Individually, these perceptions of risk tell only part of the story and require the balance of all of the organizational perceptions in order for the cognitive dissonance to be managed and mitigated.

In this context, risk managers become coordinators of business intelligence rather than arbiters of what is and is not a risk. The management of risk is a communication process that is central to the success of the enterprise rather than an overhead process that compliance so often becomes. Participation in risk management is equivalent to participating in the development of business strategy. The desire not to lose (rather than the misguided view of being averse to "daring") is the underlying motivation for the process.

THE RISK PERCEPTION CONTINUUM

The risk perception continuum (Figure 1) summarizes the categories of risk and how they can be placed in an operational context. Using Eccles and Puschaver's concept of the three categories of risk, an organization can assign one of three different perceptions to determine the source and value of risk information:

Figure 1. The risk perception continuum

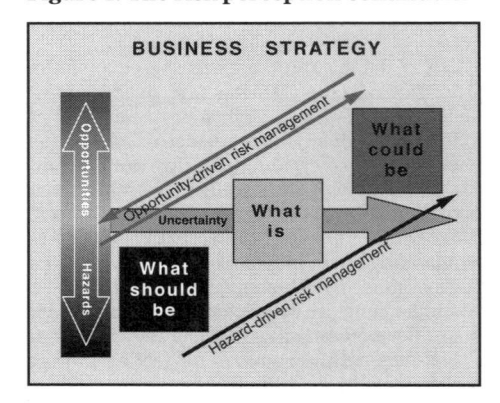

- *What Should Be* is the perception of risk that comes from external standards. These are "best practices" for both operational and business managers. The measures involved determine the degree to which an organization is aligned with these practices in the context of what the organization wants to achieve. For example, alignment with "best practices" for a data center is likely to be more important for a financial institution than an advertising agency.

It is tempting to place compliance functions in this area and track these issues as hazards. This is a mistake on two levels. First, the risk management process is central to the success of the organization and needs the oversight of the audit function. Putting them in the same unit creates a conflict of interest, one that is clearly identified in the Committee of Sponsoring Organization's (COSO) enterprise risk management framework. Second, compliance is a legal and regulatory function. One does not assess the risk of not complying. The primary audiences

Risk Management: Beyond Compliance

CASE STUDY
JP Morgan—Managing the Risk of Outsourcing
The risk management process can be scaled to encompass the entire organization, a specific business unit, or a large project. A year prior to outsourcing 40% of its technology, JP Morgan initiated a predictive risk management program that converged the perceptions of technology and business managers and established an IT risk profile for each business unit.
- The IT self-assessment process was conducted quarterly on a global basis, and provided the bank with a portfolio view of IT operational risk across all business units.
- The risk profiles allowed the bank to negotiate service levels based on an understanding of where the internal IT group was supporting the business strategy and where improvements were necessary.
- The IT self-assessment process was transferred to the successful vendors and the business units continued to contribute their perceptions, resulting in a shared process between the vendors and the bank.
- Perhaps the most important result of the process was a better understanding in the business units of IT capabilities and capacities. The organization gained an understanding of the technology that provided a competitive advantage (and should therefore be retained in the bank) and of the infrastructure and shared applications that could be turned over to external vendors.

for this information are regulators and external auditors, and the ability to adhere to these requirements is really the baseline for participating in the marketplace.
- *What Is* comprises the uncertainty of the operating environment of the organization. This is the area where quantitative analysis and hedging are done to determine the upside and downside of a deal. It is here that both business and operational managers have the greatest impact on the management of risk, and it is here that the communication of the different perceptions of risk is most critical. The convergence of these perceptions constitutes valuable business intelligence.

The classic example of managing risk in this manner is the HR hiring process. The MD of equity trading in an investment bank may have an urgent need for a large number of junior traders. The human resources department has a responsibility to ensure that the people the MD wants to hire have actually attended the universities claimed on their resumés and that they have passed a strenuous background check. The tension between these two perceptions is satisfied by the candidates signing a letter accepting their immediate dismissal should they be found to have misrepresented their qualifications. The organization embraces the risk that the contributions to the strategy will outweigh the potential for any damage that might be done during a relatively small window of time.
- *What Could Be* is the repository of the strategy of the organization and the perception of what risks need to be taken for it to be achieved. This perception is dynamic and responds to the demands of the marketplace, as well as the capabilities of the operating environment.

Perhaps the best known example of how strategy drives the management of risk in an organization is the behavior of the US space agency, NASA, following John F. Kennedy's announcement that there would be an American on the moon by the end of the 1960s. In recently released tapes of meetings between Kennedy and James Webb, the director of NASA, the impact of strategy on operational capabilities is well illustrated. Webb advises Kennedy of the vagaries of space and the need to expand the space program to include a number of interim steps necessary to gain a better understanding before anyone can go to the moon. Kennedy listens and then tells Webb that he doesn't care about space, he wants to get to the moon before the Russians.

What's interesting about this exchange is that Kennedy was defining a strategic goal that had no near-term likelihood of being achieved. He was also using that strategic goal to redefine the risk. The technical risk was unknowable at the time, but the political risk was quantifiable. Strategy organizes the operational environment and focuses it in specific directions. It requires operational managers to converge their perceptions of risk with the goals of the organization.

Figure 1 also demonstrates the difference between driving risk management from the

Approaches to Enterprise Risk Management

opportunity or strategy perspective as opposed to the hazard perspective. The latter approach tries to force standards up through the organization. Operational managers experience this as an audit process and, other than quarterly reports from the audit committee, very little of this information receives much attention from the senior executives responsible for implementing strategy.

Alternatively, risk management driven from the opportunity perspective creates a communications vehicle for the entire organization. This is a bi-directional process because, as the strategy is communicated into the operating environment, the organization responds with business intelligence.

IMPLEMENTING A RISK MANAGEMENT PROCESS

Using the organization's strategy as the context (rather than "best practices" or regulatory requirements), the first step in the process is to ask operational managers to identify the risks that must be embraced in order to achieve this strategy (operational disciplines are defined as those organizational units that do not generate income, i.e. finance, HR, IT, PR, etc.). Once identified, these activities are assessed—usually using a RAG (red, amber, green) rating—to determine the likelihood of their being achieved.

There are two important steps in this first stage of the process that are often lacking in risk management programs.

1. Operational managers are asked to predict a risk rating, usually on a quarterly basis, for the next four quarters. This provides the organization with more valuable data than point-in-time risk assessments, whose shelf-life tends to be quite short. It also provides operational managers with the ability to communicate anticipated challenges in the future and/or illustrate how current challenges will be positively addressed over time.
2. Operational managers are also asked to note whether the activities they believe must be undertaken have sufficient funding. Once this information has been collated, the organization has a map of where it is investing in managing risks central to the strategy and where it is not.

Operational managers are then asked to complete an actual vs. planned assessment at the end of each quarter. This is not an exercise to assess competency, but rather another channel for communication in the risk management process. Strategy may change, requiring a new percep-

Figure 2. Converging the perceptions of risk

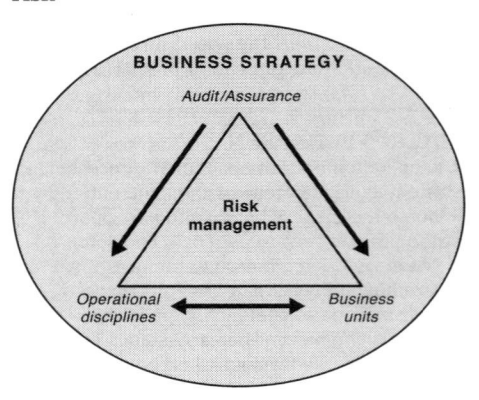

tion of risk. Operational awareness of greater or lesser challenges may impact the original risk rating. Departures from the original assessment are expected and should be viewed as business intelligence rather than as a scoring of prescient abilities.

Once the process is established with the operational managers, the second stage of the risk management process can be implemented. Here, business managers are asked to contribute their perceptions of risk to the mission-critical operational activities that have been identified. For example, if the IT department identified the rollout of a new operating system as a risk that needed to be embraced and rated it as an amber or a red, given the exposure in maintenance and security, the business managers might rate it as a green as they have no clear knowledge of the technical issues. Differences in the perception of risk are expected and provide an opportunity to understand risk across operational and business disciplines.

The third stage (Figure 2) in the risk management process is the audit review, which not only validates the process itself, but also uses the risk assessments as a source for audit oversight of specific operational activities. The convergence of perception between operational and business managers and the audit function provides the risk management process with the widest possible range of understanding of risks to the strategy.

Once this process is established, metrics can be applied to risk ratings, operational disciplines can be weighted in importance by business unit, and portfolio views of risk can be developed across business units.

Risk Management: Beyond Compliance

CONCLUSION
No risk management function can ensure that negative events won't happen. The complexity of the markets and the speed of change create exposures that are difficult to predict. Managing risk as a process that engages the entire enterprise in the achievement of the business strategy does, however, create a resilient organization that can better respond to difficulties that always arise.

MAKING IT HAPPEN
The operational risk management process described in this article begins with the business strategy but ultimately engages the entire organization. Senior management needs not only to endorse the process but also to participate in and use it on a continuing basis. The early stages of the process require patience, and some care should be taken in the initial implementation.
- There is often confusion in the operational disciplines about what is a risk to the business strategy and what is a best-practice or compliance requirement. Risk managers will likely need to assist operational managers in this distinction.
- Simplicity is key in the early stages of the risk management process. Many efforts collapse under their own weight when organizations attempt to accomplish too much in a short period. Risk management is about leveraging existing expertise; complex metrics can be applied once the system is robust.
- Using the risk management process as a communication process, not only for challenges but also for capacities and creative solutions, is essential in making it a robust vehicle for the generation of business intelligence.

MORE INFO
Book:
Bernstein, Peter L. *Against the Gods, The Remarkable Story of Risk*. New York: Wiley, 1996.

Article:
Kloman, Felix. "Risk management and Monty Python, part 2." *Risk Management Reports* 32:12 (December 2005). Online at: tinyurl.com/34hwowx

Report:
Puschaver, Lee, and Robert G. Eccles. "In pursuit of the upside: The new opportunity in risk management." Leading Thinking on Issues of Risk, PricewaterhouseCoopers, 1998.

Websites:
COSO (Committee of Sponsoring Organizations of the Treadway Commission): www.coso.org
Prospect theory: prospect-theory.behaviouralfinance.net and www.sjsu.edu/faculty/watkins/prospect.htm
Risk Metrics: www.riskmetrics.com
Strategic Operational Risk Management Solutions (SORMS): www.sorms.com

A Holistic Approach to Business Risk Management by Terry Carroll

EXECUTIVE SUMMARY
- The events of 2008 make it unsurprising that we are preoccupied with financial risk.
- Financial risk is part of overall business risk—business risks have financial consequences.
- As well as being viewed individually, risks should be viewed holistically.
- A holistic approach to risk means looking at each risk in the context of others.
- Managing business risk can be positive and offer opportunities.
- The credit crunch is an example for all companies, not just banks.
- There is a simple, clearly defined process for managing business risks.
- Risk pervades every element of the overall business process.
- The whole organization should be engaged in the risk management process.

INTRODUCTION
After arguably the greatest credit crisis in history, it is unsurprising that lenders, borrowers, and investors alike have become preoccupied with financial risk. Its magnitude seems to have dwarfed all other business risk considerations. It can be hard to take a pragmatic view when the strictures in the financial markets may have put the corporation at risk, but the correct perspective is for all risk to be captured in a holistic framework.

Apart from the consequences of events in the financial markets, some recent risk considerations have been imposed rather than occurring naturally. Among those that were more prevalent prior to the credit crunch were the issue of corporate manslaughter and the need to comply with burgeoning health and safety regulation.

What seems sometimes to have been overlooked is that all financial risks are business risks (i.e. a risk to the business), and all business risk has financial consequences. There are those, especially in the public sector, who seem preoccupied with budgets and spending, rather than planning. The advent of business process reengineering (BPR) in the 1980s seemed to coincide with downsizing or rightsizing, as companies trimmed or even slashed their budgets.

What BPR and business planning have in common is the need to put the horse in front of the cart. Financial transactions are the consequence of business decisions. Budgets are the consequence of business planning. Cost efficiencies should only arise from BPR where the exercise is to design or redesign the organization to deliver the current strategy in the current markets and circumstances.

In summary, all risks have potential consequences for financial and business continuity. A holistic approach means looking at each risk in the context of others, and of the business and financial risk as a whole.

RISK IS A NATURAL CONSEQUENCE OF BUSINESS
Financial risk is a subset of business risk, which is a consequence of business decisions. You cannot be in business without taking risks. Whether you accept these risks or not is a function of whether your business thinking is proactive or reactive.

No one can eliminate all business or financial risk. Either you don't have a business, or the premiums you would need to pay to eliminate risk would transcend any prospect of profit.

It could be argued that in the public sector, and with the latter's growing influence in commerce (for example through public/private partnerships), risk has become an industry in itself. The public sector does not have a profit imperative. If it is decreed that risk shall be actively managed or insured against, the cost is picked up by the taxpayer. The growth of the health and safety industry in the United Kingdom has undoubtedly saddled the taxpayer with burgeoning costs. It has impacted industry in much the same way, but with less chance to pass this on to the customer.

WHAT IS BUSINESS RISK?
"Risk is a threat that a company will not achieve its corporate objectives."[1] A typical dictionary definition would be: "Risk is the possibility of suffering harm or loss." Such a definition characteristically has implicit negative connotations. Here we are talking about a more objective approach, where risk is recognized as part and parcel of enterprise.

Approaches to Enterprise Risk Management

The management of risk is fundamentally about ownership and accountability for the management and business processes, and their possible opportunities and consequences.

The process can be characterized by four simple components:
- evaluation;
- control;
- transfer;
- constructive damage limitation (insurance or hedging).

Managing risk is a continuous process, as opposed to something that you do just once. Starting from strategy, and considered throughout the organizational processes, risk is present

materialization of this risk ultimately brought down.

We don't have enough information to be sure whether the boards of the US institutions had sufficient oversight over the nature and scale of the risks being created. We do, however, know that the financial authorities, and especially the Bank of England, had become increasingly concerned about the lack of control or regulation of what have been labeled "toxic assets" long before the problems became critical to the markets.

This is a clear lesson for the boards and executives of companies. Not just in relation to financial risk, but to business risk in general. We do not propose a new industry of risk management, but

---

CASE STUDY
The Credit Crunch and the Irresponsible Creation of Financial Risk
The credit crunch has been a highly illustrative case study in dysfunctional risk management. What brought the financial markets to their knees was the irresponsible and inadequately controlled creation of excessive risk, with little or no consideration of the consequences.

In a climate where interest rates were historically low from 2001, and with bonus-fueled incentives to grow the balance sheet, US financial institutions identified a new group of customers. These were people at the bottom of the economic food chain, living in rented property, who were persuaded that with interest rates so low it was cheaper to buy their homes than to rent them.

As interest rates rose and fixed-rate deals matured, a growing proportion of this new army of borrowers found they could not meet the repayments. Unsophisticated, many of them simply defaulted on the payments, and some even walked away. The result was what became known as subprime assets.

The problem was compounded in at least two further ways, however. The new assets had been securitized into packages that could be sold on to fund new lending, and some had even been disaggregated into their component parts, to be sold on to other investors such as hedge funds and other investment funds. So long as the returns were good nobody complained, but as the markets unraveled investors became increasingly concerned about where their money was invested.

Many of these assets were off balance sheet, and even offshore. Often they weren't regulated. When, in August 2007, BNP Paribas found that it couldn't value three of its funds because there was no longer a sound market for these esoteric assets, the whole global financial system began to crumble.

---

and has potential impacts at every step of the way. The trick is in being able to see it in a positive and opportunistic way rather than in a negative light. Ideally, the whole organization should be constructively engaged and empowered in the recognition and management of risk.

LESSONS FOR COMPANIES

In the infamous 1980s Barings case, the board either was not aware of the scale of risk being created, and/or it did not have sufficient or satisfactory controls, including the separation of functions. Nor does it appear to have had a sufficient, or a holistic, view that would have considered the burgeoning risk in the context of the whole of Barings' business, which the

we do strongly recommend that risk management should be a core business function. It does not sit apart from business planning and decision-making, but it is a close cousin of audit, and may ideally be viewed as internal consultancy, informing and improving the quality of management decisions.

Similarly, in the public sector, risk management in its many guises has come to resemble a core function that is sometimes "the tail that wags the dog." The risk management function should be woven into mainstream decision-making; it should start with, and encompass, the whole of business risk; and it should enrich and inform management rather than constrain and curtail, otherwise it misses the point.

A Holistic Approach to Business Risk Management

A SIMPLE FORMULATION

Holistic business risk management starts with strategy formulation and goes right through to business and financial planning, and ultimately implementation. At every stage, the simple question is "What are the consequences of this decision?"

For some, risk management or risk review seems to be more of an afterthought. For example, prospectuses and project plans seem always to finish with a summary and evaluation of the risks. This is done with an eye to investors or stockholders, to satisfy them that management has thought of all the significant consequences of a plan or proposal. Often it amounts to little more than a rhetorical flourish: "See, we've done the risk evaluation."

It would be better if management wove risk evaluation into every stage of planning and decision-making. It should be at the heart of all high-quality management thinking, and should be seen to enrich the quality and rigor of decisions, rather than holding them back or, worse still, being a mechanical afterthought, and only when demanded or requested.

There is a simple pattern to the consideration of risks as part of business decision-making:
- determine the risk;
- analyze it;
- evaluate it;
- manage it;
- ignore it;
- insure against it;
- control it;
- improve the management and business processes that are the basis of the risk.

A WHOLE ORGANIZATION ENTERPRISE

It has been characteristic for management to be directive rather than consultative. Managing risk in a holistic way can be time-consuming, but, like success, it touches the whole enterprise. Singular decisions were taken for US institutions to drive into subprime assets. Would it have been different if the whole organization had been engaged in the decision? It is important to see managing risk as a central business need, woven throughout the fabric of the organization.

Ultimately, the management of risk is the responsibility of the board. As the governance medium of the organization, the board approves and oversees strategy and policy. At the strategic level, some other questions and issues that arise are:
- What is risk in the context of our business organization?
- What does managing risk imply for us and our management processes?
- Where does responsibility for the management of risk lie?
- Why should we manage risk?
- What are the benefits of managing risk?
- Are we complying with legislation, good practice, standards, regulation, and sound governance?

Managing risk will always be a balance between evaluating and optimizing opportunity on the one hand, and identifying and dealing with the potential related risks on the other.

Do you need a specific department to manage risk? Might one actually create confusion within other departments? If you were establishing your organization from scratch today, would you set up a specific function called risk management? Ideally, it should be woven as an integral part into the management and business processes. The mature organization instinctively scans for, and is aware of, risk in everything it does.

SO HOW DO WE DO THIS?

World class organizations have world class management practices and processes. By all means set up a risk management function, but it should be a servant to, not a constraint on, the organization. It should be participative, engaging, and integrated with the internal audit process, in the nature of an internal consultancy.

It should be engaged end to end in the entire management processes—from strategy formulation to implementation and delivery. It should especially facilitate management, and indeed the whole enterprise, to make the consideration of risk fundamental to every business decision in a positive, objective, and contributory way, rather than as a constraint on enterprise.

Where such risk evaluation results in a decision to insure against risk, rather than manage it, this should also be the consequence of objective evaluation rather than defensiveness. Excess insurance is a brake on enterprise, and has financial consequences for the bottom line. Where it comes in the form of derivatives or hedges, it can sometimes create more rather than less risk if there is not a "total balance sheet" approach.

CONCLUSION

Risk management was born out of the insurance industry. It has become endemic in the public sector, with consequent burgeoning costs. It has had negative rather than positive results. All great entrepreneurs are risk-takers. The best either have a sound, intuitive awareness of risk and its balance with enterprise, or are secure

Approaches to Enterprise Risk Management

enough to lead the evaluation of possible consequences, so as to enrich rather than inhibit business decisions.

Now is the time to see the management of risk as a holistic business process that is inherent in every decision. As opposed to being seen to hold back enterprise, the consideration and evaluation of risk should be seen as enriching the quality of business decisions. It is, however, sensible to capture the risk evaluation alongside the decision. You make the decision including the risk consequences, rather than despite them.

As well as being woven into the management and business processes, holistic risk management should embrace as much of the organization as is practicable. What-ifs, constructive challenge, and objective review should be celebrated rather than shunned. Financial transactions are the consequence of business decisions. Negative risk outcomes and their financial costs should not be a surprise, except where they arise from chance.

Insurance, whether through premiums or derivatives, should not merely be a safety net. It should be the result of mature identification, consideration, and evaluation of risk scenarios and consequent management decisions. That way, the net financial outcomes can be predicted with reasonable accuracy and consistency.

Those organizations that take a holistic, constructive, and proactive view of risk are less likely to be caught out, are more likely to succeed in the long run, and produce more predictable and manageable results. Where they engage as many of the staff as possible in the process, the by-products could well be better reputation and trust with investors, customers, and staff, and better long-term market value.

Above all, this objective, positive, holistic approach to business risk management empowers organizations, management, and individuals to grow through openness and mature evaluation, rather than feel constrained by a process that seems to sit apart from the core enterprise.

MORE INFO

Book:
Carroll, Terry, and Mark Webb. *The Risk Factor: How to Make Risk Management Work for You in Strategic Planning and Enterprise*. Harrogate, UK: Take That Books, 2001.

Article:
Carroll, Terry. "A risky business." *Exec* online magazine (August 2007): www.execdigital.co.uk

Website:
Association of Corporate Treasurers (ACT) risk management main page: www.treasurers.org/Risk+Management

NOTES

1 Harris-Jones, J., and L. Bergin. *The Management of Corporate Risk—A Framework for Directors*. London: Association of Corporate Treasurers, 1998.

Risk—Perspectives and Common Sense Rules for Survival by John C. Groth

EXECUTIVE SUMMARY
- "Risk" generally implies the potential for loss (gain), an unfavorable (favorable) outcome, or danger (safety).
- Uncertainty is different. Many characterize "uncertainty" as the doubt as to the outcome. Uncertainty may stem from lack of knowledge about a potential outcome, or from variability in the outcome that has nothing to do with available knowledge.
- People argue over the definition of risk and what kind of risk is relevant in the pricing of assets. Our approach defines risk as whatever risk influences investor behavior and the resultant pricing of assets.
- An increase in the perceived risks of any asset results in a decline in its value. Most economic models view this as a nonlinear relationship.
- There are "controllable" and "uncontrollable" risks. Managers need to identify the uncontrollable risks and make conscious decisions concerning exposure to such risks.
- "Unnecessary risk" is risk that can be eliminated without adversely affecting expected returns. Exposing your company to unnecessary risks garners no reward and adversely affects company value.
- Managers should employ common sense rules of risk management for survival. Esoteric models should supplement rather than displace these rules.
- Survival in an uncertain environment with exposure to risk argues for a strategy of preserving the right of choice and commitment, and avoiding positions that force a course of action.
- Managers will benefit from awareness of, and a strategy for, risk and uncertainty resolution versus capital commitment with time.

INTRODUCTION
We are fortunate to live in a world characterized by risk and uncertainty. Absent risk and uncertainty, with work, diligence, and access to information we could know each event that was to transpire. We would lose the opportunity for expectations, dreams, surprises, good fortune, and much more. We might as well have these "good" things, since in a certain world we presumably would still have "bad" events. Conceptually, in an uncertain world we can in fact choose to avoid *some* risks and bad events, or at least mitigate the effects of these events.

Common sense guidelines or rules will assist in garnering the benefits of bearing risk, allow us to make decisions that make sense, and protect us from unacceptable consequences. For simplification, we will consider a risk relative to a situation—for example, a new product, surgery, oil exploration, negotiating the release of hostages—and refer to the whole as a "project."

First, let's look at essentials, then some common sense rules, and after that ideas for action. Surprisingly, we admit that historically people have benefited—and in the future they will continue to benefit—from ignoring everything we say here. People have taken risks without conscious evaluation or without regard to risk–return relationships. Sometimes the results have been incredibly beneficial or rewarding. On other occasions the results have been disastrous.

SOME FUNDAMENTALS
People differ in their views concerning risk and uncertainty. "Risk" generally implies the potential for loss (gain), an unfavorable (favorable) outcome, or danger (safety). A number of investors would think of risk in a semivariance or asymmetric sense: It's only risk "if it comes out bad." More generally, one thinks of risk as an outcome that may vary (favorably or unfavorably) as a result of the underlying process(es) that will generate the outcome. With respect to investments, many define risk as the chance of variability in the outcome.

Some characterize "uncertainty" as the doubt concerning the outcome. Uncertainty may stem from lack of knowledge about a potential outcome, or from variability in the outcome that has nothing to do with available knowledge.

An "outcome" that occurs at a point in time may result from chance, the influence of variables (for example a force), or a combination of both. Often the risk of a venture may have

13

Approaches to Enterprise Risk Management

its origin in one or more factors. In a dynamic rather than a purely mechanistic environment, the inherent risk of an investment may vary with time. Alterations in the origins of risk result from changes in the array or level of influence of variables that affect outcomes.

One can sometimes limit risk by influencing or even eliminating the influence of certain variables on outcomes. Generally, these efforts have costs that will affect the net outcome of circumstance.

For ease of discussion, we will combine risk and uncertainty in a practical way: With risk and uncertainty, we don't know for sure what will happen. Additionally, we will define "risk resolution" as the emergence of reality, the resultant impact on the variables that influence the outcome, and the event and the consequences that occur.

Core principle: *We do not live probabilities or expected values, or predicted or modeled outcomes. We live the events of reality that arrive with time.*

The demise of Long Term Capital Management (LTCM) in 1998, creating global financial panic, tells us that even the legends of Wall Street and the incredible talents of Nobel laureates cannot alter this principle. Shirreff (2004) illuminates a host of issues related to LTCM and other aspects of risk. The subprime debacle, as well as certain derivatives, shows that some continue to ignore fundamental principles, or harvest returns while foisting the risk and consequences of poor decisions on others. These and other historical events prompt us to share perspectives and common sense rules on risk.

COMMON SENSE RULES

Since we live events, not distributions or probabilities, applying some common sense rules will enable us first to survive, and second, to survive on favorable terms.

Identify All Sources of Risk[1]

Turn over every rock to unearth factors that may influence the outcome of the contemplated course of action. Sources of risk fall into major categories:

- *Inherent in the project*: For example, the ability to complete a project as anticipated, the outcome of events related to pursuit of the project, whether the oil is there or not, and technical issues.
- *External to the project*: For example, political and market factors that will influence the realization of the project and/or the benefits it brings. External factors may influence whether the project proceeds as planned (denied permits, blocked access, nonavailability of materials) and/or the realization of expected benefits even if the project itself is brought to completion as expected (changes in energy prices or taxation, expropriation, etc.).
- *External–inherent effects*: Forces external to the project may affect the course of the project or its outcome. A rise in the cost of ingredients used in a food processing/marketing venture with consequent effects on markets and margins is an example.
- *Inherent–external effects*: For example, the outcome of a project may alter the external environment, as when a project changes the efficiency and economics of microchip manufacturing, with a major impact on applications and markets.

Never Bear Risk Unintentionally

Under the right circumstances the conscious bearing of risk offers opportunity. Having a source of risk that "surprises" us offers the prospect of various outcomes ranging from good, through unfavorable, to bad—perhaps uncontrollably bad or even disastrous.

Remember that risk allows the possibility of good as well as bad outcomes. An outcome that stems from the unconscious bearing of risk might offer an incredibly good reward. Recognizing the possibility of good/bad outcomes is quite different from doing well accidentally. Unfortunately, danger lurks in bearing risk unconsciously—we do not get to choose if the outcome is good or bad. Absent an awareness of the risk, unless we have succeeded in getting another party to bear all known and unknown risks, the impact of unfavorable consequences falls on us.

Overlooking or inadvertently ignoring certain risks can have a disastrous impact on outcomes. A recent disclosure suggests that a major manufacturer of aircraft may have failed to consider consciously the risks attendant on signing sales contracts denominated in one currency while having significant exposure on the input and production side in another currency. Importantly, the choice to accept such risk is logical and defensible even if the subsequent chain of events proves unattractive. *To overlook risk when making decisions differs considerably from the choice to accept a risk.*

Choose, Rather than Be Compelled, to Bear Risk

Historically, the decision to assume risk, coupled with the events that transpired, has resulted in some very beneficial outcomes. *In risk exposure,*

Risk—Perspectives and Common Sense Rules for Survival

the issue is choice rather than the level of risk. We purposely offer an example from outside economics. In 1928, a daring surgeon and a patient—the true equity in the venture—took a huge risk when the surgeon performed the first hemispherectomy on a human.[2] Individuals have taken extraordinary risks in many fields and under many circumstances so that others might benefit, and we later accord them accolades or see them as an intrepid explorer or hero.

Consciously deciding to bear a risk if there is sufficient potential benefit is logical. Inadvertently bearing risk due to a lack of diligence fails the test of judgment.

exposure to certain risks seems defensible—and the world has benefited from such risk-takers.

In contrast, exposing *others* to a risk who cannot tolerate that risk or its potentially catastrophic outcome fails the test of common sense. More importantly, exposing others to risk they do not knowingly choose to bear fails the test of decency and morality.

Clearly Understand Who Is Bearing Risk
Knowledge of the origins and nature of the elements of risk is essential to follow this rule. Whatever the risk at a point in time for a particular project, someone is bearing the risk—either

MAKING IT HAPPEN
Applying the common sense rules for risk suggests the following:
- *Assess the origins of risk that may influence the potential course of action.* Classify those risks as controllable, partially controllable, or uncontrollable.
- *Focus first on the uncontrollable elements of risk.* If these factors potentially have such dire consequences as to make the outcome unacceptable, the decision is relatively simple: Get someone else to bear this risk, or abandon this course of action. Make sure that the party accepting the risk is fully able to take it on, as you don't want it to revert to you.
- *Identify the potential expected benefits of taking on the risk.* Segregate these benefits into two categories: those that are easy to quantify, and those that are hard to quantify.
- With the expected benefits identified, for controllable risks decide if you wish to bear, hedge, or transfer the risks. For partially controllable risks, evaluate whether you can afford exposure to the residual risks.
- *The quantum effect.* If you feel you have a course of action that offers the possibility of disproportionate returns—a quantum leap in terms of good effects or outcome—but you cannot rationalize the action in a risk–return context, then ignore everything I've said. Accept that you are moving from logic to feelings and commitment—and do it anyway.
- Reflect and decide if the contemplated course of action makes sense.
- Follow the common sense rules offered here.

Returning to the arena of business, *recognizing and accepting* the risk inherent in exposure to multiple currencies differs considerably from discovering later that one failed to consider the risks and potential consequences of bearing this risk.

Only Take On Risk You Can Afford to Bear
Regardless of the expected return, bear risk only if the consequences of an adverse outcome are tolerable.

Common sense argues that we avoid risks with potential outcomes that *to us* are unacceptable given the circumstances. Consciously accepting the risk of bankruptcy and ruin *to oneself* is acceptable. Indeed, a personal choice "to pursue the dream" in the face of huge risk has played an important role in the world, and it will always do so. To lose your own mind capital, or financial or physical capital, or even your life by electing

singly or divided in some fashion amongst more than one party. To illustrate, a company may feel it should not bear the collective risks of several projects during a particular time window or during certain phases of the projects. Consequently, the company may share this risk with other parties, with this shedding of the risks either permanent or transitory.

Protect Against the Reversion of Risk
If you intend to transfer risk to another party, ensure that the transfer in fact occurs. Second, protect yourself against the possibility that the risk will revert to you without your permission, or if it does, without compensation. In addition, you must assess that the party accepting the risk can tolerate/survive the risk, and also not escape the risk in a manner that transfers it back to you.[3]

The burdens of responsibility extend beyond legality. If the risk effectively reverts back to you

Approaches to Enterprise Risk Management

and you accept the consequences because of your sense of social responsibility, or moral stance, or to protect your reputation, then we commend you. Rather than become the risk-bearer of last resort, instead carefully transfer the risk to those that can and will bear the risk. After all, a default on the bearing of risk defeats the objective of transferring the risk.[4]

For various reasons, a plan for risk management across time, or during the progression of events, might include the shifting of certain risks among/between parties at different points in time or with respect to particular events and outcomes. For instance, a company may choose to avoid certain risk factors during the construction of a new facility by resorting to a turnkey contract. Naturally, confidence that the party accepting the risk can comply and deliver is of paramount importance to avoid risk reversion.

Evaluate Risk Resolution with Events and/or Time

The outcome of one or more events associated with the progress of a project can have a profound effect on the level of the resolution of risk and the remaining risk for the rest of the project path. The successful synthesizing of a substance at the laboratory level and repeated replication of the synthesis can greatly alter the remaining risk in the project. Subsequent success in attaining the expected output and quality from a pilot plant would resolve more risk and cause a drop in the residual risk of the project.

Figure 1 depicts the general notion of risk resolution with events/time, without discussion of alternative scenarios and details. However, we share an example of a core issue: the commitment of capital at risk versus the resolution of risk. This example illustrates the shifting of a major risk-reduction event to an earlier point in time to resolve a major portion of uncertainty before committing the next chunk of capital. The initial risk resolution curve is shown in the figure.

As you might expect, shifting the resolution curve to the left, as indicated by the gray arrows, often entails additional costs. The analysis and decision to pursue this path should capture the relationship between those incremental costs, the chance of an unfavorable outcome, the investment schedule, and the cost of failure.

Other approaches to coping with the pattern of investment versus time versus risk resolution exist that are important if it is impossible, or prohibitively expensive, to shift the resolution curve. For example, one party desiring to participate in the venture might find it possible to take or create an option that allows it to participate if

Figure 1. Capital invested versus time and risk resolution

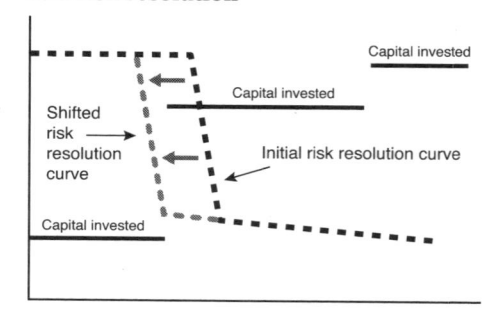

later on risk is resolved in a favorable manner. For example, a pharmaceutical company might take an option on another small company in the situation represented by the initial resolution curve, the relative bargaining positions obviously influencing the nature and terms of the option.

Divide Return and Risk Disproportionately

In many models of valuation, changes in cash returns have a linear effect on value. Changes in the required rate of return have a nonlinear effect on value. Table 1 illustrates these relationships with a present value problem. A to B to C involve changes in cash flow, with the same dollar effect on value—up or down $24.72 as the cash flows increase or decrease from the base value—highlighted with solid-line boxes.

The discount rate reflects the risk of cash flows. D, E, and F illustrate the asymmetric effects of changes in the discount rate, with different dollar effects on value. An equal increase or decrease of 1% in the rate yields an unequal change in value ($22.56 vs. $20.50).

Table 1. Value and changes in cash flow versus discount rate

	Year 10 cash flow	Change in cash flow	Discount rate	Present value	Change in value
A	$900	($100)	0.15	$222.47	($24.72)
B	$1,000	Base $100	0.15	$247.18	($24.72)
C	$1,100		0.15	$271.90	
D	$1,000		0.14	$269.74	$22.56
E	$1,000	Base	0.15	$247.18	($20.50)
F	$1,000		0.16	$226.68	

Risk—Perspectives and Common Sense Rules for Survival

Know the Way Out
The best analysis will not overcome the reality that we don't know what the future holds. Even if we choose a course of action that passes all the common sense tests, we still should always ask: How do I get out of here if...?

We hope we will not have to escape a particular circumstance. Giving some thought to that possibility will prepare us for such an undesirable outcome—even though we may take an entirely different path from those identified in this process. People are remarkably resilient and creative. Thinking through things ahead of time somehow prepares the mind to work at its best, no matter what happens.

The Common Sense Test
A final step in the analysis of a decision to be taken is the power of an important question: *Does the contemplated course of action make sense?* Step back from the details of analysis, and from any obsession with the project, and weigh it up from the perspective of an independent observer.

OTHER ISSUES

Capital at Risk
Give attention to the nature of the capital at risk: financial or tangible capital—or, more importantly, human capital. Care and diligence in exposing human capital to risk are critical, for example in pharmaceutical trials or new methods of treatment. Creatively determine how to minimize human capital at risk until events/time resolve risk in a manner that assures attractive expected benefits/risks for individual human capital at risk.

Avoid Unnecessary Risk
Unnecessary risk is risk one can eliminate without adversely affecting expected returns. Capital markets will not reward one for bearing risk that one can avoid.

Normally unnecessary risk, if present, resides on the operating side of a company. For example, in a manufacturing setting we intend that specific events with specific outcomes should occur. That unintended events or outcomes occur often arises from poor management, poor design, or choice of inappropriate technology, process design, and so on.

SUMMARY

We will enjoy or endure the events that actually occur in the future—not probabilities, distributions, or expected values. Common sense rules of risk management will protect one from many adverse consequences. Ignoring these rules, and making poor judgments, may yield disastrous outcomes, as illustrated only too well by the current debacle in subprime mortgages.

Models, derivatives, financial engineering, and any array of esoteric methods or practices do not overcome the fundamental fact that we live in an uncertain world. What others do will deprive us of choice, but we ourselves can increase the uncertainty of outcomes by our own behavior and the choices we make. Great care should therefore be taken to follow the common sense rules of risk management.

MORE INFO

Book:
Shirreff, David. *Dealing with Financial Risk*. Princeton, NJ: Bloomberg Press, 2004.

Articles:
Groth, John C. "Common-sense risk assessment." *Management Decision* 30:5 (1992): 10–16.
Groth, John C. "Environmental risk: Implications of rational lender behaviour." *Journal of Property Finance* 5:3 (1994): 19–32.

NOTES

1 Groth (1992) offers practical details on identifying and classifying risk factors.
2 The date of the first hemispherectomy on a human as well its classification as success or failure is a matter of debate, fed by issues such as the extent of the procedure as well as measures of success. The first human hemispherectomy, in 1923, is attributed to Walter Dandy, but the first complete procedure, also by Dandy, was performed in 1933. The procedure is primarily used to treat epilepsy.
3 A social conscience dictates that one not knowingly transfer risk to a third party that, because it cannot bear or tolerate the adverse outcome of the risk, or through intent, defaults and transfers the adverse outcome to society.
4 As the reader is well aware, some parties may "accept" risk for compensation with the *intent* of defaulting on the bearing of the risk and garnering (stealing) unearned returns, i.e. taking the returns without actually bearing the risk.

Integrated Corporate Financial Risk Policy
by David C. Shimko

EXECUTIVE SUMMARY
- Corporate risk is any threat to financial objectives, measured in financial terms.
- Risk is defined not necessarily as absolute risk, but relative to a benchmark.
- If risk is free, corporate departments will squander it. By putting a price on risk, it is managed when it should be.
- Corporate treasuries tend to minimize risk, probably not consistently with corporate objectives.
- Procurement risk problems often come from fixed budget levels.
- Marketing risk problems often come from giveaways in customer contracts.
- An integrated corporate risk policy defines how risk should be measured, priced, and rewarded in the corporation, leading to better corporate decisions in all departments.

DEFINING RISK—HARDER THAN IT SEEMS

Risk can be described as the threat of an adverse outcome. Many firms take the benchmark strategy of doing nothing (i.e., investing in Treasury Bills), and measure their risk in absolute terms relative to the strategy of doing nothing. Others measure their risk-taking behavior relative to what might be considered risky benchmarks. Mutual funds, for example, do not focus on the absolute risk of their portfolios; rather, they determine how far away they are from a market benchmark, such as being long the S&P 500. Corporations should explicitly determine their proper benchmarks.

For example, when a gold company hedges its exposure to gold prices, it is arguably reducing risk. However, shareholders may see this as an increase in risk, since it moves the company away from its natural gold exposure. Similarly, shareholders own all sorts of assets and diversify their risks; if a company moves away from its natural risk profile it is making the shareholder portfolio less diversified.

Most financial institutions should measure their risks relative to holding Treasury Bills, since that is an appropriate benchmark strategy for its shareholders. Furthermore, because financial institutions' risk capital levels are regulated, risk is a scarce resource that must be consumed wisely.

In all cases, shareholder preferences should be considered in establishing the risk benchmark, risk measure, and risk appetite. This is the first critical step in establishing a best practice integrated risk policy.

RISK INTEGRATION

Many treatments of risk deal with risk silos: treasury risk, insurance risk, budget risk, procurement risk, sales price risk, and marketing risk. While specialized knowledge in each of these areas informs risk management and execution, it does not address questions like the following:
- How important is one risk vis-à-vis the corporation's entire risk profile?
- Is it better to manage a risk operationally or through financial means?
- Are there natural risk offsets to consider before targeting a particular risk for elimination?
- What are the interactions among risks and the natural diversification benefit companies generally have?

The following sections consider selected risks that are shared by many corporations, within the framework that good risk management in each area must be consistent with the overall corporate standard. The overall corporate standard should include a cost for risk to prevent it from being squandered, measures of risk that are consistent with corporate objectives, consistent policies for treasury and insurance risk, best practices in procurement and marketing risk, corporate hedging policy to hedge integrated risk (not in each silo), and risk-based performance measurement to reward those who manage risk prudently.

THE COST OF RISK

Financial institutions often place an explicit cost on risk to ensure it is being taken prudently. For example, a bank may require that a transaction that risks $100 million in bank capital must earn at least $25 million in present value. This cutoff percentage (25%) can be called a risk-adjusted return on capital, or RAROC.

Bank capital is affected by market risk (changes in market prices), credit risk (default

Approaches to Enterprise Risk Management

risk and counterparty performance risk), and operational risk (people, processes, and systems). Any activity that increases risk should not be voluntarily undertaken without earning a commensurate return. The logic is as simple as net present value: if money were free, people would squander it more. When risk is free, it is also squandered. Nonbanks also need measures of the cost of risk, although the measures may be different.

The risk-based performance measurement process is designed to ensure that managers take risk prudently, by reflecting the cost of risk in assessments of their performance, and thereby affecting their compensation.

MEASURING AND REPORTING RISK

If risk is the threat of an adverse outcome, that threat should be measured against the corporation's business objective. If the business objective is to "maximize shareholder value," then the logical risk measure is the potential reduction in share price. If the business objective is to "maximize earnings while keeping an investment grade rating," then the appropriate risk measures are "earnings at risk," a probabilistic statement of how bad earnings can get, and the probability of a ratings downgrade.

Many corporations report their risks in terms of value-at-risk or, worse, Greek letters such as sigma (standard deviation) and delta (sensitivity to a pricing benchmark). Best practice firms report their risks not only in financial terms that senior managers can understand easily, but also in terms that map directly into financial goals.

TREASURY

A company's treasury usually has the best opportunity to manage risk, since it deals mostly with issues related to interest rates and foreign exchange. A treasury risk policy that requires 100% hedging may be at odds with corporate objectives. For example, a large corporation with little debt probably does not need to worry about whether its debt is financed on a fixed or floating basis. Since floating debt is usually cheaper, it may be better not to hedge. The same thing is true of foreign exchange. If the risks are small relative to the company, the question should be asked if hedging is necessary.[1] If the risks are large, hedging may be justified.

Other treasuries trade quite a lot within their hedging boundaries, creating a pocket of speculative activity within the firm. Unless the firm can demonstrate a core competence in trading foreign exchange, this does not usually contribute positively to corporate objectives.

PROCUREMENT AND BUDGETING

Fixed price budgets are the classic example of a procurement risk management policy that may be inconsistent with corporate risk policy. Budgets create the artificial incentive to hedge regardless of the cost of doing so, as long as the realized price is within budget. Other procurement policies have to do with portfolio price risk management of the company's factors of production. This subportfolio of the company must also be managed in a way that is consistent with overall corporate objectives.

The other major procurement risks include supplier performance, often modeled as a credit risk, and supply chain management, usually modeled as an operational risk. By establishing a cost of risk at the corporate level, a procurement division can make intelligent choices about which risks to take, which risks to manage, and how to manage them most efficiently.

Risk problems in procurement and budgeting can be best demonstrated in the accompanying case study.

MARKETING AND SALES

While most companies are well aware of the credit risk in their receivables, they are usually less aware of the risks in their sales contracts. For example, a product warranty creates a potentially costly obligation for the company that needs to be considered in product pricing. That calculation should include not only the expected warranty service costs, but also consideration for the risk that warranty claims may be much higher than expected.

Other sales contracts may be inadvertently giving away valuable options:
- renewal options (at the same price);
- cancellation options;
- options to increase or decrease purchase quantities;
- options to match price (for example, a most-favored nation clause);
- requirements to post collateral (financial products);
- options for additional free services.

In many environments, salespeople are rewarded on the basis of revenue. Hence, they are loath to cut price. An alternative for many of them is to continue to "throw in options" until the deal gets done, hoping they will never be valuable, but running that risk for the company. They are hoping those risks will never be quantified or attributed to the sales group.

Best practice risk management in marketing prices the various contract features considering both expected losses and risks, and charges the

Integrated Corporate Financial Risk Policy

sales department for the costs of the options it gives away.

RISK-BASED PERFORMANCE MEASUREMENT

The common theme in all the corporation's departments is that if risk has no cost, departments should not be penalized for taking it (as with the case study). If risk has a cost, it should be quantified and charged to the department to make sure they take risk only when it is appropriate (as with the marketing example). Policies that require minimizing risk are usually inappropriate (such as the treasury example), since that is not the corporate objective.

The risk-based performance measure for a company that measures risks relative to earnings would be:

Department's contribution to earnings over benchmark
− (Earnings-at-risk department contribution
× Cost of earnings risk)

For example, if a procurement is expected to cost 25 cents per share in earnings, has the risk of going up to 30 cents per share, but ends up costing 24 cents per share, its earnings contribution is 1 cent, its earnings-at-risk contribution is 5 cents, and its performance measure (assuming cost of risk of 25%) is −0.25 cents per share. If the department can cut its risk in half at no cost, its contribution is +0.38 cents per share. This performance measure gives explicit guidance on procurement risk management, and rewards procurement for finding a way to reduce risk.

Finally, risk-based performance measurement systems, like any performance measurement systems, invite abuse from those whose compensation depends on those systems. Care must be taken in the design of these systems to reduce or eliminate the risk of "gaming the system."

OVERALL HEDGING POLICY

Many firms prefer to manage their risks in silos, with separate departments for insurance risk, treasury risk, procurement risk, and pensions. This has the benefit of putting decision author-

---

CASE STUDY

A large multinational corporation operates a distribution facility in Puerto Rico. The facility maintains automobiles and light trucks, requiring the use of significant amounts of diesel over the year. The price of diesel is determined by a local index that fluctuates roughly along the lines of US gas prices. The company's procurement officer has a budget to meet for the year, and will not meet his target if diesel prices increase over the year. He has two alternatives: to try to fix a price with a small distributor, or to try to hedge the price using market derivatives. What should he do?

Answer: First, since this is a large corporation, it is likely that it does not need to manage this risk. In other words, the costs of managing risk are probably greater than the benefits. The only driver for hedging is the policy that affects the procurement officer's compensation. Therefore, the procurement officer should seek a solution whereby his budget is adjusted in line with the changes in diesel prices; if diesel prices go up $0.50, his budget should go up as well. His budget should drop if diesel prices fall, so he is not rewarded for a windfall outside his control.

Regarding the hedging methods, both are problematic. By fixing the price with a small distributor, he may be using his market clout to put the distributor in jeopardy, since the distributor may have to take the deal and will not be able to hedge. Since there are not many diesel distributors in Puerto Rico, this may not be wise, since the distributor could go bankrupt. By hedging the price with derivatives, the procurement officer will see increased trading costs, including risk of rogue trading, margining, and counterparty credit risk.

---

ity where the expertise lies, and can improve execution of policy. However, the cost is that the departments may have different objectives and may manage risk in inconsistent ways.

Some firms establish a single central hedging authority that takes ownership of all the departmental risks and decides how to hedge those risks at the portfolio level for the benefit of the company. This process tends to ensure that small risks are not managed, but large risks that cross department lines are actively measured and managed.

CONCLUSION

Risk management policy is more than a risk control policy. It sets out defined threats to corporate objectives, measures threats relative to the financial indicators that define success, and ensures consistent interpretation and pricing of risk throughout the company. A widely used measure at financial institutions is RAROC or something similar. A corporation's choice of risk measure and cost will depend on its particular circumstances.

Approaches to Enterprise Risk Management

MAKING IT HAPPEN
- Determine if risk is a scarce resource for your company.
- If it is, seek to identify risks in all parts of the firm.
- Risks are often hidden in contracts, procurement, budgeting, marketing, sales, and even risk mitigation.
- Put a cost on risk to facilitate a culture of smart risk-taking.

MORE INFO
Books:
Many good books specialize in enterprise risk management for financial institutions, but there are few titles available on enterprise risk for corporations generally.

Chew, Donald H. (ed). *Corporate Risk Management*. New York: Columbia University Press, 2008.
Damodaran, Aswath. *Strategic Risk Taking: A Framework for Risk Management*. Upper Saddle River, NJ: Wharton School Publishing, 2008.
Smithson, Charles W. *Managing Financial Risk: A Guide to Derivative Products, Financial Engineering, and Value Maximization*. 3rd ed. New York: McGraw-Hill, 1998.

NOTES
1 Copeland, Thomas E., and Yash Joshi. "Why derivatives don't reduce foreign exchange risk." *McKinsey Quarterly* (February 1996): 66–79.

Internal Auditors and Enterprise Risk Management by Ian Fraser

EXECUTIVE SUMMARY
- Organizations should implement effective risk management as a component of good corporate governance.
- Internal audit has a natural affinity with risk due to its centrality to audit and auditor expertise in monitoring and systems review.
- The key issue for determination is the parameters of the internal audit responsibility in the risk management area. Is internal audit best focused on a monitoring and review role, or might this extend to risk identification and the establishment of risk management systems?
- There is no one "best-fit" solution, and much will depend on organizational size, safeguards to protect objectivity, and the range and scope of available internal auditor expertise.

INTRODUCTION
Traditionally, internal auditors have been "policemen," and their efforts have been concentrated on the more detailed, and arguably less appealing, aspects of financial auditing within organizations. Often, therefore, internal auditors have been regarded in the past as the poor relations of their external auditor cousins. This no longer applies, however, as the purpose of many internal audit functions has evolved over time.

From a concern with (arguably) low-level financial audit, internal auditors have progressed to systems audit and an involvement with economy, efficiency, and effectiveness (the 3Es), to their contemporary focus on enterprise risk management. I generalize here, of course; not every internal audit function in every organization has been involved with each of these areas. In the public sector, for example, there has tended to be more involvement with the 3Es. This chapter is concerned with the internal audit role in connection with how enterprises manage risk.

INVOLVEMENT OF INTERNAL AUDIT WITH RISK
To an extent, the traditional role of internal auditors in connection with financial auditing gave them an initial knowledge base with which to get involved with risk management. Financial auditing has a concern with the risk of financial misstatement, whereas (although this burden falls primarily on the external auditors) audit risk is primarily concerned with the risk of issuing a wrong opinion on the financial statements. The recent external audit phenomenon of business risk auditing has pinpointed that effective financial audit (whatever the ostensible audit methodology employed) has to engage with business risks. The rationale for the latter assertion is, of course, that entity business risks, of whatever nature, ultimately affect the risk of misstatement in the financial statements. There is, therefore, a clear link between business risk and audit risk.

Thus, in one sense, it is natural for auditors (whether internal or external) to be concerned with the management of risks within organizations. External auditors tend to be involved with organizations on an occasional, rather than an ongoing, basis, and so it is difficult for them to have anything other than a relatively superficial appreciation of the business risks. Indeed, this is a valid criticism that has been made of "business risk auditing" as an external audit methodology. Arguably, therefore, there is a ready-made role for internal auditors in connection with risk.

Undoubtedly, however, the UK Turnbull Report (henceforth "Turnbull") on corporate governance was an important catalyst in the process of involving internal auditors with risk management. The Turnbull emphasis on the adoption by corporations of risk-based approaches to the establishment of internal control systems, and on the subsequent monitoring of these systems' effectiveness, created a role for high-level monitoring agencies within organizations. Internal audit functions were the clear beneficiaries of this, and Turnbull provided an opportunity for internal auditors to align their work to real business issues and to make an impact at board level. There was a clear opportunity for internal auditors to enhance their (in many cases) erstwhile humble status and to expand their jurisdiction as a professional interest group.

Approaches to Enterprise Risk Management

THE INTERNAL AUDIT RISK ROLE—WHAT SHOULD IT BE?

While it is now probably fairly uncontroversial to argue that internal auditors certainly have a role to play in relation to risk management, the parameters of the role are far less easily defined. Are internal auditors executive managers specializing in risk management, or, alternatively, are they concerned primarily with the monitoring of organizational risk management systems? There has certainly been a tendency, post-Turnbull, for internal audit functions to gravitate toward the former role. The intention of Turnbull, however, was primarily that the internal audit role should largely be focused on the evaluation of risk management and the monitoring of internal control effectiveness. While the post-Turnbull era has seen some companies assign ownership of risk management to internal audit, there is recognition of the pitfalls involved in this. With most internal auditors still receiving what is primarily a financial training, there may be a danger of non-financial risks receiving inadequate consideration.

There is also a real danger of internal audit departments losing their independent status within organizations if they evolve into risk management functions. There is evidence that when risk management initially became a priority for organizations, many internal audit heads were assigned responsibility for risk management audit. This, however, has not always been the case as distinct functions for internal audit and risk management have been established in some organizations.

CASE STUDY

Tonko—Shaping the Internal Audit Role through Experience

- Tonko is a large conglomerate group, with around 50,000 employees. It operates in several international geographies over several industrial sectors. Tonko is based in the United Kingdom and has had a strong internal audit function operating from the home country for around 25 years.
- The corporate governance and risk agendas of the 1990s saw the profile of risk management being enhanced significantly within the group, with responsibility for the area being given initially to the group's internal audit function. This appeared to be the natural home for risk management because of the prominence given to internal audit by Turnbull and by other authoritative corporate governance pronouncements. This worked well.
- Internal audit established business risk management systems and reporting mechanisms that flowed up from business units to divisions and ultimately fed into the group risk strategy. Internal audit carried out the usual monitoring role on these, making sure, first, that risks (and changes in these) were being reported on, and, second, that action was taken as appropriate.
- Internal audit also ran risk workshops at various levels to facilitate the identification of risks. Line management subsequently took action to control and mitigate the risks identified.
- Internal audit was involved in a two-way facilitation process. It was first ensured that business unit and divisional risk concepts and appetites were aligned with those of the group. At the same time internal audit made sure that lower-level concerns fed into the overall group risk evaluations and group risk register where appropriate.
- While this system worked quite well and could have continued indefinitely, some confusion was expressed about the internal audit role. It was unclear whether the internal auditors were acting as facilitators/risk identifiers or as monitors/assessors. There was also some loss of focus on basic controls in the work of internal audit.
- As a result a separate group of risk specialists was established with the remit of working with group business units and divisions in identifying risks and prioritizing them. Internal audit retained responsibility for the review and monitoring of risk management systems and for making sure that there was alignment of concepts and priorities at all group levels.
- It is not suggested that the Tonko experience is a template that should be followed by all organizations. Smaller entities, in particular, sometimes find that the combined approach works best. The size, and available skill set, of the internal audit function will be important determinants of the process.

In brief, the internal audit role might be summarized as: "The provision of objective assurance to corporate boards and senior management on risk management effectiveness; specifically, to ensure that key risks are managed appropriately

Internal Auditors and Enterprise Risk Management

and that internal control systems are operating effectively."

This is a general definition, though, and might be interpreted in various ways as far as the fine detail of responsibilities is concerned.

PROFESSIONAL GUIDANCE AND POTENTIAL DIFFICULTIES

The available professional guidance goes into more detail by emphasizing the distinction between the risk *management* and *monitoring* roles. The Institute of Internal Auditors (IIA), for example, suggests (in its position statement *The Role of Internal Audit in Enterprise-Risk Management*, available on the IIA website) that

within organizations, developing a risk management strategy for board approval, facilitating the identification and evaluation of risks, coaching management on responding to risks, coordinating ERM activities, consolidating the reporting on risks, maintaining and developing ERM frameworks."

It's when we come to this last category, however, that delineation of responsibilities may be unclear. This may be especially the case with the distinction between monitoring and advice by internal auditors on the one hand, and the exercise of a management role on the other. There has arguably been a tendency for some internal

MAKING IT HAPPEN

- Whatever the responsibilities of the internal audit (or, if it exists, risk management) function, the board has to get involved by setting the "risk appetite" of the organization and by assigning broad functional responsibilities.
- It's important that in a large or diversified organization individual divisions and business units feel involved in the process.
- It will generally be appropriate for internal audit, at a minimum, to be responsible for evaluating and monitoring risk management processes and for providing assurance on the adequacy of risk evaluation and reporting.
- *If* the independence and objectivity of internal audit are protected, and *if* the internal audit function has access to the appropriate range of expertise, *then*:
- The internal audit role might be extended to the facilitation of risk identification and the development of risk reporting frameworks.

internal auditors should be responsible for:
- "Providing assurance on the design and effectiveness of risk management processes, providing assurance that risks are correctly evaluated, evaluating risk management processes, evaluating the reporting on the status of key risks and controls, and reviewing the management of key risks, including the effectiveness of the controls and other responses to them."

But not for:
- "Setting the risk appetite, (the willingness of an organization to accept a defined level of risk), imposing risk management processes, providing assurance to the board and management, making decisions on risk responses, implementing risk responses on management's behalf, accountability for risk management."

The IIA suggests that internal functions may be responsible for the following functions as long as safeguards are put in place to protect internal independence:
- "Championing the establishment of Enterprise Risk Management (ERM)

auditors to assume more executive-type roles in the ERM area as a way of enhancing their professional jurisdiction. The Institute of Chartered Accountants in England and Wales (ICAEW) takes a broadly similar line to the IIA by emphasizing the internal audit role in assessing the various processes by which risks are *identified*, *managed*, *controlled*, and *reported*.

Overall there is certainly not one "easy-fit" solution. Various legitimate approaches to delineating responsibilities might be taken. For example, internal audit would normally be responsible for such functions as the evaluation and monitoring of risk management processes and controls. It would not normally be regarded as appropriate for internal audit to assume ownership of organizational risks or to set the risk appetite.

CONCLUSION

Effective risk management is a necessity for all organizations and is an important component of good corporate governance. Internal audit needs to be involved in the process—at a minimum it has an important role to play in the monitoring of risk management systems. In many cases

Approaches to Enterprise Risk Management

there may be sound arguments for extending this to functions such as developing reporting frameworks for risk management and facilitating the identification of risks. The size of the organization, independence safeguards, and the range of internal audit expertise are all important issues requiring consideration when determining the boundaries of external audit responsibilities.

MORE INFO

Books:
Fraser, Ian A. M., and W. M. Henry. *The Future of Corporate Governance: Insights from the UK*. Edinburgh, UK: Institute of Chartered Accountants of Scotland, 2003.
IFAC. *Enterprise Governance: Getting the Balance Right*. New York: Professional Accountants in Business (PAIB) Committee, International Federation of Accountants, 2004.
Pickett, K. H. Spencer. *Auditing the Risk Management Process*. Hoboken, NJ: Wiley, 2005.
Pickett, K. H. Spencer. *Audit Planning: A Risk-Based Approach*. Hoboken, NJ: Wiley, 2006.

Websites:
The Committee of Sponsoring Organizations of the Treadway Commission provides guidance on organizational governance, business ethics, internal control, enterprise risk management, fraud, and financial reporting: www.coso.org
Personal website by David M. Griffiths introducing risk-based internal auditing: www.internalaudit.biz
The Institute of Internal Auditors, for internal auditing standards and other professional pronouncements: www.theiia.org

Best Practices in Risk-Based Internal Auditing
by Sheryl Vacca

EXECUTIVE SUMMARY
- Agree on a common framework for the risk-based auditing and monitoring program.
- Assess risks across the enterprise and then prioritize them by looking at the likelihood of occurrence and impact for the organization.
- Develop a risk-based auditing and monitoring plan from the identified risk priorities.
- Execute a corrective action plan developed by management to mitigate risks and/or resolve risks.
- Assess the auditing and monitoring process for effectiveness.

GETTING STARTED
In designing risk-based auditing and monitoring activities, it is important that the internal auditor works closely with the organization's senior leadership and the board, or committee of the board, to gain a clear understanding of auditing and monitoring expectations and how these activities can be leveraged together to help minimize and mitigate risks for the organization. These discussions should also include leadership from the legal, compliance, and risk management functions, if they are not already a part of the senior leadership team.

This process should include performing periodic audits to determine compliance with respect to applicable regulatory and legal requirements, and to provide assurance that management controls are in place for the detection and/or prevention of noncompliant behavior. Additionally, risk-based auditing and monitoring should include mechanisms to determine that management has implemented corrective action through an ongoing performance management process to address any noncompliance.

Once the common framework for the risk-based auditing and monitoring program has been established, four key tasks must be performed:
1. Assessment and prioritization of risks, conducted enterprise-wide;
2. Development of a risk-based auditing and monitoring plan;
3. Execution of a corrective action plan developed by management to mitigate risks and/or resolve risks;
4. Periodic assessment of the overall process for effectiveness.

RISK ASSESSMENT
The Committee of Sponsoring Organizations of the Treadway Commission (COSO) helped to define "risk" as any event that can keep an organization from achieving its objectives.[1] According to the COSO model, risk is viewed in four major areas:
- operational (processes and procedures);
- financial (data rolling up to internal/external statements);
- regulatory (federal, state, local, organizational policy);
- reputation (institutional).

There are several ways in which risk assessments in these areas can be conducted. These include the use of:
- focus groups to assist in the identification of risks;
- interviews of key leadership and the board;
- surveys;
- reviews of previous audit findings, external audits conducted in the organization, and identifying what is occurring within the industry and the local market, etc.

Once risks have been identified, a prioritization process is needed to identify the likelihood of the risk occurring, the ability of management to mitigate risk (i.e. are there controls in place for risk, regardless of the likelihood of those risks of occurring?), and the impact of risk on the organization. Risk prioritization is an ongoing process and should include periodic reviews during the year to ensure that previous prioritization methods, when applied in real time, are still applicable for the risk.

It is important that senior leadership participate in, and agree with, the determination of the high-risk priorities for the audit and monitoring plan. This will ensure management buy-in and focus on risk priorities. Also, with managers involved at the development stage of the plan, they will be educated as to the type of activities being planned and the resources needed to conduct these activities. Hence, during the plan year, if there are changes, management will

Approaches to Enterprise Risk Management

understand the need for additional resources or a change in focus in the plan as the business environment and priorities may change.

DEVELOPING THE PLAN

The International Standards for the Professional Practice of Internal Audit (IIA), Standard 2120 says "The internal audit activity must evaluate the effectiveness and contribute to the improvement of the risk management processes."[2]

This is done through the development and execution of the risk-based auditing and monitoring plan.

Risk assessments and prioritization are important elements in the development of your risk-based auditing and monitoring plan. Considerations related to the plan should also include:

- Review of other business areas in the organization which may be conducting an audit or monitoring activity in this area:
  - If so, could you leverage this resource for assistance in completing the stated activity, or utilize their activity and integrate the results into the overall plan?
- Resources available to implement the plan:
  - Do you have the appropriate resources for the subject matter as needed within your department? (If not, is there subject matter expertise somewhere else in the organization?)
  - If subject matter requires outsourcing, budget considerations and overall risk priorities may need to be re-evaluated.
- Hours needed to complete the plan.
- Projected timeframes.
- Defined auditing or monitoring activities and determination as to whether they are outcome or process oriented.
- Flexibility incorporated into the plan to address changes in risk priorities and possibly unplanned compliance risks/crises which may need an immediate audit or monitoring to occur.

IIA Standard 2120.A1 identifies the focus of the risk assessment process: "The internal audit activity must evaluate risk exposures related to the organization's governance, operations, and information systems regarding the:

CASE STUDY

Scenario: An organization with multiple businesses in several geographic locations is conducting an enterprise-wide risk assessment. It is noted during the risk assessment that, due to recent financial losses, the organization is going through a consolidation of business units and reduction in workforce. This has been identified as a high-risk priority area for the auditing and monitoring plan for the next fiscal year.

In planning the audit on the risk area of business consolidation, the following considerations should be included:

- The business consolidation could be impacting the organization in various ways—customer base loss, reduced finances, loss of reputation, loss of workforce resulting in loss of controls, etc.
- The risk-based audit will focus on areas of greatest impact: loss of controls in financial areas due to the reduction in workforce.
- The timing of the audit will be negotiated to bring the most value to the organization. This might involve having a two-part audit. Part I could take place after the business consolidation and reduction in workforce have occurred. This would include assessing the consolidated business unit to determine if there are any gaps in the financial controls. For instance, segregation of duties is commonly found in situations with loss of people and consolidation of functions. Any gaps identified would become actions for management to correct before the Part II audit took place.
- Management may also want to set up its own monitoring system to ensure that its corrective actions have resolved any of the gaps identified.
- Part II of the audit would occur after a negotiated period of time with management and would allow the corrective actions to have been in place long enough for their effectiveness to be determined.

The overall purpose of this type of risk-based auditing is to work with management in "real time," to add value to the organization in regard to its strategic and best business interest, and to provide input on processes before they become "fixed." After management believes it has the "fixes" in place, then the second part of the audit will help to provide assurances that the risks identified are no longer risks and that no new gaps or lack of controls have developed around the process of business consolidation and reduction in workforce.

Best Practices in Risk-Based Internal Auditing

- Reliability and integrity of financial and operational information;
- Effectiveness and efficiency of operations;
- Safeguarding of assets;
- Compliance with laws, regulations, and contracts.

The process of risk assessment continues through the execution of the plan where the engagement objectives would reflect the results of the risk assessment. Risk-based auditing and monitoring is ongoing and dynamic with the needs of the organization.

EXECUTION OF THE PLAN—MAKING IT HAPPEN

Each activity should have a defined framework which will provide management with an understanding of the overall expectations and approach as you execute the plan. The framework for your activities should include the following actions:

- Set the purpose and goal for the activity (audit or monitoring):
  - Identify the scope from the purpose or goal, but make sure that it is objective, measurable, and concise.
  - Before conducting activities in high-risk priority areas, it is important to consider whether legal advice may be needed in establishing the approach to the activity.
- Conduct initial discussion with the business area for input related to audit attributes, timing, and process:
  - Concurrent vs retrospective status may be determined at this point. (Concurrent is "real time" and before the end point of what you are looking at has occurred. Retrospective is after the end point has occurred, i.e. the claim has been submitted or the research has concluded, etc. Milestones should be determined for rationale as to how far back to go, for example, new law, new system, etc.).
- Finalize the approach and attributes:
  - Sampling methodology will be determined largely by the scope (purpose and goal) of your activity. For example, the sample used in self reporting a risk area to an outside enforcement agency may be predetermined by the precedent that the enforcement agency has set in industry; to determine if education is needed in a risk area, a small sample only may be needed, etc.
  - Consider the audience frame of reference that will receive the results of activity, and then develop an appropriate format for reporting.
- Conduct the activity.
- Identify preliminary findings and observations.
- Provide an opportunity for findings and observations to be validated by the business area.
- Finalize the report.
- Identify processes for the follow-up after management has taken corrective action related to activity findings and observations.
  - Data collection and tracking are critical because they provide trend analysis and measurement of progress.
- Determine the key points of activity that may be provided to leadership and/or in reporting to the board.

MAKING IT HAPPEN

The development of an effective risk-based auditing and monitoring program includes several key elements:
1. Performing an enterprise-wide risk assessment that includes operational, financial, regulatory, and reputational risk (1-IIA).
2. Prioritizing risks identified through measures such as likelihood and impact for the organization.
3. Developing a risk-based auditing and monitoring plan from the identified risk priorities.
4. Determining that corrective action plans which have been developed by management to mitigate priority risks or ensure controls are in place to lower the risk level for the organization.
5. Conducting follow-up activities that validate, monitor, or audit corrective actions to mitigate and/or resolve the identified risks.
6. Re-evaluating risks on an annual basis through a risk assessment process to ensure that the priority risks of the organization have been addressed.
7. Conducting a periodic third-party review of the risk-based auditing and monitoring plan to assess whether:
   a. processes are in place to identify risks;
   b. appropriate resources are utilized to audit and/or monitor risks;
   c. a commitment to reinforcing the need for management to execute plans to mitigate risks is demonstrated by the board and senior management.

Approaches to Enterprise Risk Management

The overall process of developing the audit and monitoring plan should be documented. This would include a description of how the risk assessment was conducted and the methodology for prioritization of risks. Working papers to support the audit findings, reports, and corrective action plans should be documented and filed appropriately. Prior to the audit activity, be sure to define and document what should be considered as part of the working papers.

At the end of each plan year, it is important to conduct an evaluation of the overall effectiveness of the plan. Questions to consider may include:
- Was the plan fully executed?
- Were appropriate resources utilized for the plan's execution?
- Were the activities conducted in a timely manner?
- Did the plan "make a difference" in regard to the organization's strategy and business?
- Did the plan reach the goal of detecting, deterring, and/or preventing compliance research risks from occurring?

Annual evaluations may be conducted through self reviews or independently of the internal audit function by a third party, i.e. peer review conducted with auditors from other organizations, Quality Assessment Review conducted according to IIA standards (every 5 years), etc. However, while self reviews are less resource intensive, it is recommended that a independent review be conducted at least every other year to assess the effectiveness of your auditing and monitoring efforts. Figure 1 helps to identify the benefits of an effectively executed risk-based auditing and monitoring plan.

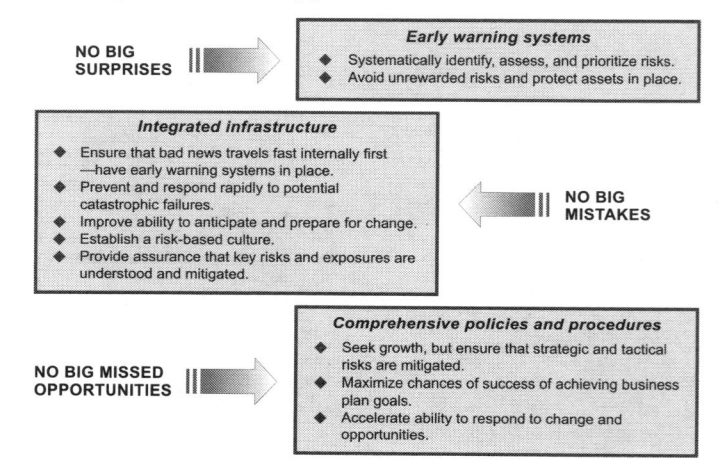

In summary, effectiveness in the development and execution of the risk-based audit and monitoring plan will be determined by the integrity and characteristics of the overall audit and monitoring process. Effective audit and monitoring activities will assist in the identification of weaknesses in controls, management's action to correct those weaknesses, and follow-up to ensure that timely mechanisms have been put in place to strengthen controls for mitigating the business risks. Additionally, risks will be detected, deterred and/or prevented with effective auditing and monitoring activities.

Figure 1. Benefits of an effectively executed risk-based auditing and monitoring plan

NO BIG SURPRISES → **Early warning systems**
- Systematically identify, assess, and prioritize risks.
- Avoid unrewarded risks and protect assets in place.

Integrated infrastructure ← **NO BIG MISTAKES**
- Ensure that bad news travels fast internally first—have early warning systems in place.
- Prevent and respond rapidly to potential catastrophic failures.
- Improve ability to anticipate and prepare for change.
- Establish a risk-based culture.
- Provide assurance that key risks and exposures are understood and mitigated.

NO BIG MISSED OPPORTUNITIES → **Comprehensive policies and procedures**
- Seek growth, but ensure that strategic and tactical risks are mitigated.
- Maximize chances of success of achieving business plan goals.
- Accelerate ability to respond to change and opportunities.

Best Practices in Risk-Based Internal Auditing

MORE INFO

Websites:
Federal Sentencing Guidelines, Chapter 8. US Sentencing Commission's webpage's at www.ussc.gov/general.htm (history and overview of the guidelines) and www.ussc.gov/GUIDELIN.HTM (guidelines and manuals). Chapter 8's provisions can be found at www.ussc.gov/2004guid/tabconchapt8.htm
General Accounting Office (GAO): www.gao.gov
Institute of Internal Auditors: www.theiia.org
Public Company Accounting Oversight Board (PCAOB): www.pcaobus.org
Sarbanes–Oxley Act 2002: www.soxlaw.com
Securities and Exchange Commission: www.sec.gov
Society of Corporate Compliance and Ethics (SCCE): www.corporatecompliance.org

NOTES

1 The Committee of Sponsoring Organizations of the Treadway Commission. *Enterprise Risk Management Framework: Draft (2003)*. Published in 2004 as *Enterprise Risk Management—Integrated Framework* and available from www.coso.org

2 Institute of Internal Auditors. *Professional Practice Standards*. 2120—Risk Management, Section A1. January 2009.

Implementing an Effective Internal Controls System by Andrew Chambers

EXECUTIVE SUMMARY
- Effective internal control gives reasonable assurance, though not a guarantee, that all business objectives will be achieved. It extends much beyond the aim of ensuring that financial reports are reliable. It includes the efficient achievement of operational objectives and ensuring that laws, regulations, policies, and contractual obligations are complied with.
- There is growing appreciation that effective internal control does not evolve naturally. It requires concerted effort on an ongoing basis.
- Often initially stimulated by the requirements of the Sarbanes–Oxley Act (2002), many more businesses are now systematically documenting, testing, evaluating, and improving their internal control processes. We show how to do this.
- In a large organization this more rigorous focus on internal control is likely to encourage greater standardization of similar processes in use in different parts of the organization.
- More effective internal control does not necessarily cost more. Aside from reducing costly risks of avoidable losses and business failures, it is often no more costly to organize business activities in ways that optimize control.
- Better internal controls may enable a business to engage safely in more profitable activities that would be too risky for a competitor without those controls.

INTRODUCTION
In some jurisdictions law or regulation may require effective systems of internal control, with serious penalties for irresponsible failure. The Sarbanes–Oxley Act (2002) requires CEOs and CFOs of companies with listings in the United States to certify their assessment of the effectiveness of internal control over reported disclosures (s302) and financial reporting (s404), with penalties of up to $1 million and ten years imprisonment for unjustified certification, or up to $5 million and 20 years imprisonment for wilful breach of the requirements (s906). The Public Companies Accounting Oversight Board's Auditing Standard No. 5 (2007) requires the company's external auditors themselves to assess the effectiveness of their client's system of internal control over financial reporting, in order to meet the audit requirements of s404 of the Sarbanes–Oxley Act.

Japan and Canada have laws broadly similar to the Sarbanes–Oxley Act. Although not reinforced by the risk of criminal sections, provision C.2.1 of the The UK Corporate Governance Code (2010) requires that the board of a company listed on the main market of the London Stock Exchange should satisfy itself that appropriate systems are in place to identify, evaluate, and manage the significant risks faced by the company; and provision C.2.2 requires that the board should, at least annually, conduct a review of the effectiveness of the group's system of internal controls and should report to shareholders that they have done so. The review should cover all material controls, including financial, operational, and compliance controls, and risk management systems. In addition, the UK Financial Services Authority's Disclosure and Transparency Rule DTR 7.2.5 R requires companies to describe the main features of the internal control and risk management systems in relation to the financial reporting process (see Schedule C).

WHAT "EFFECTIVE" MEANS
Although similar requirements exist in many countries, the principal driver for implementing an effective internal controls system should be the enlightened self interest of the company.

Effective internal control is intended to give reasonable assurance of the achievement of corporate objectives at all levels. An internal control framework should be used for the design and evaluation of an internal control system. The COSO framework is the most widely applied of three published frameworks.[1] COSO (the Committee of Sponsoring Organizations of the Treadway Commission) defines internal control as follows:

"Internal control is broadly defined as a process, effected by the entity's board of directors, management and other personnel, designed to provide reasonable assurance regarding the achievement

Approaches to Enterprise Risk Management

of objectives in the following categories:
1. Effectiveness and efficiency of operations.
2. Reliability of financial reporting.
3. Compliance with applicable laws and regulations."

Other definitions of internal control categorize the objectives of internal control differently, but fundamentally, effective internal control gives reasonable assurance that all of management's objectives will be achieved. For instance, the King Report (2002)[2] defined internal control as follows:

"The board should make use of generally recognized risk management and internal control models and frameworks in order to maintain a sound system of risk management and internal control to provide a reasonable assurance regarding the achievement of organizational objectives with respect to:
1. Effectiveness and efficiency of operations;
2. Safeguarding of the company's assets (including information);
3. Compliance with applicable laws, regulations and supervisory requirements;
4. Supporting business sustainability under normal as well as adverse operating conditions;
5. Reliability of reporting;
6. Behaving responsibly towards all stakeholders."

Before a conclusion can be reached that internal control is effective, both *results* and *processes* must be considered. For the former, the test is whether there have been any known outcomes attributable to significant breakdowns in internal control. Absence of these does not lead automatically to the conclusion that internal control is effective: it is possible that there may have been breakdowns of internal control yet to be discovered; it is also possible that serious weaknesses exist within the system of internal control that have not yet been exploited. So the second test must also be applied, which is to assess the quality of the control processes or "components."

DESIGN CHARACTERISTICS OF AN EFFECTIVE INTERNAL CONTROLS SYSTEM

The COSO internal control framework recognizes five essential components of any effective internal control system:
- The control environment: Values and culture; tone at the top; policies, organizational structure.
- Information and communication: Reliability, timeliness, clarity, usefulness.
- Risk assessment: Identification, measurement, and responses to threats.
- Control activities: Procedures followed for a control purpose.
- Monitoring: Review of internal control arrangements.

A common failing in designing and evaluating a system of internal control is to focus almost exclusively on control activities, vitally important though they are, overlooking that the other components are also essential. The Securities and Exchange Commission's rule for management's implementation of s404 of the Sarbanes–Oxley Act requires that a recognized internal control framework is applied. Usually it is the COSO framework that is used, and the framework comprises all of these five as being essential components of an effective system of internal control.

General hallmarks of an effective system of internal control include that controls:
- are designed to meet objectives which are clear;
- have regard to competitive issues;
- enable and ensure that performance is measured;
- aid the identification of risks;
- result in unsatisfactory performance being rectified;
- ensure that activities are completed in a timely way;
- mean the right people do the right jobs;
- are cost effective;
- are placed as early in the process as is practical, so that thereafter there is control;[3]
- specify and require appropriate authorization requirements;
- ensure there is an adequate audit trail;
- are "preventative" rather than merely "permissive";
- have no more movements, or steps than are necessary;
- are flexible to allow for adaptation;
- are documented.

Control activities can be categorized as follows:

Preventive controls: *To limit the possibility of an undesirable outcome being realized.* The more important it is that an undesirable outcome should not arise, the more important it becomes to implement appropriate preventive controls. Examples are when no one person has authority to act without the consent of another, or limitation of action to authorized persons (such as only those suitably trained and authorized being permitted to handle media enquiries).

Corrective controls: *To correct undesirable outcomes that have been realized.* Examples are the design of contract terms to allow recovery of

Implementing an Effective Internal Controls System

CASE STUDY 1

A multinational company took the requirement to comply with s404 of the Sarbanes–Oxley Act as an opportunity to assess the effectiveness of its internal control generally, not just internal controls over financial reporting.

First, the accounting processes that could lead to financial misstatements were identified. Second, mission-critical operational processes were identified where there were significant risks of not achieving business objectives and/or risks of misstatement. These accounting and operational processes were documented in process maps (flowcharts), using distinctive symbols to denote what were considered to be key s404 controls, other key financial controls, and key operational controls. These controls were described in a spreadsheet-based control register, supplemented where necessary by further process narrative. From this understanding of each process, deficiencies in control procedures were identified and corrected. Using predetermined, documented test scripts, each key control within a process was then tested for compliance prior to drawing a conclusion about internal control effectiveness of the process.

Initially this work was done by the internal audit function, before being transferred to become an ongoing responsibility of management, working to an annual cycle.

CASE STUDY 2

To be useful, process narrative on internal control must be sufficiently specific to indicate whether control is effective. In the three examples below, only the third is adequate. The reader of the first and second examples will be unclear as to whether it is merely the narrative that is inadequate, or that internal control is inadequate.

Control Documentation Poor

A report on duplicate invoices is produced before payments are made. It is looked at and approved by someone who plays no other part in the order-processing and invoicing procedures.

Control Documentation Average

Each day, before the payments processing run, the senior creditors clerk (SCC) investigates a report on possible duplicate invoices. The SCC signs and dates this report when the check has been completed, and sends the report to James Smith for second review and final approval. James signs and dates the report to indicate completion of his review and approval of the SCC's investigation.

Neither James nor the SCC has access to the purchase order or invoice-processing SAP modules or the manual parts of those subsystems.

Control Documentation Good

Daily, before the IT-based processing of payments, the SCC personally prints out a possible duplicate payments report from the payables module in SAP (SAP report code 9VDFZ3). This report may indicate five possible types of duplicate (refer to details in the process narrative).

The SCC investigates the possible duplicate invoices as indicated in the report by checking the accuracy of invoice data captured in the SAP accounts payable module against original invoices, making sure that each invoice is valid by reference to source documentation, such as purchase orders, as necessary.

The SCC has no responsibility for other elements of this system, not having any involvement in, or other access to, the processing of purchase orders or invoices—these access rights are blocked to the SCC by the accounts payable module.

When the SCC has completed the investigation, he signs and dates the possible duplicate payments report to indicate that the investigation has been completed. His manager then reviews the possible duplicate payments report, together with the relevant, supporting evidence and comments from SCC's investigation. If the manager is satisfied by the investigation and supporting evidence, he signs and dates the possible duplicate payments report to indicate approval of the SCC's investigation.

Approaches to Enterprise Risk Management

overpayment, or contingency planning for business continuity/recovery after events which the business could not avoid.

Directive controls: *To ensure that a particular outcome is achieved or an undesirable event is avoided.* Examples are a requirement that protective clothing be worn, or that staff be trained with required skills before working unsupervised.

Detective controls: *To identify undesirable outcomes "after the event."* Examples are stock or asset checks which detect unauthorized removals, or post-implementation reviews to learn lessons.

Performance controls: *To orientate and motivate the organization's people to focus on the achievement of targets that are appropriate for the achievement of objectives.* Examples are despatching all orders on the day of receipt of the order, or allowing that less than 2% of production should fail quality control checks.

Investigative controls: *To try to understand how the undesirable outcome occurred so as to be able to ensure that it does not happen next time, and to provide a route of recourse to achieve some recovery against loss or damage.*[4]

ASSESSING INTERNAL CONTROL EFFECTIVENESS

A widely followed approach to assessing and improving internal control effectiveness has been developed that comprises these steps (see case study 1):

1 Determine the documentation to be used, such as process maps (flowcharts), control registers, and process narratives.
2 Identify the objectives to be achieved.
3 Determine the processes that are key to the achievement of objectives.
4 Learn about each key process, documenting it in narrative, spreadsheet, and/or flowchart form.
5 Within a key process, identify and document the key controls.
6 Judge the potential of each key control to be effective, if followed as intended. Modify the control approach if necessary.
7 Design and document tests to be conducted to assess compliance with each control.
8 Conduct these tests.
9 Interpret the results of these tests. Where necessary, ensure better compliance or modify the control approach if satisfactory compliance is judged impractical.
10 Interpret the control significance of unwanted outcomes that have occurred.
11 Consider the adequacy of the control environment, information and communication, risk assessment, control activities, and monitoring.
12 Conclude on the effectiveness of internal control at the process level.

TESTING INTERNAL CONTROLS

The extent of testing is a compromise between the need for thoroughness and the testing resources available, and will vary according to the criticality of the controls that are being relied upon, the potential for the controls to be circumvented, and the results of initial testing. For controls designed to operate at intervals (such as at week, month, or year ends), initial sample

MAKING IT HAPPEN

The approach to follow:
1 Adopt and understand a recognized internal control framework.
2 Engage the board, management, and other personnel in the ownership of internal control.
3 Identify the mission-critical business processes.
4 Consider standardizing processes across the business.
5 Document those processes, highlighting the key controls.
6 Consider the effectiveness of the key controls and improve where necessary.
7 Design tests to confirm satisfactory compliance with key controls, and take remedial action as required.
8 In addition to control activities, consider whether the other essential components of an effective system of internal control are sound—for example, the control environment, information and communication, risk assessment, and monitoring.
9 Draw overall conclusions.
10 Use the results from this process as a continuous improvement tool to improve the internal control system.

Implementing an Effective Internal Controls System

Table 1. Sample sizes to be used if the control operates at the frequencies shown

Frequency of control	Sample size
Annually	1
Quarterly	2
Monthly	2
Weekly	5
Daily	20
Many times a day	25

Table 2. Sample sizes for transaction controls

Population size	Sample size
1–3	1
4–11	2
12–50	3
51–100	5
101–200	15
201–300	20
Above 300	25 max

sizes may be as in Table 1. For controls that apply to individual transactions Table 2 may be appropriate, which can also be used for interval controls that are used in multiple locations or on multiple occasions.

ONGOING MAINTENANCE OF AN INTERNAL CONTROLS SYSTEM

Changing business requirements will result in modified business processes and the risk that controls within those processes may be abandoned or made less effective. Each modified business process that is key to the achievement of a business objective should be reassessed, applying steps 3 to 6 (above), prior to releasing the new or modified business process for operational use.

For established processes, performance criteria should be established to monitor the quality of performance and the extent to which controls fail.

MORE INFO

Books:

American Institute of Certified Public Accountants (AICPA). *Internal Control over Financial Reporting: Guidance for Smaller Public Companies*. The Institute of Internal Auditors Research Foundation, 2006. Order from: www.theiia.org/bookstore

Chambers, Andrew. *Tolley's Internal Auditor's Handbook*. 2nd ed. London: LexisNexis Butterworths, 2009. See especially chapter 6.

Committee of Sponsoring Organizations of the Treadway Commission (COSO). *Internal Control—Integrated Framework*. 2 vols, 1992. Order from: www.coso.org/IC-IntegratedFramework-summary.htm

COSO. *Guidance on Monitoring Internal Control Systems*. 2009. See exposure/review link at: www.coso.org

Articles:

Sneller, Lineke, and Henk Langendijk. "Sarbanes–Oxley Section 404 costs of compliance: A case study." *Corporate Governance: An International Review* 15:2 (2007): 101–111.

Wagner, Stephen and Lee Dittmar. "The unexpected benefits of Sarbanes–Oxley." *Harvard Business Review* (April 2006). Online at: hbr.harvardbusiness.org/2006/04/the-unexpected-benefits-of-sarbanes-oxley/ar/1

Reports:

Canadian Institute of Chartered Accountants. A number of publications in the series *Control Environment—Guidance on Control*. Online at: www.rmgb.ca/publications/index.aspx

COSO. "Enterprise risk management—Integrated framework." 2004. Summary and print requests online at: www.coso.org/ERM-IntegratedFramework.htm

Financial Reporting Council (FRC), UK. "The Turnbull guidance as an evaluation framework for the purposes of Section 404(a) of the Sarbanes–Oxley Act." 2004. Online at: www.frc.org.uk/documents/pagemanager/frc/draft_guide.pdf

FRC. "Internal control: Revised guidance for directors on the Combined Code." October 2005. Online at: www.ecgi.org/codes/code.php?code_id=178. To be reviewed by the FRC in 2010.

HM Treasury, UK. "The orange book: management of risk—Principles and concepts." October 2004. Online at: www.hm-treasury.gov.uk/d/3(4).pdf

(Continued overleaf)

Approaches to Enterprise Risk Management

Reports (*cont.*):

The Institute of Internal Auditors. "Sarbanes–Oxley Section 404: A guide for management by internal controls practitioners." 2nd ed. January 2008. Online at: www.theiia.org/download.cfm?file=31866

Public Company Accounting Oversight Board (PCAOB). "Auditing standard no. 5: An audit of internal control over financial reporting that is integrated with an audit of financial statements." July 2007. Online at: www.pcaobus.org/Standards/Standards_and_Related_Rules/Auditing_Standard_No.5.aspx

Securities and Exchange Commission (SEC). "Commission guidance regarding management's report on internal control over financial reporting under section 13(a) or 15(d) of the Securities Exchange Act of 1934." June 2007. Online at: www.sec.gov/rules/interp/2007/33-8810.pdf. Subject to amendment issued August 2007: www.sec.gov/rules/final/2007/33-8809.pdf

Website:

Institute of Internal Auditors: www.theiia.org

NOTES

1 Other recognized internal control frameworks are the Canadian "CoCo" framework, and the United Kingdom's Turnbull framework.

2 King Report on Corporate Governance for South Africa (March 2002), "King II," Institute of Directors in Southern Africa. "King III Report and Code" (September 1, 2009) did not include this definition of internal control.

3 For instance, incoming cash should be controlled at the point and time of entry into the business.

4 The Institute of Internal Auditors Inc., (May 2009): Practice Advisory 2010-2: *Using the Risk Management Process in Internal Audit Planning*, para 4. The meaning PA 2010-2 gives to 'investigative controls' is not identical to the meaning we have given in this chapter.

The Effect of SOX on Internal Control, Risk Management, and Corporate Governance Best Practice by David A. Doney

EXECUTIVE SUMMARY
- The effect of the Sarbanes–Oxley Act of 2002 (SOX) has been dramatic and global. SOX enhanced the regulatory framework for investor protection and confidence.
- SOX has required or encouraged a variety of best practices related to management accountability, auditor independence, audit committees, internal control reporting, risk management, and improvement of financial processes.
- One of the important contributions of the regulatory guidance is the "top-down risk-based assessment," a robust framework for identifying and assessing financial reporting risks.
- Compliance approaches, benefits, and costs continue to evolve as practice and regulatory guidance change.

INTRODUCTION
The Sarbanes–Oxley Act of 2002 was passed in the context of a series of high-profile corporate scandals, a brief recession, and the events of 9/11. These factors were cited by President George W. Bush as a threat to investor confidence and the US economy overall. He also declared: "This law says to every dishonest corporate leader: you will be exposed and punished; the era of low standards and false profits is over; no boardroom in America is above or beyond the law."[1]

US Senator Paul Sarbanes stated that during the development of the law, a series of Senate hearings with experts from business, government, and academia resulted in a "remarkable consensus on the nature of the problems."[2] These included inadequate oversight of the accounting profession, conflicts of interest involving auditors and stock analysts, weak corporate governance procedures, inadequate disclosure rules, and insufficient funding for the Securities and Exchange Commission (SEC).

The SOX law, corresponding guidance from regulators, and evolving approaches to implementation have resulted in a variety of internal control, risk management, and corporate governance best practices.

HOLD MANAGEMENT ACCOUNTABLE
The law requires that the CEO and CFO sign certifications quarterly and annually attesting that they have reviewed the financial statements and (to their knowledge) believe them to be fair, accurate, and complete. Penalties for fraudulent certification are severe. This requirement has encouraged such best practices as:

- Disclosure committees: A cross-functional group of top-level managers that meets to discuss pending public disclosures, including quarterly and annual financial reporting.
- Representation letters: To support the certification by the CEO and CFO and ensure that material information is made known to them, a variety of senior finance and operations managers sign representation letters regarding financial reporting matters relevant to their areas of responsibility.
- Improvement of finance organization: Many companies expanded the number and quality of financial personnel, particularly with respect to US Generally Accepted Accounting Principles and SEC reporting requirements.

MAINTAIN AUDITOR INDEPENDENCE
Auditors are the primary watchdogs of the corporation. Prior to SOX, auditors performed significant consulting work for publicly traded companies ("issuers") that they audited. Further, auditors often moved into senior financial management positions in the client company. These factors created at least a perceived conflict of interest.

SOX prohibits auditors from providing many types of consulting services to issuers they audit The law also prohibits auditors from auditing an issuer if the issuer's CEO or top financial management worked for the audit firm during the past year.

EMPOWER THE REGULATORS
Prior to SOX, the audit industry was self-regulated. SOX also established the Public Company Accounting Oversight Board (PCAOB), a non-

39

Approaches to Enterprise Risk Management

profit, nongovernmental entity, to oversee the audit firms. The PCAOB sets standards and publicly discloses the results of its auditor reviews and any disciplinary action taken.

Critics also argued that the SEC, the regulator tasked with investor protection and corporate disclosure standards, was significantly underfunded and understaffed. The SEC budget was nearly doubled in the wake of SOX and remains at that level today.

of independence. Issuers are now required to disclose whether or not the audit committee has a financial expert, which has encouraged additional financial expertise on audit committees. Auditors are now required to provide more robust disclosures to the audit committee regarding alternative accounting policies and their discussions with management. Audit committees must also ensure the availability of an anonymous reporting channel for accounting or auditing

CASE STUDY
SIRVA, Inc.—Implementing a Top-Down Risk Assessment
SIRVA, Inc., is a decentralized global moving and relocation services company with revenues of $4 billion in 2007. Under new internal audit leadership in 2007, the company implemented a top-down risk assessment, new SOX compliance software, and brought the effort substantially in-house. This resulted in *annual* savings of over $3 million and brought costs into line with benchmark companies.

First, management completed a risk-ranking of each balance sheet account (and certain sub-accounts) to assess the risk of material misstatement. The ranking was also used to identify key process/location combinations ("processes"). For example, revenue and receivables might be significant (i.e. in-scope) for one location but not another.

Second, processes were risk-ranked. Higher-risk processes or topics included entity-level controls, period-end reporting, revenue, and key accounting estimates and judgments. Other transactional processes such as accounts payable, payroll, tax, and treasury were lower risk and received less assessment effort. Nearly 200 material misstatement risks (MMR) were documented by systematically considering key accounting policies and financial statement assertions for each process or account. Risks represented "what could go wrong" in relation to the account or assertion.

Third, the number of key controls tested was reduced from the prior year by 50% (from nearly 1,000 to 500) by including only those entity-level and transaction-level controls needed to address the MMR. In other words, specific risks determined which controls mattered, as opposed to merely large dollar balances, locations, or systems. Management assigned each control a risk-ranking of high, medium, or low. This ranking was based on a combination of account-specific and control-specific factors in the SOX guidance. Sample sizes used in testing were based on the ranking and the frequency of control operation.

Fourth, SOX compliance software was implemented to document the risks, controls, and tests. Comprehensive status and quality reporting was developed and discussed in weekly meetings with the global audit team and management.

Finally, multiple domestic general ledger systems were consolidated into one system. Further, two major operating platforms were consolidated into one, removing an entire financial process.

ENGAGE AUDIT COMMITTEES
Prior to SOX, former SEC Chairman Arthur Levitt stated that "qualified, committed, independent and tough-minded audit committees represent the most reliable guardians of the public interest."[3] The many scandals that resulted in SOX indicated that audit committees were not performing their financial oversight responsibilities effectively.

SOX mandated that the audit committee, rather than management, be accountable for the relationship with the auditor, including selection, compensation, retention, and review

matters (i.e. a "whistleblower hotline"). The law also expanded protection for whistleblowers and penalties for retaliation against them.

EVALUATE KEY FINANCIAL CONTROLS
The infamous SOX "Section 404" guidance requires both management and the external auditor to provide a report that includes an opinion regarding internal control over financial reporting (ICFR). This is additional to the traditional auditor's opinion on the accuracy of financial statements. It requires management to document and comprehensively test financial

The Effect of SOX on Internal Control

controls necessary to address "material misstatement risks."

Any controls that are assessed as not effectively designed (i.e. not capable of addressing the related risk, even if executed) or not operating effectively (i.e. not executed consistently) result in "deficiencies." More serious deficiencies are categorized as "significant deficiencies" or "material weaknesses" and must be reported to the external auditor and audit committee. Material weaknesses require public disclosure during the quarter in which they are identified and, if not remediated as of year-end, an unfavorable opinion on ICFR in the issuer's annual report.

The requirement to perform a comprehensive control assessment has resulted in several improvements in the art and science of financial management. For example, controls related to the "tone at the top," incentives, and conflicts of interest were often not formally assessed prior to SOX. Focus on effective controls has significantly improved. Further, the quality of the SOX assessment (for example, project management, technology use, risk assessment, and quality of presentation materials) is a good proxy for "tone at the top" in the organization and the process management skills of the finance team.

In the aftermath of SOX the focus of internal auditing efforts also shifted significantly to financial controls, as opposed to operational processes. Many issuers expanded the staffing and capabilities of their internal auditing teams to absorb incremental SOX responsibilities. The New York Stock Exchange (NYSE) listing standards now require that all listed companies have an internal audit function. Tracking deficiencies to resolution also establishes good discipline for internal audit follow-up of all issue types, as required by internal auditing standards.

MAKING IT HAPPEN

SOX regulations and implementation have provided a series of best practices to help companies improve risk, control, and governance, even if technically they are not required to comply.

- Identify and remove conflicts of interest that affect your business. These can involve auditors, management, the board, vendors, outside consultants, etc.
- Ensure that your external auditors and internal auditors are independent by having their continuing employment, performance rating, and compensation determined by the audit committee or board.
- Help to ensure that financial disclosures are transparent and fairly describe the organization's performance by using a disclosure committee and management representation letters.
- Insist on a robust top-down risk assessment of financial reporting processes. The extent of testing to perform (the primary cost-driver) can then be determined appropriately.
- Capture risk and control information in compliance database software. User-friendly software that can be customized and administered by non-IT personnel is available at very reasonable prices.
- Establish risk committees at the senior management and board level. These committees can direct risk management efforts and help the audit committee to focus on financial reporting matters.
- Develop reporting of operating metrics that are predictive of financial results and share it with the audit committee and board.
- Communicate periodically to the audit committee any significant deficiencies identified (financial or otherwise) and management's progress towards remediating them.
- Use the financial reporting effort and framework to initiate or improve an ERM program.

IMPROVE RISK MANAGEMENT

Pressure is increasing on businesses to improve risk management practices. This comes from a variety of sources, including regulators, credit rating agencies, and activist shareholders. Further, the subprime mortgage crisis which became apparent in 2007 has (arguably) exposed systemic risk management concerns.

The 2007 guidance from the SEC and PCAOB regarding SOX Section 404 established a comprehensive framework for conducting a "top-down" financial reporting risk assessment. For example, management is required to identify material misstatement risks and related controls, which then must be tested. (See the Case Study for details.)

Techniques used in top-down risk assessment are applicable to other risk categories. Under the COSO Enterprise Risk Management (ERM) framework, risks fall into strategic, operational,

Approaches to Enterprise Risk Management

legal/regulatory, and financial reporting categories. SOX compliance implies substantial coverage of financial reporting risks. The SOX compliance process also provides a framework that relates processes, risks, and controls, and the network of managers involved, which can be used to help establish an ERM program.

Many companies also use SOX-compliance database software, which may also be useful for retaining risk information to support an ERM program and as an internal audit workflow tool. For example, as internal audits are completed, the amount of risk and control information expands in such a database, across all risk types.

In response to increased expectations around risk, many audit committees have expanded their scope to include overall risk management. With SOX efforts addressing financial reporting risks, they can focus more attention on strategic and operational risks. Some issuers have also created board risk committees to address nonfinancial reporting matters.

IMPROVE FINANCIAL PROCESSES

The significant cost of the ICFR assessment required under SOX Section 404 represents a "tax" on inefficiency, providing additional incentives for process improvement. Redundant systems, processes, or locations generally require some type of incremental assessment, increasing the scope and cost of compliance. The Financial Executives International (FEI) survey of SOX 404 compliance costs in 2007[4] indicated that, for companies with average revenue of $4.7 billion, the costs in *decentralized* companies averaged $1.9 million, 46% higher than the $1.3 million in *centralized* companies. The difference is likely to be a fraction of the savings available from addressing the underlying process inefficiency.

In addition, manual control procedures involve substantially higher testing costs. For example, a manual control that operates daily may require a sample size of 30 to be evaluated by an expert. However, the same control if automated requires a sample size of just one and does not have to be evaluated each year if certain criteria are met. Leading companies track the number of manual versus automated controls and seek automation opportunities. Reducing the number of manual journal entries is another means of improving the reliability of financial statements and reducing closing-cycle time, while reducing both compliance and personnel costs.

Section 404 is one of the more contentious elements of SOX, due to the significant cost of compliance. According to a survey by FEI that included issuers with an average revenue of $4.7 billion, compliance costs were $1.7 million during 2007, or 0.36% of revenue. The total cost includes internal and external labor and auditor attestation fees.[5]

Compliance costs have continued to decline since 2004, when Section 404 became applicable for most issuers. The 2007 SEC and PCAOB guidance has provided management with additional flexibility in addressing risk and determining the timing, nature, and extent of testing procedures, further reducing costs.

CONCLUSION

SOX has resulted in dramatic changes in internal control, risk management, and corporate governance. Management and audit committees are more focused on financial reporting. The internal control and risk management best practices discussed above continue to evolve in practice. Companies continue to focus and reduce costs in their SOX 404 efforts through top-down risk assessment and compliance software, which have broader applications to other risk management efforts.

The Effect of SOX on Internal Control

MORE INFO

Book:
Farrell, Greg. *America Robbed Blind. How Corporate Crooks Fleeced American Shareholders (and How Congress Failed to Stop Them)*. Buda, TX: Wizard Academy Press, 2005.

Websites:
Committee of Sponsoring Organizations of the Treadway Commission (COSO): www.coso.org. For *Enterprise Risk Management—Integrated Framework (2004)*: www.coso.org/-ERM.htm
Institute of International Auditors (IIA): www.theiia.org. For *The International Standards for the Professional Practice of Internal Auditing*: www.theiia.org/guidance/standards-and-guidance
Public Company Accounting Oversight Board (PCAOB): www.pcaob.org
PCAOB Auditing Standard No. 5, "An audit of internal control over financial reporting that is integrated with an audit of financial statements and related independence rule and conforming amendments" (2007): www.pcaob.org/Rules/Docket_021/2007-05-24_Release_No_2007-005.pdf
Sarbanes–Oxley. The text of the Act can be found at: fl1.findlaw.com/news.findlaw.com/hdocs/docs/gwbush/sarbanesoxley072302.pdf
US Securities and Exchange Commission (SEC): www.sec.gov
"Commission guidance regarding management's report on internal control over financial reporting under Section 13(a) or 15(d) of the Securities Exchange Act of 1934." Interpretive guidance release 33-8810, etc. (2007): www.sec.gov/rules/interp/2007/33-8810.pdf

NOTES

1 Office of the Press Secretary, The White House. "President Bush signs corporate corruption bill" (Sarbanes–Oxley Act 2002): www.whitehouse.gov/news/releases/2002/07/20020730.html
2 Lucas, Nance. "An interview with United States Senator Paul S. Sarbanes." *Journal of Leadership & Organizational Studies* 11:1 (January 2004): 3–8.
3 Levitt, Arthur. "The numbers game." Speech dated September 28, 1998. Online at: www.sec.gov/news/speech/speecharchive/1998/spch220.txt
4 Financial Executives International (FEI). News release "FEI survey: Average 2007 SOX compliance cost $1.7 million." Online at: fei.mediaroom.com/index.php?s=43&item=204
5 *Ibid*. A complete cross-referenced index of SEC filers, audit firms, offices, CPAs, services, fees, compliance/enforcement actions, and other critical disclosure information can be found at: www.sarbanes-oxley.com

Enterprise Risk Management and Solvency II
by Andy Davies

EXECUTIVE SUMMARY
- The key components of ERM;
- The dangers of overcomplicating processes;
- How policies, risk strategy, and risk appetite are set;
- Capital allocation and management;
- The implications of Solvency II.

INTRODUCTION
There is a great deal that the insurance sector has to come to terms with as it addresses the implications of Solvency II. There are broad general questions such as: What does it all mean? How will it be achieved and its requirements met? How much will it cost both from a capital and a monetary perspective? What resources are required? Then there is the related issue of how the International Financial Reporting Standards will fit with Solvency II.

ENTERPRISE RISK MANAGEMENT: CULTURE IS THE KEY
Rating agencies, analysts, shareholders, and regulators are all taking more interest in capital models and enterprise risk management (ERM). Effective ERM acts as the common thread that links balance sheet strength, operating performance and business profile."[1]

In an ideal ERM model, the risk management group will work with the board and all employees to ensure that their organization has effective ERM. It is fair to say that the majority of companies today have some form of ERM, but it is also true that for many this is an area that needs further development.

ERM is not about finding the perfect model; it is about having a strong risk-management culture which ensures that risk is understood, controlled, and effectively communicated. Effective ERM should be part of an insurance company's DNA.

The key components of ERM are:
- Aligning risk appetite and strategy;
- Enhancing risk response decisions;
- Reducing operational surprises and losses;
- Identifying and managing multiple and cross-enterprise risks;
- Seizing opportunities;
- Improving the deployment of capital.

Management should consider the company's risk appetite in evaluating its strategy, setting objectives, and developing mechanisms to manage related risks. ERM provides the rigour to identify and select alternative responses to risk—such as risk avoidance, risk reduction, risk sharing, and risk acceptance. Through ERM, companies enhance their ability to identify potential events and establish responses, thereby reducing surprises and associated costs or losses.

Every company faces a variety of risks that affect different parts of the organization, and ERM facilitates effective responses to such multiple risks. By considering a full range of potential events, management can identify and proactively realize opportunities.

Finally, obtaining robust risk information allows management to assess overall capital needs effectively and enhance capital allocation.

ERM AND SOLVENCY II
Solvency II is based on three "pillars." Pillar 1 is about capital requirements and the triggers for supervisory action. Pillar 2 focuses on the supervisory activities of regulators, based on organizational and governance requirements. Pillar 3 covers additional disclosures that supervisors may need to carry out their regulatory function. Under Solvency II, the concept of an "internal model" effectively refers to an enterprise-wide risk management framework. It covers both the quantitative requirements of Pillar 1 and the organizational and governance requirements of Pillar 2.

The broad thrust of an internal model is to use an economic capital model, accompanied by the embedding and effective management of risk, driven from the board to the front line.

It is important to remember the context and immediate historical backdrop against which the insurance sector is working. It is undeniable, for example, that the industry has had problems with risk assessment and modeling in recent years. The 2005 hurricane damage payouts and the current credit crisis put significant stress

Approaches to Enterprise Risk Management

on capital and liquidity requirements for many companies. This makes discussion of capital adequacy regimes a very strong necessity, not just an academic exercise.

However, as insurance company boards try to square up to these issues—and there are many of them—there is a real danger of overcomplicating certain processes and of critical data being obscured by information overload. Having a complex model is no guarantee of success, as the crises experienced by several banks will testify. Instead, what is really critical is to ensure that the insurer's approach to risk management is simple enough for all staff to understand and engage with, and that it is also effective enough to add real value. The concept of "proportionality" is specifically enshrined within the proposed European Directive for Solvency II, so there is regulatory recognition that we do not need to over-elaborate.

Risk management will only be fully effective if people throughout the organization receive clear, consistent messages from leadership and understand what they need to do. It starts at the top, and senior management need to develop a unified view, common language, policies, and appropriate governance structures.

The recent testimony of Paul Moore, former head of Group Regulatory Risk at HBOS, makes clear the importance of culture in risk management. Moore commented that: "Being an internal risk and compliance manager at the time felt a bit like being a man in a rowing boat trying to slow down an oil tanker."[2] If the culture is wrong, then even the most sophisticated model will be ineffective.

Markel Corporation, the company for which I work, is a relatively small company with 400 employees.[3] It therefore has a very flat organization structure, enabling close interaction between board and employees. This is very helpful as all employees can be given clear and consistent messages in a common language. We are committed to creating an environment in which risk is managed effectively. The Markel style, which articulates our core values, includes statements that "we will build the financial value of our company," which implies a steady, cautious approach to risk, and "we are encouraged to challenge management...we have the ability to make decisions or alter a course quickly," which empowers discussions of strategy. As both US and UK management "walk the talk," this culture facilitates a risk-focused approach for all employees.

Figure 1 highlights that a clear articulation of risk strategy and risk appetite is an essential starting point in embedding risk management across an organization. These statements of corporate objectives act as the fundamental reference point against which all risk-taking and risk-mitigation activity within an organization should be benchmarked. They provide governance and define boundaries within which risk-based decision-making can occur, and provide a clear framework for the selection of one course of action over another.

Figure 1. Insurer of the future with integrated model

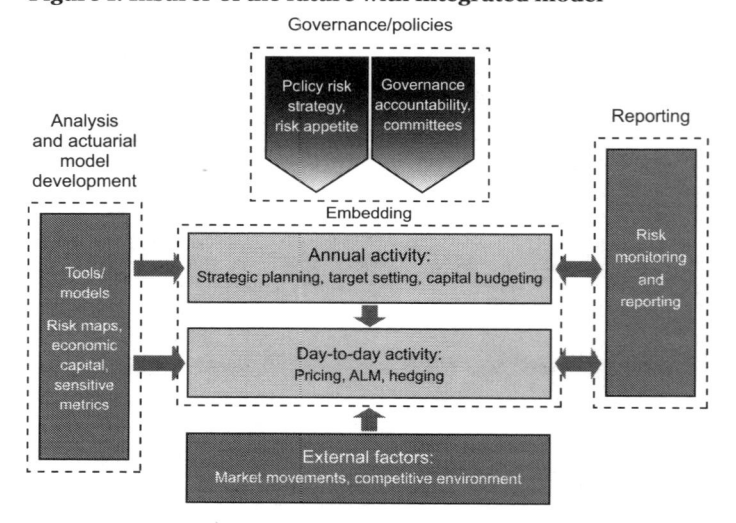

Enterprise Risk Management and Solvency II

Policies, risk strategy, and risk appetite are set at board level, and this is embedded into the annual and day-to-day activities of the business. These activities are analyzed through various risk maps, capital models, and sensitivity metrics. In addition, external factors such as market movements and the actions of competitors are communicated to the business. The model at Markel that is shown in Figure 2 splits the business into two components—underwriting and investing. As a consequence there are several key committees and meetings. These are:

- IBNR (incurred but not reported losses) and P&L meetings, at which all aspects of underwriting and reserving are discussed.
- Investment Committee meetings, where all aspects of the company's investment performance and strategy are discussed.
- And in the middle there are the Capital and Risk Committees, which look at the company's risk and capital management.

a crucial part of the business culture at Markel. They are used to identify lines of business that are not achieving profitability and required return on capital targets so that appropriate action can be taken at the earliest opportunity.

It is crucial that the results of all these meetings are embedded in the management and financial reporting and also in the capital management of the business.

Finally, the activities and results of the business are fed back to the board through effective risk management and reporting.

The results are a key driver in deciding the remuneration of underwriters. Part of our underwriters' remuneration is phased over a period of years, which thus provides a safeguard against underwriting strategies that appear profitable in the short term but ultimately deteriorate. The alignment of risk management with remuneration strategy is an essential part of the effective embedding of ERM.

Figure 2. Model used at Markel

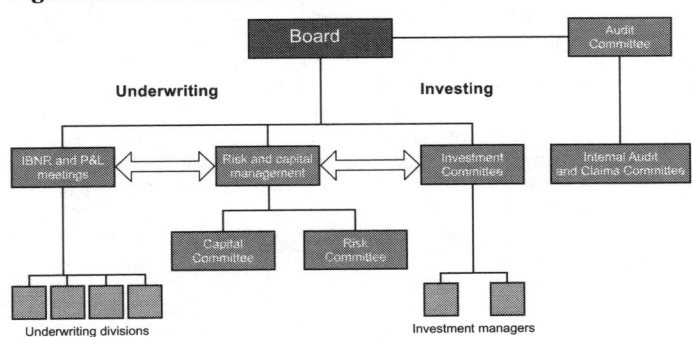

The IBNR and P&L meetings are crucial to the way Markel operates. A thorough and robust reserving process is the cornerstone of a successful organization. It is important that underwriters and management agree on the IBNR results as this ensures that there is one version of the truth. Having two sets of numbers causes confusion, wastes time, and results in poor decision-making.

The meetings need to be held on a consistent and regular basis. At Markel, IBNR meetings are held quarterly, and the P&L meetings are held on a monthly basis. The IBNR packs and P&L statements show the combined ratio and the required return on risk-adjusted capital by line of business. They include all allocated expenses so that the underwriters understand the full cost of writing their business.

The IBNR and P&L meetings are attended by senior management and underwriters and are

CAPITAL ALLOCATION AND MANAGEMENT

The standard model for the majority of companies in the United Kingdom today is a product of the Individual Capital Assessment (ICA) regime, introduced by the Financial Services Authority while it waited for Europe to refine and introduce Solvency II. The implementation of ICA has been a significant step forward in delivering more risk-based capital management and has gone a good way to help meet the challenges of Solvency II.

Figure 3 highlights that for a nonlife company the basic capital requirement is split into four risk categories:
- Insurance risk;
- Liquidity risk;
- Market risk;
- Credit risk.

Approaches to Enterprise Risk Management

Figure 3. Capital allocation

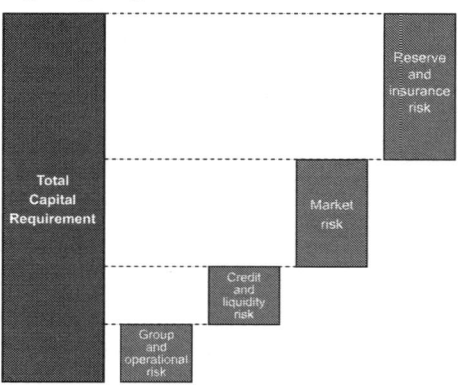

The capital assigned to these risk categories is used to produce the basic capital requirement of the company, and in most cases the capital required is calculated through a combination of stress and scenario tests and a capital model. Operational and group risk are added to the basic capital requirement to produce the company's total capital requirement.

Although this model has been successful in getting companies through the ICA regime, it will not be sufficient to meet the requirements of Solvency II. In addition, ICA models suffer from the fact that for the most part they have been developed and owned by the finance and actuarial departments in companies. As a consequence, there has been minimal embedding into the rest of the business. At Markel, our ICA process has always been multi-disciplined, with a number of stakeholders involved. However, we are embedding the process further. Individual members of the Capital and Risk Committee work with the board, underwriters, and investment managers to ensure that they understand the capital being allocated to them and the risk-adjusted returns required.

The key to effective capital management is to ensure:

- that it drives the decision-making process, ensuring optimal use of capital;
- that it is embedded into the business. It needs to be a key driver in strategy and planning, acquisitions, new lines of business, and legacy claims management. This is an area that needs a considerable amount of effort, but the benefits are considerable. This area is key to achieving the objectives of Solvency II;
- that people are rewarded by return on capital. People will take more of an interest if their bonuses are dependent on it, so ensure that the bonuses of underwriters and senior management are calculated by return on capital;
- that the model is transparent and well documented. Too many models act as a black box whose results cannot be explained;
- that financial and nonfinancial information used by the model and the capital management team is consistent with the information used by the business. Different information causes confusion, wastes time, and will result in poor decisions being made. An organization cannot have a model that operates with stand-alone information—it needs to be embedded into all aspects of the business.

The goal should be to minimize group and operational risk through effective ERM. A prudent approach is to have minimal appetite for credit and liquidity risk and a reasonable appetite for market risk.

The last and most significant risk is reserve and underwriting risk. A sound approach here is to split the capital required for reserve and underwriting risk into two components: prior-year reserve risk and current business risk. Here one allocates capital to cover the uncertainty on prior-year insurance reserves. Again, one can try to reduce this capital requirement by establishing prudent case and IBNR reserves so that reserves are more likely to be redundant than deficient.

Capital is also allocated to underwriting the current business. This capital is allocated to each product line, enabling management to set combined ratio targets that achieve the required return on risk-adjusted capital. These combined ratio targets will vary according to the volatility, length of tail, and reinsurance usage of the product line. In addition, the combined ratio target will take into consideration diversification with other classes of business.

The combined ratio targets are used to benchmark underwriting performance, and they act as a key driver in the setting of underwriter and management bonus targets.

WHAT ARE THE IMPLICATIONS OF SOLVENCY II?

The three-pillar approach of Solvency II works as follows. Pillar 1 deals with the quantitative capital requirements. It ensures that the valuation of assets and liabilities, and the calculation of capital requirements, are standardized. The areas covered are:

- Valuation of technical provisions;
- Minimum capital requirement;
- Solvency capital requirement;
- Investment rules

Enterprise Risk Management and Solvency II

Pillar 2 deals with the qualitative side of Solvency II and focuses on
- The principles of internal control and risk management;
- Individual risk and capital assessment;
- The supervisory review process.

Pillar 3 deals with disclosure requirements discipline and covers:
- Transparency and disclosure and the support of risk-based supervision through market mechanisms.

So what are the implications of Solvency II for capital management? Already we can see that there are problems.

Within Pillar 1 it is clear that the technical provision under Solvency II and International Financial Reporting Standards (IFRS) is calculated differently. This difference will be a potent source of confusion, additional cost, and wasted effort—and it needs to be resolved.

It is also clear that the communications effort required to implement Pillar 1 will not be trivial. How are the new technical provisions to be communicated and embedded in the business? How do you explain to underwriters that their loss ratio reflects discounting and a cost-of-capital adjustment? It took a long time for underwriters to understand combined ratios, so this will be a challenge.

The minimum capital requirement (MRC) set out in Solvency II fails to reward appropriate risk management due to its formulaic approach. It is also clear that in the majority of cases an internal capital model produces a lower solvency capital requirement, which means that there is a significant advantage to an organization in having its model approved. Finally, there are also significant implications for IT and data collection.

With Pillar 2 it is crucial that a company can demonstrate that it has effective ERM and that it is embedded in the business. Meeting the embedding or "use test" requires significant time and resources.

The main focus of Pillar 3 is disclosure, and therefore the implications of these disclosures need to be carefully thought through. These disclosures will include a report on:
- Governance and risk management;
- Valuation principles applied for solvency purposes;
- The internal model: methodologies, assumptions, and validation;
- Capital requirements, with an account of the company's minimum capital requirement and solvency capital requirement (SCR) and any breaches during the year, plus a breakdown of the SCR standard formula and internal model calculations.

CONCLUSION

So how does the road ahead look? It is clear that the sector has a number of challenges to overcome and that a period of hard work lies ahead. An effective ERM model, as we have argued throughout this piece, should be fundamental to any approach to implementing Solvency II and will, of itself, bring tremendous benefits to organizations that work to embed ERM in their organization.

MAKING IT HAPPEN
- A strong management culture will ensure that risks are understood, controlled, and effectively communicated. Effective ERM is a key driver in Solvency II.
- It is crucial that capital and risk management are embedded in the business. These are the DNA of an insurance company.
- Return on risk-adjusted capital should be a key driver in the remuneration of underwriters and management.
- Considerable resources and expense are still required to develop a fully integrated model; however, the capital benefits of doing so will be significant.

Approaches to Enterprise Risk Management

MORE INFO

Websites:
European Commission collection of documents on various aspects of Solvency II: ec.europa.eu/internal_market/insurance/solvency/index_en.htm
Financial Services Authority (FSA) section on Solvency II: www.fsa.gov.uk/pages/About/What/International/solvency/index.shtml
Solvency II Association training and presentations: www.solvency-ii-training.com

NOTES

1 AM Best. "Risk management and the rating process for insurance companies." January 25, 2008. Online at: www.ambest.com/ratings/methodology/riskmanagement.pdf
2 Paul Moore, HBOS, "Man in a rowing boat."
3 Markel International comprises the international operations of Markel Corporation, a US property casualty company listed on the New York Stock Exchange. It writes a variety of property, casualty, and marine insurance and reinsurance business through its two London-based platforms: Markel International Insurance Company and Markel Syndicate 3000.

Cultural Alignment and Risk Management: Developing the Right Culture
by R. Brayton Bowen

EXECUTIVE SUMMARY
- Organization culture may vary in definition from country to country, but it is essentially the sum total of the behaviors and styles of the people who drive the system.
- Organizations that properly align organization culture with business goals and objectives can realize up to 40% improvement in performance compared to peer and competitor organizations.
- Generally, 80% of acquisitions and mergers fail to perform to management's expectations, in most instances, because of a failure to understand and manage organization culture.
- Organizational members have an innate knowledge of what is and is not working within the culture of the organization and, therefore, must be engaged in the process of building the right culture.
- Culture changes within an organization require total mastery of the change management process.
- Organization culture ultimately impacts the financial performance and long-term success of an enterprise.

INTRODUCTION
The goal was to beat Microsoft at its own game. After rebuffing a takeover attempt by the giant corporation, Novell Nouveau went on an acquisition binge of its own. The strategy was to acquire a premier word-processing company that could rival Microsoft, and Microsoft's "Microsoft Word" in particular. So, in 1994, Raymond Noorda, CEO for the then second-largest software company, acquired WordPerfect Corp. for US$1.4 billion in stock. Novell was to become a "software powerhouse," delivering "stand-alone, software suites, groupware, and network applications that were to define new capabilities for information systems," according to WordPerfect's leading executive. Two years later, WordPerfect was sold for less than one-seventh of its original purchase price. The reason for the failed strategy: "The cultures were very, very different," as reported by Novell's successor CEO, Robert Frankenberg (*The Wall Street Journal*, 1996).

Taking the role of the dominator, management of Novell Nouveau assumed their ways and methods to be superior to those of WordPerfect. They eliminated the sales force, assuming the Novell Nouveau organization could assume the sales and marketing function, and went on to make a host of other mistakes. Indeed, their experience was similar to those of the majority of acquiring firms. Generally, 80% of acquisitions and mergers fail to perform to management's expectations, and the overarching factor in most instances is a failure to understand and manage organization culture.

ALIGNING ORGANIZATION CULTURES
What is Culture?
Culture can be thought of as the organizational context in which behaviors can be characterized and assessed. It is the environmental code that prompts people to act in certain ways to "fit in" at different levels and perform in "expected" ways. For example, customers entering a fine dining establishment understand they are expected to dress appropriately, deport themselves in a dignified manner, wait to be seated at an assigned table, and ultimately, pay a high price for the experience. Yet, there are usually no formal rules that are posted stating how guests are supposed to dress or how they are to behave. Once seated at their table with friends or other guests, they can adjust their behaviors to a more relaxed and interactive mode. This analogy equates to organizational cultures, wherein the overarching culture may prompt people to act one way, whereas once they settle into their own departments or business units, their behavior may change somewhat from the corporate norm. Bringing about change on an organization-wide basis requires considerable understanding of what is needed and why; and it requires superior change-management ability.

Elements of organization culture include: How people work together; how responsible they feel for the success of the enterprise; how ethically they behave; how people behave toward customers; how they feel about the quality of the company's goods and services; how prideful they

51

Approaches to Enterprise Risk Management

feel about the mission of the enterprise; and ultimately, how fulfilled people feel in having a say in the business or making a difference in people's lives as a result of the work they perform. In the end, highly constructive and productive cultures lead to optimum outcomes.

Why Change?
More corporations are coming to appreciate that relationship marketing is leading to increased sales, as compared to transactional marketing. To effect a shift of such magnitude requires a carefully planned migration of both structural and cultural change. Companies such as Globus, the German based hypermarket; DM-Drogeriemarkt, a retail chemist; Southwest Airlines and Lufthansa, both commercial airline companies; and Ikea, the Swedish multinational home furnishing retailer—all have created cultural environments that have enabled them to be enormously profitable compared to their industry counterparts. In each of these organizations, employees work as teams. Management provides prescriptive guidance rather than restrictive direction. Employees are entrusted to do the right thing and encouraged to be the best at what they do, namely, providing customers not only with quality goods and services but also with great customer experiences.

Up to 40% improvement in performance can be achieved by changing organization culture. According to Stanford Business School professor, Jeffery Pfeffer, providing training, status equalization, employment stability, and strong recognition and reward programs can propel any number of organizations to enviable levels of success.

To remain viable and competitive, even service sector entities, for example utilities, financial institutions, and government services, are recognizing the need to shift from transaction-based systems to ones that are more relationship-focused. Such changes require enormous changes in organization culture, as well as in supporting structures, i.e., operational, technological, and policy structures. Because "structure follows strategy," it is virtually impossible to make shifts in organizational culture unless changes in structure occur, as well, to support such seismic shifts.

When Is Change Necessary?
Nowhere is the need for cultural alignment more evident than in the case of acquisitions and mergers. What usually happens is that the acquiring entity assumes its culture to be superior to that of the entity being acquired, as in the case of Novell Nouveau cited earlier. Rather than identifying and optimizing the most constructive aspects of the acquired organization's culture, the culture of the acquirer subsumes the culture of the acquired organization. Consequently, the outcome is not unlike that of Novell Nouveau's in acquiring WordPerfect. Equally, compelling circumstances exist when organizations are pummeled by downturns in the economy or paradigm shifts in industry standards and/or customer preferences. Organizational transformations are required to jumpstart the business concept or power-charge employees, propelling them in a new direction. Out of the ashes of the past must arise a new phoenix, if the organization is to transform itself into a vital resource for meeting, if not exceeding, customer needs and marketplace demands. Today, Starbucks, the international brand, roaster, and specialty coffee retailer, which operates in 43 countries with approximately 15,000 stores, is being assailed by competitors offering cheaper alternative products. Under Howard Schultz, returning to the company as chairman and CEO, the company is adopting a turnaround strategy of providing customers not only with the distinctive Starbucks "experience," and innovations, but also, a can-do employee attitude. "Welcome to Starbucks! What can I get started for you?" is the greeting welcoming every customer. While it is still early in the game, the emphasis is on reigniting the emotional attachment customers have had in the past with the product and the people who are the face of the company.

Similarly, when organizations determine that their focus must shift from product sales to customer satisfaction and retention, a significant change in organization culture is required. Employees need to be trained and empowered to improve the quality of goods and services, solve problems, and earn the respect and, ultimately, the loyalty of their customers. For example, in 1993, when CEO Louis Gerstner took the reins of IBM, the company had just lost US$8 billion. His challenge was to transform IBM from a stodgy, centralized, mainframe computer company, where customers were expected to come to "Big Blue" and turf wars among departments abounded, to a fast-paced, customer-focused, well-oiled machine, where employees were expected to work as a team to meet and exceed the needs of their customers. In *Who Says Elephants Can't Dance*, Gerstner wrote, "Culture isn't just one aspect of the game. It is the game. In the end, an organization is nothing more than the collective capacity of its people to create value."

As organizations continue to grow globally, it becomes a virtual impossibility for management

Cultural Alignment and Risk Management

to be ever-present, critically focused on day-to-day operations. Instead, organization cultures must be designed that are conducive to teamwork, self-direction, ethical decision-making, and the achievement of outstanding results. Team members throughout the organizational system must share a vision and a passion that can only come from an organization culture that is carefully designed and ardently nurtured.

thinking and behavioral styles, which make up three groupings, termed the "constructive," "passive-aggressive," and "passive-defensive" styles. An "ideal" culture is "constructive" when the dominant organizational styles are "self-actualizing," "achieving," "humanistic and encouraging," and "affiliative." Summary results from completed assessments enable organizations to understand how their cultures operate

MAKING IT HAPPEN
Culture change requires a strategic perspective on why culture is important to the organization, and how it will make a significant difference in the strategic positioning and success of an enterprise. The process begins with articulation of the vision and mission of the organization. To achieve optimum performance, the culture of the organization needs to be aligned with the vision, mission, and strategic goals and objectives of the organization. The behaviors of senior leadership must model the new standard, and the change and implementation process must begin with senior leadership.
- Conduct a system-wide assessment of the organization's current culture.
- Determine where change is necessary and why.
- Profile the desired culture of the organization, ensuring that the targeted profile will bring out the best in the organization.
- Engage organizational members in the processes of assessing the current culture, profiling the desired culture, and implementing needed change.
- Incorporate the desired behavioral styles into the performance-planning and management process for both individual members, and the business as a whole.
- Continue to assess progress versus plan. Be certain to obtain feedback from key stakeholders such as customers, vendors, and investors, and make adjustments as needed to improve results.

A MODEL FOR THE IDEAL CULTURE
Organizational Awareness
Ask any employee about his or her organizational culture, and chances are the words chosen to describe the environment will range from "political," "highly competitive," "collaborative," and "team-like" to "stressful," "mission driven," even "rewarding." The collective wisdom of organizational members represents a sort of meta-knowledge about the behaviors exhibited as a result of the cultural context in which they function. These descriptors, in essence, paint a picture of how functional or dysfunctional an organization's culture is and, in turn, how successful or unsuccessful the organization is as a whole in the way it operates. Moreover, it is this collective conscience, or meta-knowledge, that contains the answers as to how the organizational culture could and should be ideally.

Dimensions of Culture
Various models exist for assessing the culture of an organization. Perhaps the most widely used survey instruments have been developed by Human Synergistics International. Their Organizational Culture Inventory®, for example, measures 12 and where improvements can be made to improve outcomes in a variety of areas, including employee/labor relations, customer relations, organizational performance, and profitability.

Blueprint for Change
The benefit of using such assessments as described above is that organizational leadership is better able to target areas for change. Knowing how the present organizational culture impacts on performance, and where enhancements can be made to improve performance can form the basis of a master plan, or blueprint for change. Moreover, by tapping into the collective conscience of the organization and enlisting the involvement of organizational members, leadership can manage the change process more effectively—simply put, it becomes a holistic process or a "bottoms-up-top-down" approach. In the end, the change effort is sustainable, because all organizational members understand what is needed and how to make it happen—more importantly, they become collaborators in the change process rather than victims or passive spectators. Any number of corporations, including American Eagle Outfitters, Disney, Men's

Approaches to Enterprise Risk Management

Wearhouse, and Hewlett Packard, have focused on organizational culture as a means of optimizing performance, while sparking the commitment and active engagement of their employees. They have adopted that strategy from day one, and it has been the foundation for success.

Further Implications

In addition to profiling the culture of an organization, management can extend the evaluative process to assessing the individual behavioral styles of organizational members. Consistent with the notion that "a chain is only as strong as its weakest link," the behavior of every member of the organizational "chain" must be aligned with the desired profile of the organization's ideal culture to ensure optimum results. Further, individual performance plans should be honed to include the behavioral norms expected of organizational members, and periodic reviews conducted to help determine how well behaviors are aligned, and where improvement in individual behavioral styles is needed.

CONCLUSION

In a global economy that is becoming more complex and conflicted, there is little room for error, and even less room for guesswork. Organizational culture is as critical an element in managing a business as information technology, or financial controls. Indeed, it is more elusive but equally powerful to ensuring the success of an enterprise. The experience of Novell Nouveau and WordPerfect proves how costly the neglect of organizational culture can be to the financial performance of a business. By way of contrast, those organizations that consciously tend to the process of building the right organizational culture have reaped rewards well beyond those achieved by their peer and competitor organizations.

MORE INFO

Books:

Bowen, R. B. *Recognizing and Rewarding Employees*. New York: McGraw-Hill, 2000.

Cameron, K. S., and R. E. Quinn. *Diagnosing and Changing Organizational Culture: Based on the Competing Values Framework*. San Francisco, CA: Jossey-Bass, 2005.

Driskill, G. W., and A. L. Brenton. *Organizational Culture in Action: A Cultural Analysis Workbook*. Thousand Oaks, CA: Sage Publications, 2005.

Gerstner, L. V. *Who Says Elephants Can't Dance: Leading a Great Enterprise Through Dramatic Change*. New York: HarperCollins, 2002.

Hennig-Thurau, T., and U. Hansen (eds). *Relationship Marketing: Gaining Competitive Advantage Through Customer Satisfaction and Customer Retention*. New York: McGraw-Hill/Irwin, 2000.

Pfeffer, J. *The Human Equation: Building Profits by Putting People First*. Boston, MA: Harvard Business School Press, 1998.

Schein, E. H. *Organizational Culture and Leadership*. 3rd ed. San Francisco, CA: Jossey-Bass, 2004.

Articles:

Barriere, M. T., B. R. Anson, R. S. Ording, and E. Rogers. "Culture transformation in a health care organization: A process for building adaptive capabilities through leadership development." *Consulting Psychology Journal: Practice and Research* 54:2 (2008): 116–130.

Clark, D. "Novell Nouveau: Software firm fights to remake business after ill-fated merger." *Wall Street Journal (Midwest ed)* 76:62 (January 12, 1996): A1, A6.

Kavita, S. "Predicting organizational commitment through organization culture: A study of automobile industry in India." *Journal of Business Economics & Management* 8:1 (2007): 29–37.

Websites:

The Howland Group, Inc.: www.howlandgroup.com
Human Synergistics International: www.humansynergistics.com

Building Potential Catastrophe Management into a Strategic Risk Framework
by Duncan Martin

EXECUTIVE SUMMARY
- Most organizations recognize the need for a strategic risk framework. Such a framework typically identifies and analyzes the key strategic risks faced by the organization, such as competitive, regulatory, technological, demographic, and environmental changes.
- If adopted at the highest level, an effective framework will drive resource allocation and, consequently, the ability of the organization to achieve its goals.
- Many organizations fail to integrate the potential impact of catastrophes into their framework. Despite investing considerable time and energy into a risk management framework, this failure can result in large, unexpected losses. For example, a business might foresee, and mitigate, the entry of a new competitor but be caught off guard by a major flood that causes equal disruption and loss in value.
- To avoid being blindsided in this way, best-practice risk management builds catastrophe risk management into the same framework as strategic (and other) risks. With resources directed at those risks that pose the greatest threat, the full spectrum of risks is measured and managed consistently, thereby underpinning long-run organizational success.

DEFINITIONS
What is catastrophic risk? In brief, catastrophic risk is: "stuff happens." More precisely, it is the risk of extreme damage and loss of life from a natural or human cause. Some unexpected, perhaps unexpectable, event occurs. Half a world away from its source in southern China, SARS kills 38 people in Toronto; a nuclear reactor at Chernobyl is driven into a state its designers never even imagined even as its operators disable critical safety features, and it explodes; events in the Middle East cause Britons to blow themselves up on the London Underground.

Strategic risk is also stuff happening, but from a business point of view. An ailing computer manufacturer trounces established consumer electronics firms by producing the killer portable music device, and then follows up with a mobile phone that is both revolutionary and beautiful; tiny car firms constrained by postwar, small island scarcity eliminate waste by worshipping quality, end up reinventing the entire manufacturing process, and brutally upend incumbents; Wall Street's best and brightest simulate endless market disruption scenarios except the one that finally happens—no bids and no offers. Result: total paralysis.

Beyond strategic and catastrophe risk, financial and operational risk are equally necessary if less glamorous parts of a fully functional risk framework. Only through the consistent identification, measurement, and management of the full spectrum of risks can an organization be sure that it meets its objectives successfully.

CORE CONCEPTS
More formally, there are four core concepts in risk: frequency, severity, correlation, and uncertainty.

An event is frequent if it occurs often. Most catastrophes are, mercifully, infrequent. Historically, there is a severe earthquake (seven or greater on the Richter scale) about once every 25 years in California. Hence, the frequency of big earthquakes in California is 1/25, or about 4% each year.

An event is severe if it causes a lot of damage. For example, according to the US Geological Survey, between 1900 and 2005 China experienced 13 earthquakes that in total killed an estimated 800,000 people. The average severity was 61,000 deaths.

Most people's perception of risk focuses on events that are low-frequency and high-severity, such as severe earthquakes, aircraft crashes, and accidents at nuclear power plants. Strategic risk also focuses on such low-frequency/high-severity changes, such as disruptive technologies or new entrants. However, a fuller notion of risk includes two additional concepts: correlation and uncertainty.

Events are correlated if they tend to happen at the same time and place. For example, the flooding of New Orleans in 2005 was caused by a

Approaches to Enterprise Risk Management

hurricane; the 1906 earthquake in San Francisco also caused an enormous fire.

Estimates of frequency, severity, and correlation are just that: estimates. They are usually based on past experience and, as investors know well, past performance offers no guarantee of what will happen in the future. Similarly, the probabilities, severities, and correlations of events in the future cannot be extrapolated with certainty from history: They are uncertain.

The rarer and more extreme the event, the greater the uncertainty. For example, according to the US National Oceanic and Atmospheric Administration, in the 105 years between 1900 and 2004 there were 25 severe (category four and five) hurricanes in the United States. At the end of 2004, you would have estimated the frequency of a severe hurricane at 25/105 or about 24% per year, but there were four severe hurricanes in 2005 alone. Recalculating the frequency at the end of 2005, you would end up with about 27% per year (29/106). That's a large difference, and would have a material impact on preparations.

Which estimate is correct? Neither, and both: Uncertainty prohibits "correctness." Uncertainty is the essence of risk, and coping with it is the essence of risk management.

Both catastrophic and strategic risk management are thus predicting and managing the consequences of rare, severe, and potentially correlated events under great uncertainty.

THINK, PLAN, DO
Integrating catastrophe risk into strategic risk management requires a common conceptual framework. Best-practice risk management is—always and everywhere—a three-step process: Think, plan, do (Figure 1).

Think
Thinking comes first. Before being able to manage risk, risk managers must know how much is acceptable to their organization, and at what stage to cut any losses.

This risk appetite is not self-evident. It is a philosophical choice, an issue of comfort with the frequency, severity, and correlation of and uncertainty around potential events. Different individuals and organizations have different preferences.

Some people enjoy mountain climbing. They are comfortable with the knowledge that they're holding on to a small crack in a wet rock face with their fingertips and it's a long way down. Others prefer gardening, their feet firmly planted on the ground, their fingertips on their secateurs

and not far from a cup of coffee. Similarly, some organizations aspire to blue chip, triple-A solidity, others to the rough and tumble of start-ups and venture capital, with the added drama of the San Andreas fault under their feet.

For strategic risk, managers attempt to simplify risk appetite down to how much money an organization is prepared to lose before it cuts its losses and changes objectives. For catastrophes, it is the frequency with which a certain event results in death—the frequency and severity of fatal terrorist attacks in London for example. In some cases, it is defined externally. For example, on oil rigs in the North Sea it is defined through legislation. Events that cause death more often than once in 10,000 years are not tolerable and rig operators must mitigate the risk of any event with worse odds than this.

Figure 1. Think, plan, do

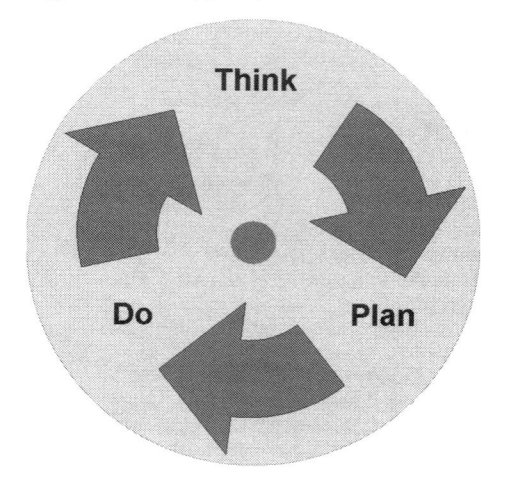

Plan
Planning is next. There are two parts: a strategic plan that matches resources and risks; and a tactical plan that assesses all the major risks identified and details the response to each one.

The first part is the big picture risk appetite. If, for example, an organization decides that the frequency, severity, and uncertainty of flooding in London are too great, the big picture is that the organization needs to leave London, incurring whatever costs this requires. The strategic big picture also has to make sense. For example, although the high command of the US Army Rangers recognizes that they operate in very dangerous environments—occasionally catastrophically so, such as in Mogadishu, Somalia—and

Catastrophe Management in a Strategic Risk Framework

CASE STUDY

Morgan Stanley was until recently a leading American investment bank. Investment banking is not for the fainthearted since it involves taking very large financial risks. Consequently, Morgan Stanley invested very large amounts in financial risk management. In general, this worked well and the firm was mostly profitable through the 1990s.

Managing financial risk is merely par for the course for investment banks. One thing that set Morgan Stanley apart from its peers was its assessment of catastrophe risk at one of its major operational hubs, the World Trade Center (WTC) in downtown New York. The corporate security manager, a decorated former soldier named Rick Rescorla, predicted the 1993 WTC bombing and had been able to convince the firm that such an attack would happen again; the firm had committed to move out at the end of its lease in 2006. On September 11, 2001, Morgan Stanley had 3,700 employees in the WTC. All but six—one of them Rescorla—got out alive, a direct result of constant practice and calm execution.

The integration of catastrophe risk into the strategic risk framework of the firm saved many lives. Few cases are this dramatic, but the point is the same: Risks are risks, regardless of source. The way we label them is entirely arbitrary. If, because of that labeling, we fail to treat all risks consistently, the consequences can be serious.

hence will on occasion lose soldiers, they have adopted a policy of "no man left behind." This helps to ensure that in combat Rangers are less likely to surrender or retreat, perhaps as a result winning the day. Consequently, governments spend a lot on flood defences, and armies spend a lot on search and rescue capabilities.

The next stage is detailed tactical planning. First, identify all the risks, strategic and catastrophic, financial and operational—all the things that might go wrong. Then, assess and compare them to see which are the most likely and the most damaging. Finally, figure out what to do, who's going to do it, and how much that's going to cost.

Many firms create business continuity plans on this basis. California's statewide disaster planning process is an excellent template for responding to catastrophes, because there's plenty of opportunity to practice: All manner of major incidents there—earthquakes, tsunamis, floods, wildfires, landslides, oil spills—occur relatively frequently. State law specifies the extent of mutual aid obligations between local communities and requires each to appoint a state-certified emergency manager. Emergency managers create a detailed disaster-management and recovery plan for their local community, reflecting local issues and needs. These plans are audited by state inspectors and rolled up into a statewide plan. To obtain the necessary resources, the plan is input to the state budgeting process.

Risk aversion does not necessarily make you safer. Many people or communities express a low risk appetite but baulk at the expense of reducing their risk to match their risk appetite. They don't put their money where their mouth is;

instead they simply hope that the rare event doesn't happen. However, in the end, even rare events do occur. The results of mismatching risk appetite and resources were devastatingly demonstrated recently as Katrina drowned New Orleans.

Conversely, a large risk appetite is not the same thing as recklessness. Technology venture capital firms quite deliberately "bet the farm" on a few firms in narrow technology domains that they believe will be highly disruptive and hence profitable. This is high risk for sure, but the extensive deliberation and diligence of the investment and management processes mitigate the risk.

Do

Doing is a combination of activities. Before an event, *doing* means being prepared. This consists of acquiring and positioning the appropriate equipment, communications systems, and budget; recruiting, training, and rehearsing response teams; and ensuring that both the public and the response teams know what to do and what not to do. A contingency plan that is not tested is likely to fail.

After an event, *doing* means keeping your wits about you while implementing your plan, managing the inevitable unexpected events that crop up, and, to the extent possible, collecting data on the experience.

Once the epidemic has broken out or the earthquake has hit, the key is not to panic. Colin Sharples, a former acrobatic pilot and now the head of training and industry affairs at a British airline, observes that instinctively "your mind freezes for about ten seconds in an emergency. Then it reboots." Frozen individuals cannot help

Approaches to Enterprise Risk Management

MAKING IT HAPPEN
In terms of implementation, there are five key principles.
- First, integration must be top down. Only senior management can both view the full holistic picture and require compliance further down.
- Second, the integration has to be genuinely "lived" by the senior managers. If employees feel that integration is merely lip service, they will not participate and the experiment will fail.
- Third, since risk appetites tend to be low with respect to very severe events, the resultant scarcity of events may drive hubris: Since it hasn't happened for a while, it probably won't or can't happen again. In industrial settings, researchers have observed that the odds of a serious accident increase with the time elapsed since the last one. Avoiding this complacency is critical.
- Fourth is the balance between sounding the alarm and having people respond. The more often an alarm sounds, the more likely it is that individuals will assume it's just a drill, or faulty, and tune it out, but if an alarm never sounds, no one will know what to do.
- Finally, many risk issues are amenable to sophisticated mathematical and computational treatments. There is a temptation to assume that just because a risk is measured, it is managed. It isn't.

themselves or others. To counter this instinct, pilots are required go through a continuous and demanding training program in a flight simulator which "covers all known scenarios, with the more critical ones, for example engine fires, covered every six months. Pilots who do not pass the test have to retrain."

Most organizations operating in environments where catastrophes are possible have similar training programs, albeit usually without the fancy simulation hardware. In addition to providing direct experience of extreme conditions, such training also increases skill levels to the point where difficult activities become routine, even reflexive. Together, the experience and the training allow team members to create some "breathing space" with respect to the immediate danger. This breathing space ensures that team members can play their part and in addition preserve some spare mental capacity to cope with unexpected events.

The importance of this "breathing space" reflex reflects a truth about many extreme situations: They don't usually start out that way, but a "chain of misfortune" builds up where one bad thing builds on another and the situation turns from bad to critical to catastrophic. First, something bad happens. For example, first a patient reports with novel symptoms and doesn't respond to treatment. Then they die…then one of their caregivers dies too. Then one of their relatives ends up in hospital with the same symptoms…and so on. A team with "breathing space" can interrupt this chain by solving the problems at source as they arise, allowing them no time to compound. In this case, a suspicious (and perhaps even paranoid) infectious disease consultant (the best kind) might isolate the patient and implement strict patient/physician contact precautions before the infection was able to spread.

For most organizations, the critical learning point is not to create a continuity or contingency plan and then let it sit on a shelf. A plan that gathers dust is a dead plan—only living plans can save lives.

CLOSE THE LOOP
When the *doing* is over and the situation has returned to normal, risk managers must close the loop and return to *thinking*. The group has to ask itself: "So, how did it go?" Using information collected centrally and participants' own experience, each part of the plan is evaluated against its original intention. This debrief can be formal or informal, depending on what works best. Sometimes it might even be public, such as the Cullen inquiry into the disastrous Piper Alpha North Sea oil platform fire in 1989 that cost 165 lives.

Where performance was bad, the group must question whether the cause was local: training, procedures, and equipment; or strategic: the situation was riskier than the organization wants to tolerate, or is able to afford. These conclusions feed into the next round of *thinking* and *planning*.

PITFALLS
The main pitfall in the integration of catastrophe risk into strategic risk management is an insufficiently holistic process. Usually, this stems from the separation of strategy development, risk management, and, in many cases, insurance. In many organizations strategy development is the sexiest assignment and is jealously guarded by its departmental owners. As a result, sometimes strategic plans can be insufficiently informed

Catastrophe Management in a Strategic Risk Framework

by risk assessment. Since they tend to communicate in jargon and equations, risk management departments often do not help themselves. Sometimes, insurance is not a component of the risk management scheme; it is part of the finance area, and an obscure part at that. As a result, decisions on which risks to cover and to what degree may be taken without consideration of the organization's overall risk appetite. This lack of integration of the risk assessment process can ultimately lead to inconsistent treatment of risks and misallocation of scarce resources.

MORE INFO
Books:
Abraham, Thomas. *Twenty-first Century Plague: The Story of SARS*. Baltimore, MD: Johns Hopkins University Press, 2005.
Cullen, Lord W. Douglas. *The Public Inquiry into the Piper Alpha Disaster.* London: The Stationery Office, 1990.
Junger, Sebastian. *The Perfect Storm: A True Story of Men Against the Sea.* London: HarperCollins, 2007.
Perrow, Charles. *Normal Accidents: Living with High-Risk Technologies.* Princeton, NJ: Princeton University Press, 1999.
Pyne, Stephen. *Year of the Fires: The Story of the Great Fires of 1910*. London: Penguin, 2002.
Singer, P. W. *Corporate Warriors: The Rise of the Privatized Military Industry*. Ithaca, NY: Cornell University Press, 2004.

Article:
Stewart, James B. "The real heroes are dead." *The New Yorker* February 11, 2002. Online: www.rickrescorla.com/All The Heros Are Dead.htm.

Websites:
California Governor's Office of Emergency Services: www.oes.ca.gov
Federal Emergency Management Agency: www.fema.gov
London Resilience: www.londonprepared.gov.uk

Real Options: Opportunity from Risk
by David C. Shimko

EXECUTIVE SUMMARY
- Common examples are the right to make, expand, contract, defer, or cancel an investment or contract.
- Value real options by considering the value of the asset or contract with and without the ability to adjust.
- In some cases, the Black–Scholes model can be used to approximate the value of real options directly.
- Real options generally increase in value as uncertainty about the future increases.
- Real options can be proprietary or shared, simple or compound, restructurable or not.
- Real options have real value; many corporate valuations cannot be explained except for the presence of real options.

WHAT IS A REAL OPTION?
The origin of the term "real option" derives from financial options. For example, the right to buy a house for a fixed period of time at a fixed price is a call option,[1] except that the underlying asset is a real asset, not a financial asset. Business people and economists discovered that many business processes involve options, and that financial mathematics can be brought to bear to value those options. Some popular examples include:
- the right to make an investment, such as the option to build a plastics plant in China;
- the right to expand or contract an investment based on changes in market conditions, such as a plant design that accommodates changes in production rates at very low cost;
- the right to defer an investment, such as the right to wait for better market conditions to develop a property;
- the right to accelerate an investment;
- the right to cancel a contract;
- the right to produce or not to produce a product, such as the right of a petroleum refinery or electricity power plant to produce or not produce fuel or power;
- the right to choose how to undertake an investment, such as a gold producer's right to choose the mining strategy that maximizes its value.

"Option" and "optimize" share the same root, the word "opt"—meaning, of course, "to choose." Therefore, the value of a real option can be thought of as the value of any right to choose, when compared with following a strategy where no such right is conferred. This suggests the mathematical relation:

Value of real option = Value of strategy with decision rights
− Value of strategy without decision rights

In some cases, the option value may be computed directly, as shown in Example 1.

Example 1
A company has a one-year option to acquire an oil-producing property for $100 million. The present value of the drilling profits is currently estimated to be $100 million, and the oil reserves are currently being depleted at the rate of 2% per year. The present value assessment varies according to the price of oil, with a percentage volatility (standard deviation) of 15% per year. If the interest rate is 4%, what is the value of the option?

To value the option, it is helpful to see how the real option resembles a standard financial call option. The owner of an equity call option has the right to buy a stock at a predetermined price (the strike price) for a predetermined period of time. The stock pays dividends which the option holder will not receive if the option is unexercised. Stock volatility makes the option valuable—the more volatile the stock, the greater the value of deciding to buy later at a fixed price. In the case of the oil option, the "stock value" is the present value of the profits, the "volatility" is the percentage variation in the present value, the "strike price" is the acquisition price of the property, and the "dividend" is the depletion of the oil reserve.

As a first approximation, an analyst might use the Black–Scholes formula of stock option pricing to value the real option. Using any online

Approaches to Enterprise Risk Management

calculator, and the inputs below, the resulting call option value is $6.82 million.

Stock price	US$100
Dividend	2%
Exercise price	US$100
Volatility	15%
Interest rate	4%
Time	1 year
Call option value	US$6.82

Some real options fit the Black–Scholes framework nicely, but most real options have degrees of complexity that are not captured by the option pricing model.

Example 2
A developer owns a piece of land that is currently used as a parking lot. The present value of the parking lot revenues is $5 million. He can convert the land into an apartment building and net an additional $5.5 million in present value. Or he can convert the parking lot into an office building and net an additional $6 million in present value. What is the value of the property in this case?
1 US $5 million, since it currently being used as a parking lot.
2 US$11 million, since the office project is more profitable than the apartment project.
3 The value of the highest current net present value (NPV) usage of the land.
4 None of the above.

The answer is clearly not 1; a parking lot is worth more than the present value of its current income since it has demonstrated valuable alternative uses. Answer 2 is tempting, but it is wrong if there are any other projects more valuable. Answer 3 may be correct, but also could be incorrect because of the use of the word "current." It may have a more valuable use in the future and, under some conditions, it would be worthwhile to wait to develop the land until that possibility materializes.

The correct answer is generally 4, since the value of the land is equal to *or higher than* its current value in the highest use. The reason for this is that conditions change over time. If the property owner waits a year, they may find that residential real estate grows faster than commercial, or vice versa. At some point, however, it is optimal to make the irreversible decision as to how to convert the property. In those cases, the value of waiting is zero.

Because the property owner has the right to wait to invest, this confers additional value to investment until the moment when it is no longer optimal to wait, and the option is exercised.

PROPERTIES OF REAL OPTIONS
In many situations, increased project risk reduces project value. This is particularly true when a company has constrained capital and increased risks put the company's survival in jeopardy.

Real options have the opposite effect. Like financial options, they generally increase in value the more uncertain the values of the underlying variables. They generally increase in value the longer the time an option can be deferred. And they increase in value as the cost to exercising falls.

Real options also tend to mitigate project risk, since the project owner has the right to modify strategy midcourse. This can help avoid the worst outcomes for the project, providing a kind of operational hedge against downside risk.

VALUING REAL OPTIONS
When an option pricing formula cannot be applied, there are two other ways to value real options: One using backward induction (best for decision trees) and one using simulation (best for problems with continuous input price changes). As an example of option valuation using backward induction, consider the following game, similar to the American television show *The Price is Right*.

Backward Induction
The contestant is given $50 and has to make a decision whether to keep the $50 or pay $50 to choose one of three boxes. One box has a valuable prize worth $100, but the other two boxes have nothing. After choosing a box, the host reveals an empty box and offers the contestant a chance to switch. What is the value of the player's option to switch?

The tree in Figure 1 summarizes the decision problem.

Figure 1. Decision problem summary

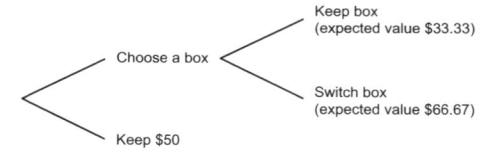

Choose a box
— Keep box (expected value $33.33)
— Switch box (expected value $66.67)
Keep $50

If the contestant always keeps their box of choice, the expected value is 33.33 since there is a 1/3 chance of getting $100. If they switch after seeing an empty box, there is a 2/3 chance they changed an empty box for a valuable one, and a 1/3 chance they changed a valuable box for an empty one.

Real Options: Opportunity from Risk

CASE STUDY
In 1998, the NYSEG's Homer City power plant, an 1,884 megawatt coal-fired plant located on the border of New York and Pennsylvania, sold for a price of $955 per kilowatt of capacity. Similar plants, Dunkirk and Huntley, sold for about a third of that price. What was the difference? Was it a problem of irrational exuberance on the part of the bidders, or was there something else going on?

It turns out that because of its location, the Homer City plant had the option of delivering power into New York, and into Pennsylvania and Ohio, giving it the opportunity to benefit from price discrepancies in the three regions. At one hour's notice, the plant could decide to sell in whichever market had the higher price. This real option owned by the NYSEG accounted for roughly two thirds of the market value of the plant. This case was analyzed by Robert Ethier.[3]

Using backward induction, we confirm that switching is the best strategy, and since the value of that is greater than $50, the value of the game is $66.67. The value of the game without the right to switch is $50, since it is optimal not to play the game. Therefore, the value of the option to switch in this case is $16.67 (= 66.67 − 50).

Simulation
More generally, real options are valued using stochastic modeling and some form of optimization theory. For example, plastics can be produced from natural gas or from naphtha. To value a plant that has the option to choose its feedstock, it is necessary to simulate price fluctuations in natural gas and naphtha and determine how the company would optimize its feedstock strategy depending on the prices realized. This problem is complex because switching is costly and cannot be accomplished instantaneously.

Clearly, there is always value in having the ability to switch feedstocks; however, that value may be very small if the costs of switching are high or the volatility of feedstock prices is low. Generally we can say that the value of the switching option is the difference in value between the plant that can switch its feedstock and the value of the plant that cannot.

NPV AND REAL OPTIONS
Many companies make avoidable NPV mistakes. According to the textbook approach, for example, a manufacturing firm should update its production methods if the present value of the benefits exceeds the present value of the costs. This is not necessarily correct. If new and better innovations are being made available over time, management may find an even better renovation alternative. If they repeatedly renovate every time they make a small gain, they will have lost the opportunity to have made a big gain on the best possible renovation.

For this reason, the NPV rule must consider the value of the option to wait to renovate. The NPV rule can be adjusted by including the lost option as a cost or by requiring the present value of benefits to exceed a predetermined multiple of the present value of the costs. This problem was first analyzed rigorously by McDonald and Siegel (1986).[2]

ADVANCED REAL OPTIONS
The options discussed so far were proprietary to a particular economic agent. In some cases, real options are shared, introducing an element of game theory into their valuation. For example, the option to enter a new market may be shared by one's competitors, and the value of the option depends on competitor strategy. Also, some options are compound rather than simple; in these cases, one exercises an option to obtain another option, which adds a layer of analytical complexity, but the financial intuition remains the same.

MAKING IT HAPPEN
- Identify an aspect of a business where managers respond differently to different market conditions. It may be evidence of the existence of a real option.
- Value the option by considering how the company behaves with and without the flexibility.
- Evaluate the cost/benefit of increases or reductions in flexibility using the same framework.
- Apply this methodology to other corporate situations, and the valuation of acquisitions and divestitures.

Approaches to Enterprise Risk Management

MORE INFO

Books:

Copeland, Tom, and Vladimir Antikarov. *Real Options, Revised Edition: A Practitioner's Guide*. New York: W. W. Norton, 2001.

Kodukula, Prasad, and Chandra Papudesu. *Project Valuation Using Real Options: A Practitioner's Guide*. Fort Lauderdale, FL: J. Ross Publishing, 2006.

Mun, Jonathan. *Real Options Analysis: Tools and Techniques for Valuing Strategic Investments and Decisions*. 2nd ed. New York: Wiley, 2005.

Schwartz, Eduardo S., and Lenos Trigeorgis. *Real Options and Investment Under Uncertainty: Classical Readings and Recent Contributions*. Cambridge, MA: MIT Press, 2001.

Trigeorgis, Lenos. *Real Options: Managerial Flexibility and Strategy in Resource Allocation*. Cambridge, MA: MIT Press, 1996.

Website:

Links to articles, papers, and other resources on real options: www.puc-rio.br/marco.ind/ro-links.html

NOTES

1 A financial call option is the right to buy a security at a predetermined price for a predetermined time period. A put is the right to sell a security at preset terms.

2 McDonald, Robert, and Daniel Siegel. "The value of waiting to invest." *Quarterly Journal of Economics* 101:4 (1986): 707–728.

3 Ethier, Robert G. "Valuing electricity assets in deregulated markets: A real options model with mean reversion and jumps." February 1999. Viewable on the New York State Library website at www.nysl.nysed.gov

Understanding Reputation Risk and Its Importance by Jenny Rayner

EXECUTIVE SUMMARY
* Reputation is a critical intangible asset; it is an indicator of past performance and future prospects.
* Reputation is based on stakeholders' perceptions of whether their experience of a business matches their expectations.
* Knowing your major stakeholders, how they perceive you, and what they expect of you is vital in managing reputation risk.
* Everyone working for an organization bears some responsibility for upholding its reputation.
* Reputation risk is anything that could *impact* reputation—either negatively (threats) or positively (opportunities).
* Risks to reputation should be integrated into the business's enterprise risk management (ERM) framework so that they receive attention at the right level and appropriate actions are taken to manage them.

INTRODUCTION
Reputation is the single most valuable asset of most businesses today—albeit an intangible one. A 2007 global survey[1] rated damage to reputation as the top risk, although half the respondents admitted that they were not prepared for it. Hard-earned reputations can be surprisingly fragile in the globalized, technologically interconnected 21st century. The trust and confidence that underpin them can be irrevocably damaged by a momentary lapse of judgment or an inadvertent remark.

That is why understanding reputation risk has become a key focus for businesses in all sectors. It is now recognized that reputation risks need to be managed as actively and rigorously as other more quantifiable and tangible risks.

REPUTATION AND ITS VALUE
Reputation is an accumulation of perceptions and opinions about an organization that reside in the consciousness of its stakeholders.

An organization will enjoy a good reputation when its behavior and performance consistently meet or exceed the expectations of its stakeholders. Reputation will diminish if an organization's words and deeds are perceived as failing to meet stakeholder expectations, as illustrated by the reputation equation below.[2]

Reputation − Experience = Expectations

Reputation has intrinsic current value as an intangible asset. Although reputation will not appear as a discrete balance sheet item, it represents a significant proportion of the difference between a business's market and book values (less any quantifiable intangibles such as licenses and trademarks). Since intangibles usually represent over 70% of market value, reputation is often a business's single greatest asset.

Reputation also plays a pivotal role in a business's future value by influencing stakeholder behavior and, hence, future earnings potential and prospects. A good or bad reputation can affect stakeholder decisions to maintain or relinquish their stake—be they investors, customers, suppliers, or employees. The "corporate halo" effect of a reputable business can help to differentiate products in a highly competitive sector, may allow premium pricing, and can be the ultimate deciding factor for a prospective purchaser of services. A strong reputation can help to attract and retain high-quality employees and can deter new competitors by acting as a barrier to market entry. Reputation can also shape the attitude of regulators, pressure groups, and the media towards a business and can affect its cost of capital.

Perhaps the greatest benefit of a good reputation is the buffer of goodwill it provides, which can enable a business to withstand future shocks. This "reputational capital," or "reputation equity," underpins stakeholder trust and confidence and can persuade stakeholders to give a business the benefit of the doubt and a second chance when the inevitable unforeseen crisis strikes.

DEFINING REPUTATION RISK
Reputation risk should be regarded as a generic term embracing the risks, from any source, that

Approaches to Enterprise Risk Management

can *impact* reputation, and not as a category of risk in its own right. Regulatory noncompliance, loss of customer data, unethical employee behavior, or an unexpected profit warning can all damage reputation and stakeholder confidence.

Reputation risk is not only about downside threats, but also about upside opportunities. Climate change, for example, is a potential business threat, but many firms have spotted and exploited the flip-side opportunity for competitive advantage by developing green technologies and promoting themselves as environmentally friendly, thereby enhancing their reputation.

Reputation risk can therefore be defined as: "Any action, event, or situation that could adversely or beneficially impact an organization's reputation."

IDENTIFYING REPUTATION RISKS

The most crucial stage of the reputation risk management process is *identifying* the factors that could impact reputation. Risks have to be recognized and understood before they can be managed. Considering the seven drivers of reputation is a useful starting point, as these are also fertile sources of threats and opportunity to reputation (see figure below).[3]

Figure 1. The seven drivers of reputation

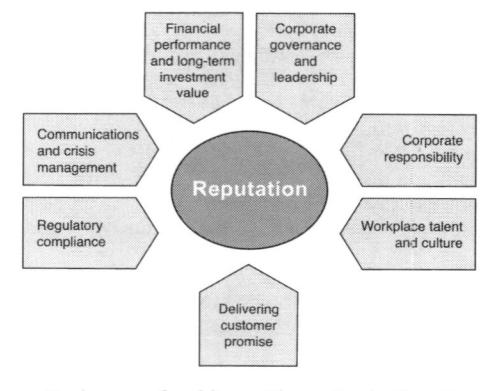

Businesses should consider not only the risks under their direct control, but also risks in the "extended enterprise" relating to suppliers, subcontractors, business partners, advisers, and other stakeholders. Could the values, business practices, or activities of its partners expose the business to reputation risk by association?

One way of approaching this is to consider the expectations of each major stakeholder group against the drivers of business reputation to develop a "heat map" of potential trouble spots and zones of opportunity. Major mismatches between expectations and experience can be analyzed to highlight areas where action is needed to bridge the gaps.

Asking the following questions may also help to uncover reputation risks:
- What newspaper headline about your business would you least (or most) like to see? What could trigger this?
- What could threaten your core business values or your license to operate? Such risks can seriously damage reputation and lead to an irreversible loss of stakeholder confidence.
- Could there be collateral risk arising from the activities of another player in your sector? If so, the reputation of your own business may be vulnerable and come under intense stakeholder scrutiny.
- Could reputation risk exposure arise from an acquisition, merger, or other portfolio change? A mismatch of values, ethos, culture, and standards resulting in inappropriate behavior could seriously damage reputation. Conversely, if the acquisition target enjoys a superior reputation, it could provide a competitive edge.

EVALUATING, RESPONDING TO, MONITORING, AND REPORTING RISKS

Once risks to reputation have been identified, they can be evaluated, appropriate risk responses developed, and the risks monitored and reported.

Risks to reputation can be *evaluated* in the usual way by considering the likelihood of the risk occurring and the impact if it does. The reputational impact of such risks should be considered explicitly, alongside financial or other impacts. This can be done by the use of a word model which explains reputational impact in a way that is relevant and meaningful for a given business. Table 1 provides an example of a four-point reputation impact scale that caters for both threats and opportunities.

In assessing reputational impact, the view of relevant stakeholders should be considered to ensure that the impact is not underestimated. That is why understanding stakeholders and what they regard as current and emerging major issues lies at the heart of reputation risk management.

Reputational impact can sometimes be quantified in monetary terms—for example, expected reduced income resulting from loss of customers or license to operate; or impact on share price or on brand value. The true ultimate impact can be difficult to estimate as the immediate consequence may be only a relatively small financial penalty (for example, a fine for pollution).

Understanding Reputation Risk and Its Importance

Table 1. Sample reputation impact assessment criteria

Low	Moderate	High	Very high
• Local complaint or recognition • Minimal change in stakeholder confidence • Impact lasting less than one month	• Local media coverage • Moderate change in stakeholder confidence • Impact lasting between one and three months	• National media coverage • Significant change in stakeholder confidence • Impact lasting more than three months • Attracts regulator attention or comment	• National headline/international media coverage • Dramatic change in stakeholder confidence • Impact lasting more than 12 months or irreversible • Public censure or accolade by regulators

However, the event may, over time, have an insidious effect which erodes the business's reputation (for example, because of a perception that the business is not concerned about the environment).

Response plans should be developed to manage the more significant risks that present unacceptable exposure to the business. The gap between experience and expectation can be bridged by improving the business's performance or behavior and/or by influencing stakeholder expectations so they are more closely aligned with what the business can realistically deliver. As reputation is based on stakeholder perception, focused and clear communication to stakeholders is vital so that their perception will accurately reflect business reality.

A business may have done everything possible to anticipate and guard against reputational threats, but if a crisis strikes and the business response is inappropriate, its reputation may still end up in tatters. Having an effective and well-rehearsed generic crisis management plan that can be quickly adapted and implemented to suit specific circumstances is therefore a key component of an effective reputation risk management strategy.

Once risks to reputation have been identified and responses agreed and implemented, the risks can be regularly *monitored* by management to ensure that responses are having the desired effect. Finally, the up-to-date status of the risks should be *reported* at the right level to inform decision-making and enable external disclosure to stakeholders.

ROLES AND RESPONSIBILITIES

The board of a business is the ultimate custodian of a business's reputation. However, managing reputation risk successfully requires a team effort across the business from executive and non-executive directors, senior and middle managers, public relations staff, risk and audit professionals, and key business partners.

CASE STUDY
Citigroup

In September 2004 the Financial Services Agency (FSA), Japan's bank regulator, ordered Citigroup to close its private banking business in the country following "serious violations" of Japanese banking laws. An FSA investigation found that inadequate local internal controls and lack of oversight from the United States had allowed large profits to be "amassed illegally." The bank had failed to prevent suspected money laundering and had misled customers about investment risk. The punishment meted out by the FSA was particularly severe as a previous inspection in 2001 had exposed similar compliance weaknesses, which Citigroup had not corrected.

Citigroup's then chief executive, Charles Prince, visited Japan in October 2004 in an attempt to repair the company's tarnished image. Bowing, he apologized for the activities of his senior staff, saying that they had put "short-term profits ahead of the bank's long-term reputation." He pledged to improve oversight, change the management structure, increase employee training on local regulations, and set up an independent committee to monitor progress. He said: "Under my leadership, lack of compliance and inappropriate behavior simply will not be tolerated and we will take direct action to ensure that proper standards are upheld and that these problems do not reoccur."

That same month French retailer Carrefour fired Citigroup as a financial adviser on the sale of its Japanese operations to prevent its own reputation from being tarnished by association.

Approaches to Enterprise Risk Management

MAKING IT HAPPEN
The key components of reputation risk management are:
- Clear and well-communicated business vision, values, and strategy that set the right ethical and stakeholder-aware tone for the business.
- Supporting policies and codes of conduct that guide employee behavior and decision-making so that goals are achieved in accordance with business values.
- Extension of the business's values and relevant policies to key partners in the supply chain.
- Dialogue and engagement to track the changing perceptions, requirements, and expectations of major stakeholders continuously.
- An effective enterprise-wide risk management system that identifies, assesses, responds to, monitors, and reports on threats and opportunities to reputation.
- A culture in which employees are risk-aware, are encouraged to be vigilant, raise concerns, highlight opportunities, and act as reputational ambassadors for the business.
- Transparent communications that meet stakeholder needs and build trust and confidence.
- Robust and well-rehearsed crisis management arrangements.

Everyone employed by and indirectly working for a business should be expected to uphold the business's values and bear some responsibility for spotting emerging risks that could impact reputation. The telltale signs of an imminent crisis are often missed because personnel are not risk-aware: a spate of customer complaints, safety near-misses or supplier nonconformances, a sudden rise in employee turnover, or pressure group activity. These can act as crucial early warning indicators which allow a business to take corrective action and avert disaster.

CONCLUSION
A good reputation hinges on a business living the values it claims to espouse and delivering consistently on the promise to its stakeholders. Being "authentic," being "the real thing," has never been so important. Pursuing short-term gain at the expense of long-term business reputation and stakeholder interests is no longer acceptable practice.

Successfully managing reputation risk is both an inside-out and an outside-in challenge. The inside-out component requires business leaders to establish an appropriate vision, values, and strategic goals that will guide actions and behaviors throughout the organization. The outside-in component requires the business to scan the external environment continuously and canvass stakeholder opinion to ensure it is on a track that will secure the continuing support, trust, and confidence of its stakeholders.

Active and systematic management of the risks to reputation can help to ensure that perception is aligned with reality and that stakeholder experience matches expectations. Only in this way can a business build, safeguard, and enhance a reputation that will be sustainable in the long term.

Understanding Reputation Risk and Its Importance

MORE INFO

Books:
Atkins, Derek, Ian Bates, and Lyn Drennan. *Reputational Risk: Responsibility Without Control? A Question of Trust.* London: Financial World Publishing, 2006.
Fombrun, Charles J., and Cees B. M. van Riel. *Fame and Fortune: How Successful Companies Build Winning Reputations.* Upper Saddle River, NJ: FT Prentice Hall, 2003.
Larkin, Judy. *Strategic Reputation Risk Management.* Basingstoke, UK: Palgrave MacMillan, 2003.
Rayner, Jenny. *Managing Reputational Risk: Curbing Threats, Leveraging Opportunities.* Chichester, UK: Wiley, 2003.

Article:
See articles in *The Geneva Papers on Risk and Insurance Issues and Practice* 31:3 (July 2006). Find issue in "Archive" at: www.palgrave-journals.com/gpp

Reports:
Coutts and Company. "Face value: Your reputation as a business asset." London: Coutts and Company, 2008.
Economist Intelligence Unit. "Reputation: Risk of risks." White paper, 2005.
Resnick, Jeffrey T. "Reputational risk management: A framework for safeguarding your organization's primary intangible asset." Opinion Research Corporation, 2006. Online at: www.carma.com/Reputational_Risk_White_Paper.pdf

Websites:
The John Madejski Centre for Reputation, Henley Business School at the University of Reading—search on "Madejski" at: www.henley.reading.ac.uk
Reputation Institute: www.reputationinstitute.com

NOTES

1 Aon's Global Risk Management Survey, based on responses from 320 organizations in 29 countries.
2 Oonagh Mary Harpur in Chapter B4 of *Corporate Social Responsibility Monitor.* London: Gee Publishing, 2002.
3 Rayner, 2003.

ERM, Best's Ratings, and the Financial Crisis
by Gene C. Lai

EXECUTIVE SUMMARY
- The objective of ERM should be to maximize the wealth of all stakeholders, including stockholders, policy-holders, creditors, and employees.
- To have a successful ERM process, a company needs to have an effective risk culture, and have the support of the CEO and other executive officers, such as the CRO or CFO.
- The ERM process should include capital modeling tools, and hold high-quality and sufficient capital.
- An effective ERM will have a positive impact, not only on the best capital adequacy ratio (BCAR) but also on Best's overall ratings.
- In addition to the traditional ERM, and recent improvements such as dynamic hedging models, an effective ERM needs to consider the systemic risks that made some insurance companies insolvent in the recent financial crisis.

INTRODUCTION
The recent financial crisis has raised some questions, such as why enterprise risk management (ERM) was not able to prevent some large insurance companies from either becoming insolvent (for example, AIG) or from suffering large losses of their market value (for example, Lincoln National), and whether rating agencies properly perform their jobs.[1] It is critical that insurance companies have effective ERM programs, and that rating agencies provide adequate ratings to protect insurance companies from bankruptcy. Initially, many insurance companies adopt ERM because rating agencies consider ERM as part of their rating. Adopting ERM for the sole purpose of fulfilling the requirements of a rating agency may not be the best practice. A recent survey conducted by Towers Perrin showed that 32% of companies name identifying and quantifying risk as their main purpose. We believe these companies are moving in the right direction, but more improvements to the current ERM process are needed.

EFFECTIVE ERM
To have an effective ERM, a company needs to have an effective risk culture. To achieve an effective risk culture, a company needs to start from the chief executive officer (CEO) and other senior executive officers (including the chief financial officer (CFO) and/or the chief risk officer (CRO)).

ERM usually involves a process that identifies and assess risks, determines a response strategy and techniques, and implements and monitors the risk-management program for the enterprise. The objective of an ERM program is to maximize the wealth of the stakeholders—including stockholders, policy-holders, creditors, and employees—sustainably over the long term. It should be noted that wealth maximization is not equivalent to risk minimization. Risk and return are trade-offs. Insurance companies need first to establish their risk tolerance level and minimize unnecessary risk.

Some major categories of risk are credit risk, market risk, underwriting risk, operational risk, and strategic risk. Detailed items for each category of risk can be found in one of Best's articles.[2] In terms of credit risk, insurance companies should pay special attention to counterparty risk if they hold credit default swaps (CDSs). The recent collapse of AIG provides a good lesson for insurance companies that do not know the counterparty risk.

As a result of recent events such as September 11, 2001, the financial crisis which started in 2008, and major hurricanes in 2004 and 2005 (including Katrina, Rita, and Wilma), longevity issues have increased the risk profile of insurance companies. Insurance companies have to take action to deal with the increased uncertainty and volatility that they face. In addition, the regulatory changes regarding EU Solvency II and principles-based requirements have also resulted in improvements to the traditional risk management programs. Recent developments in ERM include catastrophe modeling, dynamic hedging modeling, and an enterprise-wide view of risk for insurance companies. Catastrophe modeling aims to deal with the rapid escalation of natural disasters caused by global warming, because it has been more difficult to predict catastrophic events. While the retirement of the baby-boomer generation presents opportunities

Approaches to Enterprise Risk Management

for insurance companies to manage retirement savings, it also creates capital market-based risk. Insurance companies have developed some products that guarantee certain returns on the invested assets. The guarantees create additional risks related to capital market performance. To reduce the risk of the guarantees, insurance companies have developed and implemented sophisticated hedging models to protect both the policy holders and these companies against adverse movements in the capital markets. The recent financial crisis has shown that the hedging programs are far from perfect. Many insurance companies have suffered from rating downgrades and potential bankruptcy. The new emphasis on ERM today is a heuristic approach, rather than a silo approach. Not only the risk of an individual unit, but also the risk correlations among the units, are critical to the success of ERM. More importantly, ERM today should pay more attention to systemic risk, which can be defined as the risk of collapse of an entire financial system or capital market. One reason for the recent failure of the financial systems is that ERM does not consider the systemic risk.

to policyholders." One of the most important factors of Best's rating is balance sheet strength. Best uses the BCAR to proxy balance sheet strength. BCAR is defined as the ratio of adjusted surplus to net required capital (NRC). The main components of adjusted surplus are reported surplus, equity adjustments, debt adjustments, and other adjustments. NRC includes fixed-income securities, equity securities, interest rate, credit risk, loss and loss-adjustment-expense reserves, net written premiums, and off-balance-sheet items. The BCAR formula also contains an adjustment for covariance, reflecting the correlation between individual components. BCAR is similar to the calculation of the National Association of Insurance Commissioners' (NAIC's) risk-based capital, but BCAR includes some important risk factors that are not considered by the NAIC's risk-based capital. BCAR can make adjustments to respond to various market issues such as rate changes, the stage of underwriting cycles, and reinsurance. It should be noted that more than two-thirds of an insurance company's gross capital requirements of BCAR comes from the company's loss reserve and net premiums

CASE STUDY
ERM and the Ratings of USAA and its Subsidiaries
In December 2008, AM Best confirmed it had given USAA and its subsidiaries (hereafter USAA) the financial strength rating (FSR) of A++ (superior) rating, issuer credit rating (ICR) of "aaa," and the debt rating of "aaa." The ratings reflect "USAA's superior capitalization and strong operating results through focused business and financial strategy." Diversified sources of earnings, capital accumulation, and strong ERM are also key factors for superior ratings. In addition, good catastrophe management, a sound reinsurance program to preserve the finance capital, and a conservative investment strategy were mentioned. The USAA case demonstrates that Best's ratings reflect the effectiveness of USAA's ERM.

ERM, BCAR, AND AM BEST RATINGS
There are different rating agencies that rate insurance companies. Among them AM Best is deemed as one of the most important. This chapter therefore focuses on the relationship between ERM and AM Best ratings. AM Best expects each insurance company to customize its ERM process to their integrated risk profile and risk management needs in order to maintain acceptable ratings. The ERM process should include capital modeling tools (such as dynamic financial analysis) to maintain appropriate capital. The process also needs to include a discussion of the impact of the company's ERM on its rating in its annual meetings.

The objective of AM Best's rating system is to "provide an opinion of an insurer's financial strength, and ability to meet ongoing obligations

written. Less than one-third of the gross capital requirements comes from investment risk, interest risk, and credit risk. After Best calculates a company's initial BCAR, it performs various sensitivity tests including the catastrophe and terrorism stress tests.

While BCAR is a critical quantitative model to measure financial strength and serve as a consistent baseline for Best ratings, it is not the sole basis for determining the final ratings. A corporate culture of risk awareness and accountability in daily operations, operating performance, business profile, and the quality of capital are also very important considerations for Best's ratings. ERM has an impact on a company's financial strength, operating performance (such as relative earnings and loss-ratio volatility), business profile (for example, catastrophe and

ERM, Best's Ratings, and the Financial Crisis

terrorism risk exposures), and the quality of capital. Thus, an effective ERM has an important impact on the Best rating. An insurance company with a strong ERM can be allowed to lower its BCAR, compared with another company with a relatively weak ERM. It is even possible that an insurance company can keep its BCAR lower than the guideline level, on a case-by-case basis, and vice versa.

ERM AND THE FINANCIAL CRISIS

This section does not intend to examine the causes of the recent financial crisis, but to discuss whether an effective ERM can mitigate the negative impact of the financial crisis on insurance companies. In the insurance industry, AIG is now 80% owned by the US government. MetLife and Prudential, among other insurance companies, may seek aid from the government. Why did ERM fail to prevent these companies from near collapse? Here are some possible answers. First, even though the concept of ERM has been popular for more than 10 years, insurance companies had not very seriously implemented ERM until recently. The current process is not perfect; while it considers the correlations among individual risks, it fails to consider the systemic risk facing the whole financial system, and the counterparty risk of derivative securities. To prevent future failures, the ERM approach needs to recognize that the solvency approach may not be appropriate in a financial crisis environment. Insurance companies need to have more capital than BCAR requires, because additional capital is difficult to obtain during a financial crisis. Second, CROs need to resist the temptation to sell complex products without really understanding the consequences of selling those products. The CDSs of AIG are an example. Finally, insurance companies should focus on their core business—underwriting business—rather than investing in exotic derivatives.

CONCLUSION

ERM has become more and more important in recent years. The recent financial crisis makes ERM even more critical to the success and survival of an enterprise. To have a successful ERM process, a company needs to have support from the CEO and other executive officers such as the CRO or CFO. The ERM process should include capital modeling tools, and hold sufficient high-quality capital. An effective ERM will have a positive impact not only on the BCAR but also on Best's overall ratings. In addition to traditional ERM, and recent improvements such as dynamic hedging models, an effective ERM needs to consider the systemic risks that made many insurance companies insolvent in the recent financial crisis.

MORE INFO

Books:
Moeller, Robert. *COSO Enterprise Risk Management: Understanding the New Integrated ERM Framework*. Hoboken, NJ: Wiley, 2007.

Articles:
AM Best Company. "Risk management and the rating process for insurance companies." *Methodology Report* (January 25, 2008).
Kenealy, Bill. "Sifting through the ashes to assess ERM's value—In a collection of essays, actuaries ponder the role of risk management in the financial crisis." *Insurance Networking News* (March 2009).
Mueller, Hubert, Eric Simpson, and Edward Easop. "The best of ERM—AM Best's enterprise risk management (ERM) criteria further confirm ERM as a central tool for insurers to manage their risk, capital, and strategic decisions more effectively." *Emphasis* (March 2008).
Mosher, Matthew C. "Special report: AM Best comments on enterprise risk management and capital models." AM Best, February 2006.
A collection of essays: *Risk Management: The current financial crisis, lessons learned and future implications*. Society of Actuaries, Casualty Actuarial Society, and the Canadian Institute of Actuaries, 2008. Online at: www.soa.org/library/essays/rm-essay-2008-toc.aspx

NOTES

1 In addition, Prudential Financial Inc. and Hartford Financial Services Group Inc. reported losses of more than $1 billion in the second half of 2008.

2 See "Risk management and the rating process for insurance companies." *Best's Methodology* (January 25, 2008).

Human Risk: How Effective Strategic Risk Management Can Identify Rogues
by Thomas McKaig

EXECUTIVE SUMMARY
- Corporations and high-level risk management are built around the people in organizations—and people are fallible.
- The need to evaluate human risk is clear: Stories abound of rogue employees in large and small organizations who have destroyed their entire firm.
- At the extreme, rogue firms, such as Enron, can destroy shareholder value and employees' lives.
- Building a quality-based organization helps to drive out rogues, but that's not the only way.
- Control measures need to be in place.
- Legal measures, the spotlight of publicity, and backing up corporate policies with firm action are all effective tools.

INTRODUCTION
Best practices in strategic risk management are intended to prevent weaknesses within corporations causing damage or even pulling down the firm. However, effective strategic risk management tools and techniques became harder to implement as business operations grow, become more complex, and operate in multiple locations. The controls that might have once been deemed acceptable in keeping employees within corporations on the same page begin to be less effective in cases of corporate restructurings that split businesses into smaller business units, and where employees are prodded into making deeper contributions to the bottom line.

Technology has not necessarily been a savior in this type of situation. Although technology has provided a platform for enhancing competitive advantage for business, it has also been a tool used by smart, capable, yet ill-intentioned employees to steal and distort overall results.

In the age of managerial cutbacks and increased workloads, a lot of things can happen that go unnoticed by overburdened managers. Interview techniques intended to keep rogues out of the workplace are—in spite of all the high-end questionnaires and intensive interview techniques that may be used—oftentimes ineffective, as potential employees are extremely savvy about modern interview techniques. Players in the job market are often familiar with the drill. Job hunters pass through many revolving interview doors, allowing them to hone their skills on how to dupe the interview process. Some interviewers may be incompetent or show poor judgment. HR departments are not foolproof, and it is only realistic to accept the fact that rogues in the workplace are here to stay. HR people will sometimes catch potential wrongdoers at the gatepost through psychological tests and other forms of due diligence involving intuition and criminal checks. But don't count on it.

Newspapers are full of stories about accountants who pad the books and give kickbacks to friends and family. Unhappy workers can damage product on the assembly line. A fired employee can show up at the workplace intent on payback for the injustice he or she feels they have suffered (in the United States this is called "going postal"). A multinational manager away from the watchful eyes of the home office can withhold information and deliver selective reports. Expense accounts can be padded. Goods can be pilfered from warehouses.

Given the current economic and political shocks, the last thing a company needs is to find itself in the news on account of the excessive creativity of one or more of its employees. Managers must face the fact that rogues will enter their organizations. So the question becomes: What can be done about it before the damage is done?

Keep in mind that human risk is about more than employees stealing from a firm; it can include individuals making unsound business decisions because nobody told them otherwise. Mistakes can be just as bad as deliberate fraud, as the following case shows.

AT THE EXTREME
At the extreme end of the spectrum, there is a widespread pattern of "pushing the boundaries" of everything from accounting rules to disclosure rules for public companies, lax internal controls, managements that focus on doing deals rather

Approaches to Enterprise Risk Management

CASE STUDY
An Invitation to Rogue Employees

The example of a small Costa Rican bank serves to illustrate this point. At the height of the opening of Costa Rica's financial markets to foreign financial institutions in 1995 there was a rush to change operations practice. In the pre-free market era, Costa Rican banks could do as they pleased and were immune to punishment even when there were banking scandals and losses that were large for Costa Rica's fragile economy during the 1980s and 1990s. Old-style banks, accustomed to getting away with providing poor customer service and having lax internal controls, found that their business environment was changing with the pending legislative changes, set to open Costa Rica's financial markets to the world.

With poor leadership at the helm, and a lack of almost any strategic management initiative, employees were forced to take on new and undefined roles in their bank. Most of these were ill-suited to employees who were given inadequate training and guidance for their new tasks.

As part of rising to the challenge of this expected competition from foreign banks, and in light of the assumed effectiveness of recently ordered ATM machines, the bank we are considering decided that a lean and mean (and ill-informed) policy of rampant firing would be an acceptable cost-saving measure. Half of the bank's staff lost their jobs, and those who remained quickly became demoralized. The newly installed bank machines did not function properly. Friday afternoon payday waits grew to two hours from the already unacceptable 15–30 minutes.

Internal communications broke down. In place of the usual courteous conversations, vitriolic emails flew from one cubicle to the next—seeding the environment for "surprise actions" from a growing league of unhappy, overworked, and demoralized employees. With no controls in place, an inexperienced bank teller authorized a loan of $US1 million to a long-standing customer—based solely on the fact that the teller liked the man and felt that he could be trusted with the money. For a small bank with a net worth of $US37 million, this inappropriate loan decision was the start of a string of poor management decisions that led to its implosion. Throughout this process the business culture undermined any attempts to implement benchmarking studies or best-practice management solutions. The "generous" employee was not fired and kept his duties with a severe reprimand. The future of the bank was sealed, and eventually it went down.

---

than managing, outright fraud and theft, and incentive systems that reward the wrong actions.

Enron followed this pattern. The case of Enron shows how a combination of intellectual laziness and groupthink by a large number of employees, consultants, and analysts allowed a group of greedy and ambitious individuals to get away with massive fraud. Enron was not a case of one or two people at the top undertaking a complex scheme unbeknown to others, but rather a case of many individuals who knew what they were supposed to do, but didn't do it. This was a case of analysts who never really questioned how Enron made its money, of accountants who didn't ask simple questions, and of employees and board members who saw dubious things but were afraid to stand up and ask the questions they should have.

STRATEGIC RISK MANAGEMENT: A VIEW

What is risk management, and how does it apply to the actions of employees? According to Kent D. Miller, "'risk' refers to variation in corporate outcomes or performance that cannot be forecast ex ante."[1] The key element here is to recognize that there is true uncertainty about human risk, or indeed any risk. The fact that an organization has survived to today without major scandal does not guarantee that it is safe in the future.

So what to do? According to Miller, effective risk management responses frequently include avoidance (which we have noted is almost impossible with the case of human risk), control (to be addressed in a moment), and cooperation and imitation (which can be achieved through quality initiatives).

QUALITY INITIATIVES CAN HELP

An organization is only as good as its parts—in this case the human parts. One fractured link in the chain means one vulnerable corporation. The quality aspect of management can be evoked to work hand in hand with problem prevention, but it is all too often overlooked.

Typically quality applies to (but is not limited to) reducing or eliminating defects in manufactured products. Beyond this, management also needs to invoke quality principles that smooth the internal environment. When intra-corporate

How Effective Strategic Risk Management Can Identify Rogues

MAKING IT HAPPEN
- Learn to live with the uncertainty of any risk, especially human risk.
- Place renewed emphasis on what is already being done, including audits (financial and performance), internal financial controls, and clear financial reporting.
- Vigilantly tweak and enforce the control mechanisms already in place. Think about expanding and/or adding controls.
- Revisit your own role as a highly visible manager. Are corporate controls short-sighted, or are they clearly structured so as to prevent deceit, fraud, and rogues from doing future damage?
- Identify high-risk areas in your firm—from inventory to treasury areas. Think about safety and security measures in addition to internal controls.

communication channels are damaged, the ensuing misinformation may foster rogue behavior within the organization. Many quality experts cite training, transparency, empowerment, and clear communication as vital steps in building a quality organization.

Whether dealing with production issues or those relating to customer service, quality initiatives espoused by management thinkers like Armand V. Feigenbaum, J. M. Juran, Philip B. Crosby, and Frank Gryna can help a business. Firms that include quality as a core value, and reinforce this value through everyday practice, have experienced reductions down to zero of defects on production lines, lower worker turnover, higher levels of worker empowerment through training, more worker satisfaction, greater productivity, and a positive outlook on the company. Valuing people as the key drivers of both quality and performance is important to a firm and can go a long way toward identifying rogues and frustrating their efforts.

Quality starts with managers. Being an ethical role model is a key function of any leader. And the good news is that nothing special has to be done to become such a positive model. However, when leadership falters it can open the door to a rogue hit, doing as much damage to the corporation as a rogue wave can do to a ship at sea. You have to work at good leadership.

But the emphasis on quality alone is not enough. Control mechanisms, including both financial and performance audits, are important for preventing and uncovering potential problems. The really effective tools are punishment and brandishing the legal arsenal available to the company. Such measures reassure the public. A corporation just can't hunker down to avoid embarrassment. Swift and fair measures will fill the void of those strategic management initiatives that fail to catch rogue employees and will serve as a heavy reminder to others who may be about to embark on a negative course of action.

To many, the idea of punishment seems to be a return to management's dark past in the days of command and control. This is not the case. Taking corrective action, including negative reinforcements and punishments, is a legitimate function of managers, just as much as positive reinforcements are. Corrective actions can include firings, admonishments, wage deductions, and suspension without pay. People in authority are chary about digging in their heels to fight for what is ethically and obviously right for fear of being politically incorrect, or worse, manifestly insensitive. Many in decision-making positions prefer a course of inaction because they lack the gumption required to stay the course. If a manager has documented proof (paper or electronic) of wrongdoing by an employee, and particularly in a unionized environment, there is little that a union can do to "rescue" the employee from receiving the appropriate reprimand, short of the union condoning such rogue behavior.

CONCLUSION

A manager faces many risks—from industry-wide risks such as currency and interest rate risks, to department-specific risks such as accounting and treasury risks. Most of these risks can be quantified, though we are finding out that many of the numbers assigned to these risks are little more than educated guesses. Unfortunately the identification, measurement, and quantification of human risk are difficult and challenging. In spite of our best efforts, and in spite of pundits who spout an arsenal of "proof" to the contrary, reliable numbers cannot be assigned to human risk. Nor can risk be completely eliminated from an organization. But quality initiatives and control mechanisms can go a very long way to minimize exposure.

Approaches to Enterprise Risk Management

MORE INFO

Books:

Crosby, Philip B. *Completeness: Quality for the 21st Century*. New York: Dutton, 1992.

Feigenbaum, Armand V. *Total Quality Control*. 4th ed. New York: McGraw-Hill, 2004.

Gryna, Frank, M. *Quality Planning & Analysis: From Product Development Through Use*. 4th ed. New York: McGraw-Hill, 2000.

Hill, Charles W. L., and Thomas McKaig. *Global Business Today*. 2nd Canadian ed. Whitby, ON: McGraw-Hill Ryerson, 2009.

Juran, J. M., and Frank M. Gryna (eds). *Juran's Quality Control Handbook*. 4th ed. New York: McGraw-Hill, 1988.

Mintzberg, Henry. *Managers Not MBAs: A Hard Look at the Soft Practice of Managing and Management Development*. San Francisco, CA: Berrett-Koehler Publishers, 2004.

Articles:

Becker, David M. "Testimony concerning new regulatory tools to control the activities of rogue individuals in the financial services industries." Given before the Subcommittee on Oversight and Investigations and the Subcommittee on Financial Institutions and Consumer Credit, US House of Representatives, March 6, 2001. Online at: www.sec.gov/news/testimony/ts042001.htm

Boak, Joshua. "Rogue trader rocks firm: Huge wheat futures loss stuns MFGlobal." *Chicago Tribune* (February 29, 2008). Online at: archives.chicagotribune.com/2008/feb/29/business/chi-fri_traderfeb29

Clark, Andrew. "From ethical champion to rogue interloper—BP's American nightmare: Accidents and allegations of market fixing destroy environmentalist image." *Guardian (London)* (November 16, 2006). Online at: www.guardian.co.uk/business/2006/nov/16/ethicalbusiness.oilandpetrol

Gunther, Will. "In the crosshairs: Limiting the impact of workplace shootings." *Risk Management* 55 (November 2008). Online at: findarticles.com/p/articles/mi_qa5332/is_11_55/ai_n31162724

Johnston, David Cay. "Staff says IRS concealed improper audits and rogue agent." *New York Times* (May 1, 1998). Online at: tinyurl.com/aqf9tr

KPMG. "An approach to mitigating rogue trading risks." KPMG LLP, 2008. Online at: www.us.kpmg.com/Rutus_Prod/Documents/12/19429NSS_RogueTrader_screen.pdf.

Malakian, Anthony. "Internal controls need to be tightened." *Bank Technology News* (April 2008). Online at: www.americanbanker.com/btn_article.html?id=20080327QJ4HD229

Prince, C. J. "To catch a thief: Employee fraud hits growing businesses hardest. Here's what you can do to make sure there's not a thief among you." *Entrepreneur Magazine* (September 2007). Online at: www.entrepreneur.com/magazine/entrepreneur/2007/september/183068.html

Website:

CBC News coverage of the Conrad Black affair: www.cbc.ca/news/background/black_conrad

NOTES

[1] Miller, Kent D. "A framework for integrated risk management in international business." *Journal of International Business Studies* 23:2 (1992): 311–331.

Best Practice
Risk Measurement and Management

Managing Operational Risks Using an All-Hazards Approach by Mark Abkowitz

EXECUTIVE SUMMARY
- Operational risk management (ORM) enables an enterprise to understand, prioritize, and control risks that threaten its well-being and the livelihood of its partners.
- Although traditionally stove-piped within an organization, different operational risks share many common elements, providing an opportunity to consolidate ORM into a single all-hazards approach, one that is holistic and systematic.
- The key to effective ORM is to recognize and mitigate those risk factors that erode our margin of safety, so allowing situations to spiral out of control.
- A key first step is for an organization to perform an ORM physical, enabling the identification of reasonably foreseeable risks, benchmarking the current status of the ORM program, revealing gaps where the organization is vulnerable, and developing cost-effective strategies to address these gaps.
- Based on recent historical events and changing conditions in our world, bringing ORM to the forefront of an organization is more important now than ever before.

OPERATIONAL RISK MANAGEMENT: A DEFINITION AND A STRATEGY

For the purpose of this discussion, Operational Risk Management (ORM) is considered to be the policies, methods, practices, and institutional culture that enable an enterprise to understand, prioritize, and control risks that threaten the well-being of the organization, its business partners, communities in which it operates, and society at large.

The cost of *poor* operational risk management can be excessive, considering that the occurrence of undesirable events can lead to fatalities and injuries; property loss; business interruption; clean-up, remediation and disposal; fines and penalties; future inspections; new regulations; long-term human health effects; environmental degradation; damaged investor, insurer, supplier, and customer relations; and loss of public confidence. By contrast, the cost of *good* operational risk management may be limited to investment in risk management benchmarking and needs assessment; resources allocated to control high-priority risks; and ongoing costs associated with ORM performance monitoring and evaluation.

THE NEED FOR AN ALL-HAZARDS APPROACH

In many organizations, the approach to dealing with operational risks is stove-piped, with different entities having responsibility for different hazards. For example, environmental health and safety worries about toxicity exposure, legal is concerned with liability, human resources focuses on occupational health, executive management has its eye on business continuity, risk management addresses insurance, and research and development cares about design failure. As a result each group has its own priorities, separate resources are used to address each problem, and there is limited coordination. Yet, while each threat may seem quite different, when one takes a closer look at how these events evolve, there is remarkable similarity; that is, a pattern or "recipe" for disaster emerges. This situation begs for the adoption of a single "all-hazards" ORM approach, a process that is holistic and systematic in nature.

RISK FACTORS

Within a recipe for disaster, each ingredient can be thought of as an underlying risk factor that erodes our margin of safety. Once this margin of safety is exceeded, the situation is liable to spiral out of control. Therefore, management control of risk factors is at the crux of an effective ORM program. In attempting to manage these risk factors within an organization, it is helpful to group them into the following categories:

Design and construction flaws: If there is a flaw in the design process and it is not discovered in time, the system is prone to failure. Even when the design is valid, problems can still arise if the materials used to fabricate the system components are faulty or the components are not assembled properly.

Deferred maintenance: It is human nature to choose to deal with problems at a later time, especially if the system is not actually malfunctioning. Unfortunately, decisions to defer

Approaches to Enterprise Risk Management

maintenance often lead to the failure of a key system component before the repair can be made, causing a serious accident to occur.

Economic pressures: Organizations typically manage a limited budget. When these resources are too scarce or spending is not controlled adequately, pressure intensifies to implement strict cost-cutting measures. This can lead to shoddy workmanship, the purchase of inferior quality materials, elimination of the use of backup operating and safety equipment, or management ignoring problems that arise.

Schedule constraints: When a deadline has been imposed, and the activity has fallen behind schedule, pressure to make up ground can cause the responsible party to turn a blind eye to important details. This situation often leads to the elimination of critical tasks, personnel trying to accomplish tasks in parallel that should be done in sequence, or not pursuing certain considerations in sufficient depth to understand their impact on safety fully.

Inadequate training: Because of a lack of adequate training, individuals who are prone to make mistakes may be placed in positions of responsibility. This in turn can either initiate or intensify a crisis situation. When there are personnel shortages, individuals may be thrown into an important decision-making role while covering for others, performing a function for which they were not properly trained. Because individuals tend to forget what they were originally taught and since processes change over time and require new learning, lack of retraining can also be a problem.

Not following procedures: When engaged in a repetitive activity, complacency can set in, and individuals tend to drift away from following formal protocols. Consequently, they either neglect to perform certain steps or invent other ways to accomplish the same task, often not considering the possible safety hazards caused by their actions. Failing to follow procedures can create a hazardous situation, one that is exacerbated by coworkers whose actions are based on assuming that those procedures are being followed.

Lack of planning and preparedness: Because of the luxury of time and the fact that a disastrous event may not have been experienced in recent memory, people tend to place a low priority on being adequately prepared for a crisis situation. All too often, little forethought is given to the variety of disaster scenarios that could reasonably occur and how to deal with them effectively. Even in circumstances where significant effort has been devoted to planning and preparedness, the product of this effort can be a written plan that is not practiced or updated, rendering it of little value when a calamity arises. Lack of planning and preparedness is one of the most common risk factors at play when something goes wrong.

Communication failure: Communication failures can occur at various stages, altering an outcome in different ways. When communication fails between members of the same organization, critical information is not shared, such as when one group decides to shut down a critical protection system for maintenance while another group is carrying out a dangerous experiment. Poor communication between organizations is also problematic. Finally, lack of communication with the public or the provision of inaccurate information can place people at risk either because they do not know the hazards they are facing, or because they are not properly advised on how to protect themselves. Along with lack of planning and preparedness, communication failure is the most common risk factor at play when something goes wrong.

Arrogance: Arrogance can rear its head in many forms, but usually appears as either the person in charge being driven to succeed for individual gain without sufficient regard for the safety of others, or an experienced individual who has become overconfident in his or her ability to deal with any problem that might present itself. In either form, arrogance can have serious repercussions.

Stifling political agendas: Government policies can have a powerful effect on the propensity for disasters. If these political agendas are hard-nosed, with little room for dialog and compromise, affected parties can feel that they have little recourse other than to resort to extreme and often hostile measures.

It is important to note that we, as humans, are involved in each and every one of these factors. While this implies that we contribute to the cause or impact of every disaster, it also means that we have an opportunity to control these factors more effectively to achieve a better future outcome.

GETTING STARTED

A key first step is for your organization to have an ORM physical, essentially a comprehensive review of how operations are performed, what risks are present in performing these operations, and how these risks are presently being managed. This engages the organization in identifying "reasonably foreseeable" risks, benchmarking the current status of the existing ORM program, identifying program gaps where the

Managing Operational Risks Using an All-Hazards Approach

organization carries the greatest liability, and suggesting strategies and tactics that can be implemented to close these gaps. Having a risk physical is important regardless of whether the organization's ORM program is relatively new or fairly mature.

CASE STUDIES
ORM Failures and Successes
There are several historic events that bring the failures and successes of operational risk management into focus. How could the event have been prevented? What could have been done to mitigate the impacts? What management controls have been implemented since the event occurred? Could it happen again? These are all legitimate ORM questions that, through hindsight, allow us to learn from experience and apply these lessons to deploying more effective ORM in the future.

Hurricane Katrina
During August 2005, Hurricane Katrina slammed into the United States, hitting the coastal areas of Florida, Louisiana, and Mississippi. A combination of storm surge, wave action, and high winds resulted in the destruction of buildings and roads in the affected areas. The impact of Katrina on New Orleans was unusually severe; portions of the city were left under 20 feet of water due to failure of the earthen levees and floodwalls that had been constructed to safeguard the city from this type of event. Hurricane Katrina caused nearly 2,000 fatalities and an estimated economic loss of $125 billion, in addition to displacing hundreds of thousands of people from their homes and workplaces. The destruction and loss of life in New Orleans, while initiated by the storm itself, cannot be attributed entirely to Katrina. Numerous failures of the city's flood protection system due to poor design and construction, deferred maintenance, and a lack of funding left New Orleans susceptible to a hurricane of Katrina's magnitude. As the city filled with water, the hurricane's effects were compounded by insufficient emergency planning and preparedness, and the inability of responders to communicate.

Alaska Pipeline and Denali Earthquake
A major earthquake struck the Alaska mainland on November 3, 2002, along the Denali fault, which passes directly under the Trans-Alaska Pipeline. Had the pipeline ruptured, it would have resulted in spillage of up to a million barrels of crude oil a day in an environmentally sensitive area. Yet not a drop of oil was released. This potential catastrophe was averted due to successful ORM in both the design of the pipeline system and the quality of the maintenance, surveillance, and emergency preparedness. The pipeline design team, using extensive field data, devised a system such that it could survive a major earthquake should one occur during the pipeline's projected 300-year operating period. As a result, a $3 million upfront investment in geological studies and corresponding design considerations helped to prevent an environmental disaster that could easily have topped $100 million in remediation costs. Concurrently, a comprehensive surveillance and maintenance system was implemented, capable of identifying problem locations in real time and dispatching crews accordingly. Moreover, emergency response was facilitated by a well-organized incident command system, contingency planning, and a training program.

MAKING IT HAPPEN
- Designate ORM as a core business practice within the organization by establishing the program at the vice-president level. The VP should be responsible for defining ORM policies and procedures, and for providing oversight of program activities.
- Organize an ORM committee, which reports to the VP, with membership that includes representatives from each element of the organization that has a designated ORM responsibility.
- Perform an ORM physical, and use it as a basis for defining program priorities, allocating resources, and implementing management control strategies.
- Monitor and evaluate ORM performance to determine whether program objectives are being met.
- Maintain ORM as a living process that is part of the culture of the organization.

Approaches to Enterprise Risk Management

CONCLUSION

We can ill afford not to recognize the new age of operational risk management, one based on a holistic and systematic approach to identifying reasonably foreseeable risks, establishing priorities, and adopting practical, achievable, and cost-effective control strategies. As history has taught us, we remain vulnerable to the occurrence of catastrophic events whose prevention or mitigation is within our control. Moreover, changing conditions in our world are posing new challenges that will require making tough risk-related choices.

Adopting an all-hazards ORM approach does not mean that we will never suffer another tragedy. However, the prospect of that happening is less likely to occur once investments in prevention and mitigation have been made. The bottom line is that we can, and should, do much better at being a master rather than a victim of risk. All it takes is a more organized approach to managing the risks that affect our daily lives, coupled with a greater tolerance for unfortunate events that will sometimes occur no matter how hard we try to avoid or prevent them.

MORE INFO

Books:
Abkowitz, Mark D. *Operational Risk Management: A Case Study Approach to Effective Planning and Response*. Hoboken, NJ: Wiley, 2008.
Garrick, B. John. *Quantifying and Controlling Catastrophic Risks*. San Diego, CA: Elsevier, 2008.

Websites:
Risk World: www.riskworld.com
Society for Risk Analysis: www.sra.org

Business Continuity Management: How to Prepare for the Worst by Andrew Hiles

EXECUTIVE SUMMARY
- No organization is immune from disaster.
- Business continuity management (BCM) is an integral part of corporate governance.
- A business continuity plan (BCP) can protect your brand, reputation and market share.
- The prerequisite discipline of risk and impact assessment reveals critical dependencies and threats to them, enabling preventative measures to be taken.
- Risk and impact assessment identifies and prioritizes mission-critical activities and the timeframe in which they must be resumed; it can also provide new risk insights to improve your business performance.

INTRODUCTION
Over five years even a well-managed organization has an 80% chance of suffering an event that damages its profits by 20%.[1]

The cause could be equipment downtime, failure of utilities or supply chain, terrorism, fire, flood, explosion, or adverse weather. Whatever the cause, without a business continuity plan (BCP), the result is the same: damage to reputation, brand, competitive position, and market share. Sometimes this damage, and subsequent losses, are severe enough to lead to permanent closure.

Yet such loss can be minimized, or even avoided, by implementing a business continuity management (BCM) system which includes developing a BCP.

Quite simply, those organizations that have a BCP tend to survive a major adverse incident, while those without a BCP tend to fail.

WHAT IS BCM?
According to one definition, BCM is: a "holistic management process that identifies potential impacts that threaten an organisation and provides a framework for building resilience and the capability for an effective response which safeguards the interests of its key stakeholders, reputation, brand and value creating activities."[2]

Information and communications technology (ICT) disaster recovery is an important and integral part of BCM—but only one part. BCM covers all mission-critical activities (MCAs)—operations, manufacturing, sales, logistics, HR, finance, etc.—not just the technology.

THE BC PROJECT
BCM starts as a project, but, once the BCP has been developed, audited and exercised, it becomes an ongoing program needing regular maintenance and exercise.

The project activities are illustrated in Figure 1.

Figure 1. BCP project structure

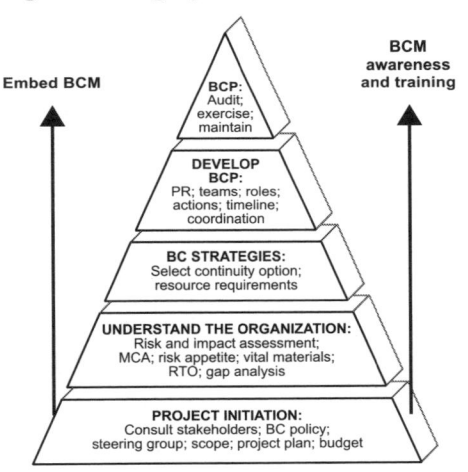

(Pyramid diagram, from bottom to top:
- PROJECT INITIATION: Consult stakeholders; BC policy; steering group; scope; project plan; budget
- UNDERSTAND THE ORGANIZATION: Risk and impact assessment; MCA; risk appetite; vital materials; RTO; gap analysis
- BC STRATEGIES: Select continuity option; resource requirements
- DEVELOP BCP: PR; teams; roles; actions; timeline; coordination
- BCP: Audit; exercise; maintain
With side arrows: Embed BCM and BCM awareness and training)

MAKING BC HAPPEN
Phase One
The BC project should start with a clear understanding of the needs of the stakeholders and the support of the board. BC policy needs to be set.

A high-level steering group needs to be set up to decide priorities and define the scope of the project. For instance, is the objective to be "business as usual"—or will it just cover the 20% of goods or services that generates 80% of the profits? Will it cover all customers, or just the most important ones? Does it embrace all locations, or just head office? How far does it go down into the supply chain? Will it cover only local disasters, or is it to cope with wide-area disasters—hurricanes, major floods, etc.?

85

Approaches to Enterprise Risk Management

GLOSSARY
BC: Business continuity
BCM: Business continuity management
BCP: Business continuity plan
BIA: Business impact assessment
DRP: A plan for the continuity or recovery of information and communications technology (ICT)
MCA: Mission-critical activities
Risk appetite: The level of loss that an organization is prepared to tolerate
RTO: Recovery time objective
RPO: Recovery point objective (of data or transactions)

Next, a project plan should be developed, identifying the milestones and deliverables of the project. These include:
- risk and impact assessment;
- agreeing BC strategies;
- developing the BCP and implementing contingency arrangements;
- audit and exercising the BCP.

A budget can be established for Phase One from a knowledge of how many sites are to be covered, how many people are to be interviewed, how many processes are to be included at each site, and an assessment of time for research and report-writing.

Risk and impact assessment can be broken down into subactivities:
- identification of assets and threats to them;
- weighting threats for probability and impact (in cash and non-cash terms);
- identification of MCAs and their dependencies;
- establishing the recovery time objective (RTO) for each (the maximum acceptable period of service outage);
- establishing the recovery point objective (RPO) for each (the time-stamp to which data and transactions have to be recovered);
- identifying the resources needed for recovery and the timeframe in which they are required;
- identifying any gaps between the RTO, RPO, and actual capability (for example, the IT backup method may not permit recovery within the RTO);
- establishing the organization's appetite for risk;
- making recommendations for risk management and mitigation;
- making recommendations to close any gaps revealed.

The risk and impact assessment is usually conducted by analysis of building plans and operational layouts; review of reports on audit, health, safety, and environmental and operational incidents; interview of key personnel; and physical inspection.

Once these activities have been completed, possible contingency arrangements can be considered. The instinctive reaction is to replicate existing capability—but there may be more cost-effective options.

Holding buffer stock could cover equipment downtime. Increased resilience and "hardening" of facilities may reduce risk to an acceptable level. Items or services could be bought in, rather than undertaken in-house. Contracts could be placed with commercial BC service vendors for standby IT, telecommunications, and work area recovery requirements.

The risk and impact assessment then forms the basis for a cost–benefit analysis of the contingency options and allows a BC strategy to be recommended and agreed.

This report, incorporating the findings and recommendations from the risk and impact assessment, forms a natural closure to Phase One. Usually there is a natural break while recommendations are considered and the budget for Phase Two is agreed.

Phase Two
Once the BC strategy has been agreed, the BC plan can be started, bearing in mind what constraints may be placed on your organization by emergency services, public authorities, regulators, and landlords and other occupants (if you occupy a building with more than one tenant).

Incident and emergency management plans (for instance, evacuation, fire, bomb threat, etc.) need to be consistent with the BCP, and there needs to be escalation processes from them into the BCP. Triggers should also be identified for escalation from customer complaints, failure of service-level agreements, problem and incident management processes, etc., into the BC process.

The BC organization may not necessarily mirror the normal organization—for instance, multidisciplined teams may be appropriate—and the BC manager or coordinator may not usually hold the level of authority they are accorded under disaster invocation.

Typically the board will be separated in two: one to manage the ongoing business, the other to deal with the disaster situation. The emergency, crisis or business continuity management team

Business Continuity Management: How to Prepare for the Worst

Table 1. Partial example of a BC organization

BC Management team	IT team	Base site recovery team
Leader: BC management team leader Alternate	*Leader:* TBD Alternate: TBD	*Leader:* TBD Alternate: TBD
Members: CFO Alternate COO Alternate PRO Alternate Marketing director Alternate Estates manager Alternate: TBD Admin support: TBD	*Members:* Applications manager Alternate PC servers/LAN manager Alternate Data/voice communications manager Alternate: TBD Admin support: TBD	*Members:* Office services manager Alternate PC servers/LAN Alternate: TBD Data/voice communications Alternate: TBD Damage assessment/salvage Alternate Loss adjuster: TBD Admin support: TBD
Reports: BC manager Alternate		
Roles: Consider group (corporate) impacts. Manage recovery. Coordinate all team action. Consider safety and security and environmental issues. Decide on priorities. Reassure media and authorities.	*Roles:* Recovery of all platforms, systems applications, and data at standby site: TBD Data/voice communications recovery at standby site: TBD	*Roles:* Damage assessment, limitation, and salvage Recovery at base site Recovery of operational capability at base site IT, data/voice communications recovery at base site
TBD – to be determined		

(BCMT) will include board-level decision-makers. These include members from business and support units, and the BC manager (effectively the project manager for recovery) will report to them.

Business and support unit teams, including ICT, will report on recovery progress and seek clarification, information, and support from the BC manager. The BC manager will resolve any priority clashes within their authority and refer others to the BCMT.

Table 1 is a partial example of a BC organization. Additional BC teams will be created as necessary to cover each MCA, business or support unit. The overview at Table 1 needs to be amplified by detailed action plans covering each BC team.

The BCP coordinator is not necessarily the same person who will be BC manager once the BCP is completed. The BCP coordinator's role is to ensure that all BCPs are completed consistently and comprehensively.

The BCPs should not be scenario-based, since the disaster is unlikely to fit neatly into any scenario envisaged. Instead, they should be based on a worst-case scenario: total loss of MCAs. However, if they are developed in a modular fashion, only that part which is relevant need be invoked if a lesser disaster happens.

The BCP coordinator will draft a BCP for the BCMT and for their BC activities, including BCP invocation procedure, and will provide advice and guidance to the business and support unit BC coordinators.

Next, a template BCP should be developed that can be used for each team. Once they have had training, BCP development coordinators for each business and support unit complete these. A support program can be created for their guidance as they develop their BCPs.

Each BCP should spell out assumptions so they may be challenged (for example, an assumption that more than one site will not suffer a disaster at the same time; or that skilled people will be available post-disaster).

The minimum content should include:

- prioritized MCAs and a credible action plan for their recovery within RTO and RPO;
- lists of team members, alternates, roles, and contacts;
- resource requirements and when and how they are to be obtained;

Approaches to Enterprise Risk Management

CASE STUDY
Buncefield
Buncefield Oil Storage Terminal supplied fuel to London Heathrow from pipelines transporting fuel from the north of England. It was owned by Hertfordshire Oil Storage Ltd, a joint venture between Total and Texaco. Other businesses were attracted to the site—Marylands Industrial Park—because of its low cost.

Around 06:00 hours on Sunday, December 11, 2005, an explosion occurred, measuring 2.4 on the Richter scale; it was heard as far away as France and the Netherlands.

The Buncefield incident was the biggest explosion, and the accompanying fire was the biggest fire, in peacetime Europe. Twenty-five different fire services tackled the blaze with 600 fire fighters.

The explosion and subsequent fire:
- destroyed some 5% of UK petrol stocks and destroyed 20 fuel tanks;
- injured 200 people; 2,000 were evacuated;
- damaged more than 300 houses and required 10 buildings to be demolished;
- caused all the schools in the county to be closed;
- cost local businesses and local authorities £1 billion: it impacted 600 businesses and prevented 25,000 staff from getting to work;
- disrupted global air traffic schedules and local transport;
- caused businesses to suffer disruption of supply;
- caused many organizations to invoke their BC plans;
- made big retailers reassess their supply chain issues;
- forced companies to make public statements to protect their share value;
- created major environmental impact from millions of gallons of burning oil, which required more than three million gallons of contaminated firewater with up to 40 different contaminants to be disposed of; it took 500 tankers five weeks to move it.

Other impacts were equally devastating:
- By January 10, 2006, data recovery and communications restoration was still ongoing.
- By January 11, 2006, 75 businesses employing 5,000 people were still unable to use their premises.
- Insurance cover was inadequate to cover losses.
- In August 2006, 2,700 claimants sued for a billion pounds in a case that will cost £61 million.
- Supermarket chain Sainsbury's closed three stores damaged by fire.
- Brewers Scottish & Newcastle lost £10 million of stock.
- Retailer Marks & Spencer closed a food depot, disrupting deliveries to retail outlets.
- Fujifilm, 3Com Corporation, and Alcom buildings were damaged.
- Andromeda Logistics' distribution centre was evacuated: operations resumed on December 12 from their alternative distribution center.
- Shares in British Petroleum, a bystander, briefly dived.
- ASOS (As Seen On Screen), an online fashion retailer, lost its new warehouse with £5.5 million stock (19,000 orders were refunded).
- British Airport Authority rationed aviation fuel at Heathrow: airlines diverted to other European airports to refuel.
- Broadcasts on BBC radio and television news urged motorists to avoid panic buying of fuel.
- The HQ of XL Video, a video producer for trade shows, events, television, and concerts suffered structural damage. They had 12 projects to load on the Monday morning. Their BCP diverted projects: all shows were shipped on December 12.
- IT outsourcing company Northgate Information Solutions Ltd had backups ready for collection at 07:00 hours daily, but the fire happened at 06:00. Local tax payments went uncollected, and billing information for utility companies was lost.

Hertfordshire County Council's crisis management plan worked: it had been used at the two rail incidents at Potters Bar and Hatfield and been thoroughly tested in October 2005.

Business Continuity Management: How to Prepare for the Worst

- contact details of internal and external contacts;
- information on relevant contracts and insurance;
- reporting requirements;
- instructions on handling the media;
- any useful supporting information (such as damage assessment forms; maps and information about alternate sites; detailed technical recovery procedures).

Once the BCPs have been developed they can be audited, reviewing each BCP for comprehensiveness, clarity, and accuracy. This also ensures that interrelationships between BCPs are reflected in the counterparty BCP.

Rigorous exercises probe BCP effectiveness under different disaster scenarios and provide realistic training for BC team members.

Lessons from BC audit and tests should be incorporated into the BCPs. Where this has not yet been done, a list should be provided at the beginning of the BCP stating what weaknesses were found to exist; who is responsible for rectifying them; and the timeframe for doing so.

The BCP may take many forms: hard copy; handheld devices; memory sticks, etc. Whatever the format, it should be kept secure, and steps should be taken to ensure that only the current version can be held.

CONCLUSION

Wise executives have long known the importance of risk and impact assessment and the need for contingency planning. With today's threats, this has never been more important. Buncefield proved the need to:

- develop a BCP to protect reputation, brand, and share value and market share;
- communicate to key stakeholders;
- communicate to emergency services and staff;
- keep investors and customers informed;
- have alternative sites for operations and for a control center;
- read and understand the emergency plans of the local authorities;
- ensure that key standby resources are in place, such as information (status, contacts); accommodation (operations and work area); and reserves (stock, spare equipment, etc.).

Buncefield cost local businesses £70 million, much of it uninsured. It is imperative to check insurance cover. The impact of a major disaster could last for months, or even years.

MORE INFO

Books:

Hiles, Andrew. *Business Continuity: Best Practices—World-class Continuity Management*. Brookfield, CT: Rothstein Associates, 2007.

Hiles, Andrew. *The Definitive Handbook of Business Continuity Management*. 2nd ed. Chichester, UK: Wiley, 2007.

Hiles, Andrew N. *Enterprise Risk Assessment and Business Impact Analysis: Best Practices*. Brookfield, CT: Rothstein Associates, 2002.

Von Roessing, Rolf. *Auditing Business Continuity—Global Best Practices*. Brookfield, CT: Rothstein Associates, 2002.

Websites:

Association of Contingency Planners: www.acp-international.com
Business Continuity Institute: www.thebci.org
Continuity Central: www.continuitycentral.com
Disaster Recovery Institute International: www.drii.org

Standards:

BS 25999 Business Continuity Management (UK)
HB 221 Business Continuity Management (Australia)
NFPA 1600 Emergency Management and Business Continuity (USA)

NOTES

1 Oxford Metrica, www.oxfordmetrica.com
2 British Standards Institute/Business Continuity Institute Publicly Available Specification 56.

Countering Supply Chain Risk
by Vinod Lall

EXECUTIVE SUMMARY
- Business strategies such as outsourcing, lean manufacturing, and just-in-time lead to efficiency gains but at the same time expose the supply chain to higher risks.
- There are different sources of risk in a modern supply chain. Recognizing and appropriately managing these risks is necessary for a glitch-free functioning of the supply chain.
- Supply chain risk management strategies must be holistic and integrated with the whole supply chain environment.
- Firms must have dedicated budget line items for supply chain risk management activities.
- Failure mode effects analysis (FMEA) can be used to assess supply chain risks.

INTRODUCTION
In March 2000, a fire at a Philips semiconductor factory damaged some components used to make chips for mobile phones. Ericsson and Nokia—two of Philips' major customers—responded to the event in very different ways. Ericsson decided to let the delay take its own course, while supply chain managers at Nokia monitored the situation closely and developed contingency plans. By the time Philips discovered that the fire had contaminated a large area that would disrupt production for months, Nokia had already lined up alternative suppliers for the chips. Ericsson used Philips as a sole supplier and faced a severe shortage of chips, leading to delay in product launch and huge losses to its mobile phone division.

Today's global supply chains are complex and lean while efficiently delivering products and services to the marketplace. These supply chains involve a rigid set of transactions and decisions that span over longer distances and more time zones with very little slack built into them. As a result they are susceptible to several types of risk. These risks include operational risk due to demand variability, supply fluctuations and disruption risk due to natural disasters, terrorist attacks, pandemics, and breaches in data security. Such risks disrupt or slow the flow of material, information, and cash, and put billions of dollars at stake due to stock market capitalization, failed product launches, and the possibility of bankruptcies. In the above example, Ericsson lost 400 million euros after the Philips semiconductor plant caught fire; another example occurred when Apple lost many customer orders during a supply shortage of memory chips after an earthquake in Taiwan in 1999. Supply chain executives and managers must visualize and have a clear understanding of these risks along the entire supply chain, starting from the sourcing of raw materials to the delivery of the final product or service to the consumer. Once these risks are identified, they need to be scored on the likelihood of occurrence, and their impact must be quantified. Resources must then be used to mitigate or eliminate elements of high risk.

TYPES OF SUPPLY CHAIN RISK
Supply chain risks can be classified into different types depending on their origin. These include supply risk, demand risk, internal risk, and external environment risk.

Supply risk: These are the risks on the supply/inbound side of the supply chain. Supply risk may be defined as the possibility of disruptions of product availability from the supplier, or disruptions in the process of transportation from the supplier to the customer. A supplier may be unavailable to complete an order for a number of reasons, including problems sourcing necessary raw materials, low process yield due to increased scrap, equipment failure, damaged facilities, or the need to ration its limited product among several customers. Transportation disruptions occur while products are in transit and add to the delivery lead time. They may be caused by delays in customs clearance at borders, or problems with the mode of transportation, such as the grounding of air traffic.

Demand risk: Demand risk is the downstream equivalent of supply risk and is present on the demand/outbound side of the supply chain. It may be due to an unexpected increase or decrease in customer demand that leads to a mismatch between the firm's forecast and actual demand. Increase in customer demand leads to depletion of safety stocks, resulting in stockouts, back orders, and the need to expedite. A fall in customer demand leads to increased costs of holding inventory and, inevitably, price reductions. Other sources of demand risk are dependence on a single customer, customer solvency, and failure of the distribution logistics service provider.

Internal risk: This is the risk associated with events that are related to internal operations of the firm. Examples include fire or chemical spillage leading to plant closure, labor strikes, quality problems, and shortage of employees.

External environment risk: These risk elements are external to and uncontrollable from the firm's perspective. Examples include blockades of ports or depots, natural disasters such as earthquakes, hurricanes or cyclones, war, terrorist activity, and financial factors such as exchange rates and market pressures. These events disrupt the flow of material and may lead to plant shutdown, shortage of high-demand items, and price increases.

STRATEGIES FOR SUPPLY CHAIN RISK MANAGEMENT

Strategies for managing risk must be a part of supply chain management and must include processes to reduce supply chain risks that at the same time increase resilience and efficiency. Firms typically use basic strategies of risk-bearing, risk avoidance or risk mitigation, and risk transference to another party. The goal of risk-bearing is to reduce the potential damage caused by the materialization of a risk, and to be successful requires that early warning systems be installed along the supply chain. The main goal of risk avoidance is to reduce the probability of occurrence of a risk by being proactive, while under risk transfer the potential impact of risk is transferred to another organization such as an insurance company.

MITIGATING SUPPLY CHAIN RISKS

A firm could use strategic and tactical plans under four basic approaches to mitigate the impact of supply chain risks. These approaches include supply management, demand management, product management, and information management. The task of managing supply chain risk is difficult as approaches that mitigate one risk element can end up exacerbating another. Also, actions taken by one partner in the supply chain can increase the risk for another partner.

Supply Management

Supply risks can be reduced by building a web of internal and external sources. Strategically, firms should focus their core competencies on new products and ideas and the engineering necessary to reduce time-to-market. They should continue to manufacture strategic, high-value, long-life products that have relatively low demand volatility while outsourcing non-strategic, low-value manufacturing and logistics services. It is important to be very selective in building a strong web of vendors and closely managing the vendor network. For each new product, the firm must capitalize on the varying expertise of its vendor network and use expected time-to-market, quality level and price to select a vendor from the network.

Tactical plans under supply management focus mostly on supplier selection and supplier order allocation. For this, firms should develop a profile of their supply bases to get a more complete picture of the supply side of the chain. This profile should include a wide range of supplier information including the total number of suppliers, the location and diversity of suppliers, and flexibility in the volume and variety of supplier capacities. Analysis of these data will help firms identify vulnerabilities in their supply chains so they can strategize, create contingency plans, conduct trade-off analysis of issues such as single sourcing, and, if needed, identify and line up backup sources.

Demand Management

Strategic plans under demand management focus on product pricing, while tactical plans are used to shift demand across time, across markets, and across products. One product pricing strategy is called the "price-postponement strategy," whereby the firm decides on the quantity of the order in the first period and then determines the price in the second period after observing updated information about demand. Shifting demand across time is known as "revenue management" or "yield management," whereby firms usually set higher prices during peak seasons to shift demand to off-peak seasons. One technique for shifting demand across markets is called "solo-rollover by market;" this involves selling new products in different markets with time delays, leading to non-overlapping selling seasons. To shift demand across products, firms use pricing and promotion techniques to entice customers to switch products or brands.

As with the supply side, firms must also develop a profile of the demand side to analyze the outbound side of the supply chain. Analysis of the demand side will identify dangers such as those associated with overreliance on a single distribution center to serve a large market, or the risks of having a highly concentrated customer base.

Countering Supply Chain Risk

Supply Chain Reserves Management
Firms can deal with supply chain risks by holding reserves of inventory and capacity in the supply chain. Managers must decide carefully on the optimal location and size of these reserves as an undisciplined approach may lead to increased costs and hurt the bottom line.

backlogs, etc. This offers more opportunities to all parties to respond quickly to sudden changes in the supply chain and requires the implementation of information technology solutions that interface business data and processes end to end.

The collaborative planning, forecasting, and replenishment (CPFR) model is often used to

MAKING IT HAPPEN
It is critical to have an easy-to-use tool to identify and manage supply chain risk. FMEA is a well-documented and proven risk management tool that is used to evaluate the risk of failures in product and process designs. It can be used to evaluate supply chain risk using the following process steps:
- **Step 1**. Identify the categories of supply chain risk.
- **Step 2**. Identify potential risks in each category.
- **Step 3**. Use a rating scale of 1–5 to rate the opportunity, probability, and severity for each risk. The opportunity score for a risk is the frequency with which it occurs. One-time risk events receive an opportunity score of 1, while commonly occurring risk events are assigned an opportunity score of 5. The probability score is the score for the expected likelihood that a risk event will actually happen, so high probability scores are used when the probability of a risk event occurring is large. The severity score indicates the level of impact if the risk materializes. Low-risk events cause a minimum impact on the supply chain and receive a low severity score. Risk events that have a significant impact on the supply chain in terms of cost, time, and quality are assigned a high severity score.
- **Step 4**. For each potential risk, calculate the risk priority number (RPN) as RPN = opportunity × probability × severity.
- **Step 5**. Use Pareto analysis to analyze risks by RPN. Pareto analysis is a formal technique used where many possible courses of action are competing for the attention of the problem-solver. The problem-solver estimates the benefit delivered by each action and then selects the most effective action.
- **Step 6**. Develop action plans to mitigate risks with high RPN.
- **Step 7**. Use another cycle of FMEA to reassess the risks.

Product Management
Firms can look at their internal networks and develop a profile of their products, processes, and services. Analysis of data in this profile can help to determine if there is a good mix of products and services and if there are risks in processes such as those used for fulfilling orders.

Information Management
Information technology tools can be used to understand and manage risk better by providing visibility into planned events and warnings for unplanned events in the entire supply chain. Firms must manufacture low-risk products first and use improved forecasts to produce the riskiest products very close to the selling season. This requires the use of reliable data and better forecasting methods. Key members in the supply chain must have easy and timely access to accurate information on such measures as inventory, demand, forecasts, production and shipment plans, work in process, process yields, capacities,

induce collaboration and coordination through information sharing between supply chain partners such as retailers and manufacturers. Under CPFR, the manufacturer generates an initial demand forecast based on market intelligence on products, and the retailer creates its initial demand forecast based on customer response to pricing and promotion decisions. Both parties share their initial demand forecasts and reconcile the differences to obtain a common forecast. Once both parties agree on the common forecast, the manufacturer develops a production plan and the retailer develops a replenishment plan.

CONCLUSION
The pursuit of new markets for products and of new sources for components is making supply chains longer and more complex. With this expansion comes increased risk, which may result in disruptions to the supply chain. These disruptions may be unexpected and statistically rare, but they must be understood, identified, and managed.

Approaches to Enterprise Risk Management

MORE INFO

Books:
Chopra, Sunil, and Peter Meindl. *Supply Chain Management: Strategy, Planning & Operations*. 3rd ed. Upper Saddle River, NJ: Prentice Hall, 2006.
Sheffi, Yossi. *The Resilient Enterprise: Overcoming Vulnerability for Competitive Advantage*. Cambridge, MA: MIT Press, 2007.

Websites:
Council of Supply Chain Management Professionals: cscmp.org
Supply-Chain Council: www.supply-chain.org

A Total Balance Sheet Approach to Financial Risk by Terry Carroll

EXECUTIVE SUMMARY
- Because the oil price rose rapidly and the wider commodities market followed suit, inflation rose to its highest level for many years. Following a protracted boom, property prices have been savaged. Only interest rates have remained comparatively benign.
- Protecting or insulating yourself or your company against financial risks is known as "hedging." Most businesses use a transaction-driven approach. The generic name often used by bankers for these hedging instruments is "treasury products."
- Bankers can provide a derivative-based hedge to reduce or neutralize an interest rate, inflation, or commodity price risk. A derivative is a financial instrument whose value changes in relation to an underlying variable such as interest rates, commodity prices, or house prices.
- Price increases and currency fluctuations, as well as interest rate movements, can be hedged. The most common source of long-term capital, fixed by nature, is retained profits. A mismatch between, say, fixed-rate assets and variable-rate liabilities may cause you to want to hedge or renegotiate more fixed-rate liabilities to produce a better match and more overall certainty, with, by definition, lower overall risk.

INTRODUCTION
We are living in some of the most volatile times in the history of the global financial markets. One of the reasons is exactly because they have become truly global. As banks seek to restore profitability, they may increase their offering of "treasury products" to customers. This article argues that these should be considered only in the context of a total balance sheet approach rather than transaction by transaction.

MANAGING INCREASED FINANCIAL RISK
We have seen a period in which the oil price rose to $147 a barrel and then fell back dramatically. The wider commodities market followed suit. Inflation rose to its highest level for many years before easing back. Property prices have been savaged, following a protracted boom. Only interest rates have remained relatively benign compared to the extremes of the past.

Volatility has been traded as a market index for many years, but in 2008 alone it hit several spikes. It has become a fact of life. Markets are now driven mainly by fear—fear of being caught out when prices fall or fear of not being in the market as prices rise. Add to that the power of short sellers and you have a scary scenario for borrowers and investors, whether individuals or corporate.

Protecting or insulating yourself or your company against financial risks is known as "hedging." The principle of hedging is easily understood—it's like an insurance premium.

In practice, the instruments generally used are known as "derivatives." These are poorly understood and, given the recent financial mess, probably viewed with fear or trepidation.

This article attempts two things: first, to put forward a more objective approach for companies wishing to improve their financial efficiency at a managed level of risk; and second, to demystify financial risk, making it a more approachable topic for the average manager or director.

WHAT IS A DERIVATIVE?
A derivative is a financial instrument whose value changes in relation to an underlying variable, for example: interest rates, the rate of inflation, commodity prices, share or bond prices, house prices, etc. Its most general use is for the purpose of "hedging" a given risk, i.e. neutralizing or taking the opposite position to a given risk, such as commodity prices, exchange or interest rates.

The problem with derivatives is that although they were created for the primary purpose of insuring against financial risks, the proportion of derivatives trading done for speculative purposes now dramatically outweighs that for ordinary trade purposes.

MOST HEDGING IS TRANSACTION-BASED
In this article we shall be proposing a "full balance sheet approach" to the management of financial risk. Most businesses currently use a transaction-driven approach. This could result in overall risk being increased rather than decreased.

Approaches to Enterprise Risk Management

By a transaction-driven approach, we mean that each transaction or set of similar transactions is individually hedged. This is the most common situation, whether the use of derivatives is recommended by a bank or requested by the customer. The generic title often used by bankers for these hedging instruments is "treasury products."

Trading and managing the use of derivatives is a highly skilled and often complex process. They are usually created and dealt with by the treasury or special products division of a bank. In the United Kingdom, these "rocket scientists," as they are sometimes known, are usually based in the City of London, embedded within the financial markets.

If you wish to hedge a risk, your bank will usually put you in touch with such a treasury specialist. Alternatively, the bank may make the first move. Not surprisingly, banks have increasingly been offering these products in the climate of increasing volatility for all the commodities and financial facilities that companies use.

A TRANSACTION-BASED APPROACH CAN ACTUALLY INCREASE OVERALL RISK

There is an important difference between the profit and loss account approach and the balance sheet approach to improving financial efficiency. Any accountant or banker worth their salt can look at the profit and loss account and come up with suggestions on how to improve profitability or reduce risk. If you fear interest rate, inflation, or commodity price risks, your banker can provide you with a derivative-based hedge to reduce or neutralize that risk. Accountants like certainty, so that they can sleep easy at night.

The danger of this approach is that it can actually increase the risk of loss for the company. Take a simple example:

Suppose you have a commercial property—the business premises for example—that you own and plan to keep for the long term. It is by nature, therefore, a fixed asset. It has a fixed notional return, i.e. its long-term value to the business. You wouldn't think of financing it out of short-term overdraft. You want a long-term debt, ideally, to finance it. This may well be at an interest rate linked to bank base rate.

Your bank draws your attention to the possibility that interest rates may increase. Wouldn't you like to hedge that risk? Their treasury products division can sell you an interest rate hedge that swaps the variable-rate risk into a fixed-rate risk, thereby insulating you against the cost of rising interest rates.

Now consider two worrying circumstances. The first is that interest rates actually fall. In those circumstances you have not only lost the value of the "premium" you paid, i.e. the cost of the derivative contract, but you've also lost the opportunity to gain from the interest rate falls, because you're now effectively stuck with a stream of fixed-rate payments.

So the first and most important consideration is not to use hedging on a transaction by transaction basis, because you may actually be increasing the overall risk profile of the company.

Take another example: sterling is falling against the dollar and, because commodities are usually priced in dollars, the effective cost you are paying for your raw materials is increasing. So you decide to hedge against the risk of a rising dollar. But suppose you also sell much of your finished product overseas. Whether or not you are invoicing in dollars—but especially if you are—the currency you receive will be exchanging into more and more pounds. This could be counterbalancing your raw material price increases.

Of course, you could decide to hedge the raw material currency risk alone and profit from the widening margins in sterling. But again, if the currency rates swing round the other way, your sales income in sterling will be falling and you won't benefit from the fact that raw material prices are also falling. This again illustrates the importance of looking at both sides of the trading account or balance sheet.

A HOLISTIC OR FULL BALANCE SHEET APPROACH

So, the first point we are making is that when you are looking at your trading, before entering into a hedge on one side of the transaction, i.e. the buying or selling side, you should also consider what is happening on the other side. You can hedge price increases and currency fluctuations, as well as interest rate movements.

There is also a range of products that can make the holistic hedging approach even more effective. As well as swapping variable interest rate payments for fixed, you can also buy what is called a "cap" or a "collar." A cap protects you from interest rate increases above a certain level but enables you still to benefit if rates fall; and a collar gives you protection from interest rate fluctuations both up and down, outside a given band of rates, and may be cheaper.

Having considered trading transactions on both sides of the equation (such as the inflation of selling prices matching out the inflation of raw material costs), the most significant and generally underexploited area is the balance sheet.

A Total Balance Sheet Approach to Financial Risk

Many of you will have come across fixed-rate mortgages for home purchase. Although 25-year fixed-rate mortgages have been available in recent years, few have been taken out to date. Normally fixes are for up to five years. The problem is that, on a 25-year mortgage term, after five years you are exposed to the risk of rising rates again. In other words, you don't have a perfect hedge.

And so with balance sheets. It would seem to be folly to fund long-term fixed assets from overdrafts, but that is exactly what some businesses effectively do. By taking the whole balance sheet perspective, you can not only ensure that you reduce overall financial risk, but you can also increase profitability without increasing risk.

EFFECTING THE FULL BALANCE SHEET APPROACH

You may still wish to seek the help of a treasury specialist, but here you want them to look at the whole balance sheet.

To take the earlier example: you may have funded the purchase of a commercial property that you intend to use and keep indefinitely, by borrowing on a five-year term at a margin over bank base rate. There is certainly logic in swapping this into a fixed rate if you think interest rates may rise, but this can also be a gamble because if they fall, you are not gaining the benefit.

Furthermore, the most common source of long-term capital, fixed by nature, is retained profits. So, suppose that your retained profits are at least as great in value as the cost of the property. Given that both are retained for the long term, they could be said to match each other. This leaves the cash that you have borrowed on a variable rate free to fluctuate. If you also generate spare cash on the other side of the balance sheet, then, in order not to increase the overall financial risk in the balance sheet, either this should be invested at a variable rate, or, if it is at a fixed rate, then the cost of the debt should be swapped to variable.

When you put all those assets and liabilities together in the balance sheet, you have not only reduced the financial risk in the balance sheet, but you have also significantly improved the certainty of the net cost or profit arising from those matched transactions.

THE CONCEPT OF DURATION RISK

The final piece of the jigsaw is known as "duration." In simple terms, duration is the length of the life of the particular asset or liability. The importance of this is as follows.

Most people understand the likely folly of borrowing short to lend long. You wouldn't borrow money for six months to buy your house. You might borrow money for 25 years with a fixed rate for the first five to give you relative certainty, but because of the constant risk of rising interest costs it is no surprise when people are looking to refix the rate for another two, three, or five years—for example, when the first fixed rate runs out. It may cost more, but that is the price of certainty.

So, the final piece is duration, and we bring this together with the whole balance sheet approach. First, you analyze your whole balance sheet by looking at each of the assets and determining which liabilities are funding which assets. If you have a mismatch between, say, fixed-rate assets and variable-rate liabilities, you may want to hedge or renegotiate more fixed-rate liabilities to produce a better match and more overall certainty, with, by definition, lower overall risk.

The next stage is to look at the average duration (or maturity/life) of the assets and the same for the liabilities. If there is a mismatch, either you will have greater overall certainty and lower risk because the average duration of the liabilities is longer than that of the assets, or you may have greater overall risk and less certainty if the balance is the other way. In the latter case, you may wish to increase the average duration of the liabilities, perhaps by refinancing.

CONCLUSION

We have introduced some complex concepts here, but this is for at least two important reasons: first, if you have, or know of, a risk that you face and choose to do nothing about it, that decision alone increases the risk to the corporation. Hedging through the use of the increasingly sophisticated range of derivative-based products can both reduce risk and increase either or both the overall return and the certainty of costs or return.

This can only be guaranteed if you use the full balance sheet approach or look at both sides of the transaction. If you allow yourself to be persuaded to hedge individual transactions, you may by definition actually be speculating and, worse still, increasing the overall risk profile of the business.

Any worthwhile treasury products specialist at your bank should understand all the principles and concepts introduced in this article and would find it hard to disagree with the overall premise. Business finance should be about improving returns and the certainty of returns and reducing or neutralizing risk. Never has this been truer than in these increasingly volatile times.

Approaches to Enterprise Risk Management

MORE INFO

Books:
Choudhry, Moorad. *Bank Asset and Liability Management: Strategy, Trading, Analysis*. Singapore: Wiley, 2007.
Van Deventer, Donald R., Kenji Imai, and Mark Mesler. *Advanced Financial Risk Management: Tools and Techniques for Integrated Credit Risk and Interest Rate Risk Management*. Singapore: Wiley, 2005.

Article:
Roy, Sayonton. "Asset liability management in risk framework." Online at: www.coolavenues.com/know/fin/sayonton_1.php3

Website:
RiskGlossary.com—see entry for "asset–liability management": www.riskglossary.com

Quantifying Corporate Financial Risk
by David C. Shimko

EXECUTIVE SUMMARY
- Standard pro forma cash flow analysis considers risk in a crude way, usually with a subjectively determined upside and downside to cash flows.
- Stochastic analysis generates a large number of scenarios to give a better understanding of risk interactions, business linkages, optionality, and contracts designed to mitigate risk.
- Simple models can be built in spreadsheets, but one must take care to model financial assets, commodity prices, interest rates, and exchange rates appropriately.
- Stochastic pro formas can lead to better capital budgeting, valuation, and risk management decisions, particularly when risk is important to decision-making.
- Even the most sophisticated models are still subject to model risk; and they do not likely capture all the risks affecting an enterprise.

EXAMPLE OF A STOCHASTIC PRO FORMA

Consider the case of a company that has experienced six months of cash flows this year and wants to forecast the next six months. The usual way to do this is to predict a cash flow growth rate—expected, high, and low—and to base the analysis on these choices. A sample cash flow projection might be illustrated graphically in Figure 1.

In reality, of course, several different cash flow patterns might emerge for the last six months of the year. Using the same risk model, we could run a large number of simulations and see what the outcomes might be. Eight possible outcomes are plotted in Figure 2.

Clearly the stochastic analysis, albeit more realistic, is not as simple and not as attractive at first blush as deterministic analysis. And there are many situations where stochastic analysis is not needed. Yet there are certain results that one can get from stochastic analysis that cannot be gained from deterministic analysis. Table 1 gives some examples.

Stochastic analysis is needed in situations where risk assessment is required, where the future company decisions depend on an unknown variable, where options are present, and when the company wants to study risk mitigation strategies.

Stochastic modeling of the income statement can be done at the aggregate level as it has been demonstrated here, or the components can be broken down into smaller components, such as the prices of products, inputs, interest rates, foreign exchange rates, and the like. The benefit of breaking down the income statement into its market-driven components is that we can find much more information on market-quoted prices and rates. This historical information is usually used as a starting point in determining how best to model these prices and rates.

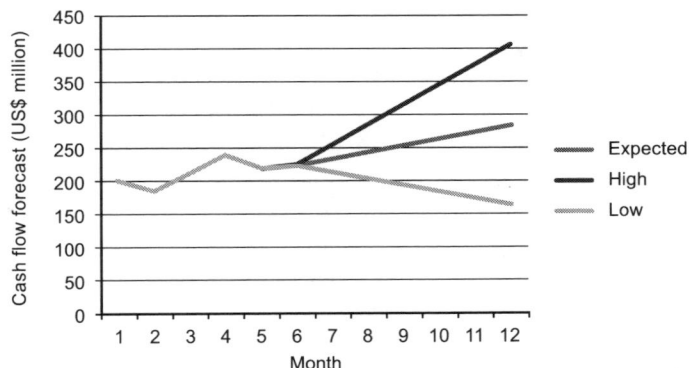

Figure 1. Deterministic cash flow forecast for last six months

Approaches to Enterprise Risk Management

Figure 2. Stochastic cash flow projection for last six months

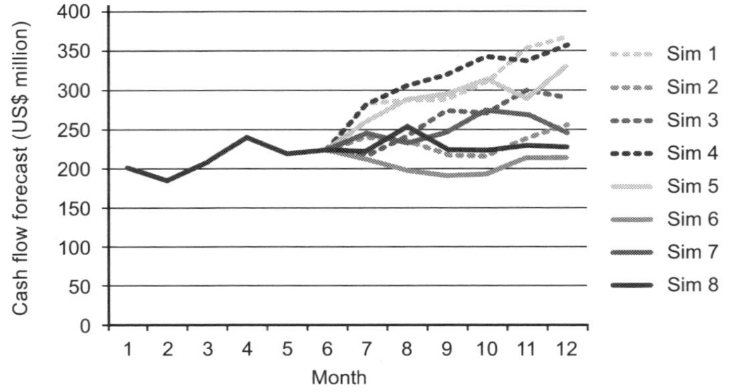

[Line chart showing Cash flow forecast (US$ million) from 0 to 400 on y-axis, Month 1 to 12 on x-axis, with eight simulation lines (Sim 1 through Sim 8)]

Table 1. Incremental analyses produced by stochastic pro formas

Analysis	Sample question
Probabilities of outcomes	What is the likelihood we will need to borrow?
Risk of outcomes	What is the most likely range for annual cash flows at year-end?
Interactions	If we invest more in capital expenditures only when cash flows are up, how do we reflect that in the analysis, and what impact does it have?
Options	Our loan contracts have floating rates, but the rates are capped. How does this affect the probabilities of different cash flow levels?
Worst case	We probably won't have the worst case revenues and the worst case costs in the same year; how does that reflect on our expectation of the worst case?
Events	There's a 10% chance we get a major contract that will increase our cash flows significantly. How do we incorporate this in the model?
Risk mitigation	The treasurer wants to lock in foreign exchange rates for our foreign buyers. How will this affect cash flow volatility?
Capital structure	What is our capacity to make interest payments on debt with 99% certainty?

MODELING MARKET RISK

Risk analysts need to spend significant time and effort to model the risk of the inputs to their stochastic models correctly. Incorrect specifications for market prices will lead to incorrect results. There are several models available to model market price risk. The choice of the best model generally is made by looking at the market's historical performance and making judgments about market price behavior.[1]

For example, if our risk model depends on fluctuations in the stock market index, a popular approach is to represent the index as following a random walk in percentage terms. Thus, any given day's return is normally distributed with a constant mean and standard deviation, and statistically independent from the previous day's return. This approach was popularized in the Black–Scholes (1973) and Merton (1973) papers on option pricing. The random walk works reasonably well, except that with specialized knowledge one could argue that the average return should not be constant, the volatility should not be constant, and there are sometimes events which cause stock prices not to be normally distributed. For this reason, the S&P 500 index may reasonably follow a random walk, but the stock of a small pharmaceutical company will not, since it is prone to occasional major events such as FDA drug approval or discovery of legal liability.

Other market prices, such as interest rates, do not follow random walks. Overly high and overly low interest rates tend to correct over time to equilibrium levels. Although that equilibrium level may change over time, the general character of interest rates is that they are *mean-reverting*—i.e., they revert to a long-run mean over time. The same is true of commodity prices. High commodity prices stimulate production, which causes future prices to fall. Low prices discourage production, causing future prices to rise. Therefore, interest rates and commodities need to be modeled in a similar way. Some currencies exhibit mean-reverting behavior and some do not.

Finally, every market price may have unique characteristics. The volatility of natural gas and heating oil changes by season. Power prices spike rapidly when generation fails and bounce back immediately as generation comes back on line. Careful modeling of critical market price inputs will lead to the best models of stochastic results.

MODELING RISK INTERACTIONS
It is not enough to have good models of security prices, interest rates, foreign exchange rates, and commodity prices. We must also understand how those prices and rates interact. For example, higher security prices are generally correlated with low interest rates. The Australian dollar exchange rate is correlated to gold prices, due to the importance of gold mining in its economy. In many cases, simplistic correlation is fine to establish a linear relationship between changes in the risk variables. However, in other cases, the correlations may not be linear, requiring a more subtle approach. For some firms, that subtlety will be important enough to build a precise model of the interaction between two risks of importance to the company.

MODELING EVENT RISK
Every corporation is subject to risks from significant events, such as losing a major lawsuit, or obtaining a patent on its proprietary technology. Also, the company can be affected by market-related events, such as the bankruptcy of a key supplier. In many modeling situations, these events play an important role in determining the probability distributions of future cash flows.

It is tempting to think of event risks as being random outcomes, independent of everything else in the model. This is the biggest mistake a modeler can make. The credit crisis of 2008, for example, showed vividly how default risks across investment banks were correlated, owing to the similarity of their risk-taking activities.

AGGREGATING CASH FLOW RISKS TO THE INCOME STATEMENT
Once all the drivers of the income statement have been modeled, they are compiled to the income statement in the same way that a pro-forma income statement would normally be generated. For example, suppose a refinery in Brazil buys crude oil in dollars, sells products in reais, shuts down production when it is not profitable to produce, and runs the risk of operational failures according to some statistical model. In this case, the modeler could build stochastic formulas for the price of crude, the price of products, the dollar foreign exchange rate, the shutdown policy of the firm, and the unplanned outage rates due to operational risk. The result is a determination of net income for each particular simulated environment. These net income numbers can be simulated as many times as required to determine the volatility of cash flows, the value of the shutdown option, and the answer to any of the questions posed above.

MODELING RISKS OTHER THAN CASH FLOW
Some risks may not affect cash flows but could affect earnings, such as a mark-to-market liability. In these cases, similar risk models can be built to model earnings risk, or to model the likelihood of a credit downgrade. Stochastic models can be simple or extremely complex, but they all are built fundamentally to make deterministic models more realistic and able to answer questions related to risk, risk management, optionality, capital structure, and much, much more.

CONCLUSION
Stochastic pro-forma analysis answers many financial questions that cannot be addressed with usual deterministic pro-forma analysis. The case study demonstrates how hedging and capital structure may be evaluated using stochastic pro formas. Other applications include evaluation of real options,[2] the study of credit ratings, and the development of probability statements around cash flow or earnings.

Like any other type of analysis, poor assumptions lead to poor conclusions. Good simulation models take a great deal of care in specifying the correct models for all the risk drivers and the interactions between them. Finally, more realistic risk-based models lead to better corporate financial decisions.

MAKING IT HAPPEN
- Begin with a project or corporate pro forma.
- Consider every assumption and ask if it is vulnerable to risk.
- Produce a risk model to simulate all the assumptions consistently and simultaneously.
- Use this model (stochastic pro forma) to design best and worst cases.
- Simulate outcomes of all key financial variables and communicate the risks.

Approaches to Enterprise Risk Management

In the final analysis, however, even a very sophisticated model is still a model, and is therefore subject to model risk. Thus, the model may not fully identify or quantify all risks that affect an enterprise, and can thereby lead to a false sense of security. Accordingly, decision-makers should consider model risk as one of the components of any financial decision based on stochastic pro-forma analysis.

CASE STUDY

An ethanol-producing company may be reluctant to issue more debt because of the high volatility of its cash flows and the increased risk of being put into bankruptcy.

A bank has proposed a transaction where the company would reduce its risk by selling its ethanol to customers at a price agreed today—i.e., entering forward contracts. If it did so, the bank would lend additional funds at the same rate. The company is reluctant to accept the bank's proposal because the sales price falls below the level at which the company thinks it can sell ethanol, costing the company $2 million per year. How can the company compare the benefit of higher debt with the cost of selling at a distressed price? And how can the company and the bank determine an appropriate level of additional debt?

A stochastic pro forma analysis could be done for the company before and after the proposed transaction. Before the transaction, the average earnings before interest and tax (EBIT) is estimated at $100 million with a standard deviation of $50 million. Shown in Figure 3 are five outcomes simulated over an eight-year period. The current annual debt service is $49 million.

Figure 3. Current EBIT stochastics

By selling its ethanol forward, the company expects to lose $2 million per year, but to reduce the standard deviation to $25 million. The resulting stochastics demonstrate that the company can now prudently afford to make higher interest payments without having much risk of failure to pay (Figure 4).

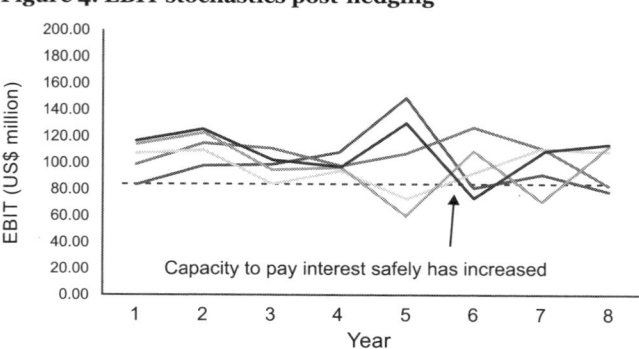

Figure 4. EBIT stochastics post-hedging

Quantifying Corporate Financial Risk

The company can afford to pay $65 million in interest safely, after hedging its results. Should the company accept the hedging program? The answer depends on taxes. If the ethanol company is not in a tax-paying situation, it has lost an expected $2 million per year in value, so it should not hedge unless there are other reasons to do so. A taxpaying firm in the 40% bracket, however, will be able to deduct the interest expense from taxable income, saving $6.4 million per year (40% of 65 minus 49). The taxpaying firm should hedge, barring other considerations that might cause the firm not to want to hedge.

MORE INFO

Articles:

Black, Fischer, and Myron Scholes. "The pricing of options and corporate liabilities." *Journal of Political Economy* 81:3 (1973): 637–654.

Merton, Robert C. "Theory of regional option pricing." *Bell Journal of Economics and Management Science* 4:1 (1973): 141–183.

Websites:

Most of the literature in "stochastic processes" is extremely technical and not suitable for the average business reader. Even "stochastic processes in finance" tends to lead to models of security prices and interest rates for building value-at-risk models and option pricing models.

The topic "financial statement simulation" in an internet search engine leads to simulation software providers, such as Palisade, Finance 3.0, and @Risk. These providers offer written materials to supplement their software services. In addition, the reader is invited to request additional materials from the author.

NOTES

1 Analysts should never expect that historical price behavior will represent future price behavior—only to realize that there is usually no better source of information for modeling purposes.

2 See the article on "Real Options: Opportunity from Risk" in this volume (pp. 61–64).

To Hedge or Not to Hedge by Steve Robinson

EXECUTIVE SUMMARY
- How currency risks are created and managed and the types of risk inherent in international trading.
- The techniques for managing currency risks.
- A framework for selecting appropriate techniques in specific business situations.
- An outline and illustration of the use of the main financial derivatives.

INTRODUCTION
Business has become increasingly international, and companies cannot ignore the impact of currency changes on cash flows, profitability, and their asset and liability position. No company is wholly immune—the cash received from exporting is affected by the relationship between the currency used by the customer to pay and the currency in which the cost of providing the product or service is denominated.

Many commodity prices have been volatile, rising and falling dramatically in recent years—driven by exploding or plummeting demand from fast-developing countries. Copper, tin, wheat, platinum, and of course oil, have risen dramatically, and this has had a significant impact on costs for many industries. Declines can be equally sudden, although falling costs often take more time to work through to market prices.

A spectacular result was the sudden collapse of several airline businesses in late 2007 and early 2008. Among them was EOS, a business-class only carrier operating mainly between London and New York, which started only in 2005. Also, Oasis Hong Kong Airlines, an innovative long-haul discount operator between Hong Kong, London, and Vancouver, MAXjet Airways, and some smaller low-cost US carriers, have all ceased trading very suddenly. Although other factors, such as reduced business travel and turbulent financial markets, have had an impact, the price of aviation fuel is the main cost driver, closely followed by the impact of currency changes—airlines pay all their costs in US dollars.

The risks extend beyond the trading sphere. Many banks have had to write down the value of their assets—largely complex "trading" securities. Finance is a global industry, and companies borrow and invest in many currencies. It is not sufficient that only financial people know how currency risks are created and managed.

WHAT ARE THE RISKS?
Currency risk is the net potential effect of exchange rate movements on the cash flow, profit, and balance sheet of a business. There are three types of currency risk:

Economic, Strategic, or Competitive Risk
Economic exposure covers the indirect risk to the profitability and cash flow of a company that arises from changes in exchange rates. It is likely that ultimately a resultant transaction exposure will arise.

An illustration, relating to the US dollar, the euro, and sterling, could be holidays. For British holidaymakers, holidays in the euro zone and the US dollar zone become more expensive if sterling weakens. The UK holiday industry could benefit from the euro exchange rate if more British stayed in the United Kingdom for their holidays.

Translation Risk
Translation risk arises when amounts denominated in foreign currency are converted to domestic equivalents for financial reporting purposes. There is no immediate cash impact. Translation can affect both the profit and loss account and the balance sheet. Increasingly, converging accounting standards under International Financial Reporting Standards (IFRS), which do not apply to unquoted companies, are removing some previous distortions. The most common accounting policy is to convert trading profit and loss numbers at an average exchange rate during the accounting period, and to convert assets and liabilities at the year-end rate.

Profit and Loss Statement Translation
The profit and loss translation is only a paper figure initially, but it may become a real transaction exposure if cash interest or dividends need to be paid. A company with a large proportion of its income, or of its cash, in other currencies, will have a translation issue, but this can be helped

Approaches to Enterprise Risk Management

by effective communication to investors, persuading them that short-term currency fluctuations will not necessarily lead to reduced long-term stockholder value creation.

Balance Sheet Translation
The foreign currency assets of the company are not exposed to currency fluctuations unless they are to be sold and the cash converted to another currency. Liabilities denominated in foreign currencies will represent a real exposure when they are due for repayment.

The impact of translation on the gearing level has to be evaluated to ensure that no covenants are breached, even if only technically. A very simple way around this is to match investment in foreign currency assets with loans dominated in equivalent currencies.

The practical difficulty is how far the company can go to protect reported earnings, while incurring a cost that will impact on the bottom line. It is also possible that a real transaction exposure could be created by a currency borrowing. Also to be considered is the impact of a fair value adjustment, on both the profit and loss bottom line and on reserves in the balance sheet.

Transaction Risk
This risk is that exchange rate movements affect the value of foreign currency cash flows. It is the only risk that has a direct and immediate impact on cash, and arises when a transaction is entered into to convert from one currency to another.

The most common trading situation creating this exposure is the sale or purchase of goods or services on extended payment terms in foreign currencies. Another common situation arises when dividend or interest payments are paid or received.

This type of risk is usually predictable and quantified, making the protection or hedging process straightforward. Really successful management of currency exposures needs to cope with transactions that have not yet been identified but are likely to occur.

SPECIFIC SITUATIONS
Price List Exposure
Scenario: An exporting company publishes a price list in a local currency. It is commercially impractical to change prices in less than six months.
Risk: A potential exposure is created for up to six months, plus any extended payment term. Actual exposure arises when an invoice is issued.
Possible solutions:
- Small print "right to impose surcharges" clauses. This is legally possible, but commercially highly damaging. Airlines have had to resort to this, but it is easier for them given the high profile of oil price movements and the fact that almost all of the competitors are doing it!
- Hedging a proportion of projected sales, from the date of publication of the price list, is advisable. What proportion is a risk management decision, dependent on the corporate attitude to risk, the corporate memory of past situations, and the degree of volatility between currencies.

Capital expenditure: This investment is usually planned and committed over a long period. There may be no actual transaction exposure until purchase contracts are awarded, so the exposure can be identified, quantified, and handled by a hedging technique.

Tender to Control Exposure
Scenario and risk exposure: Companies that regularly submit tenders for the supply of goods and services are exposed from the date of submitting the tender to the date(s) cash is received. Until an order has been received, this is potential exposure; after that event there is real exposure, and from the invoice date transaction exposure exists.
Possible solutions:
- Using historic data for guidance, assess the success rate from tender to contract. Apply that rate—with a value weighting—to all tenders issued, hedging the proportion that's likely to be successful. Additionally, where good market intelligence exists, add in those contracts likely to be won.
- Treat the exposure after winning the contract as a transaction, and hedge using an appropriate technique.
- Try to offset as many costs as possible by buying in the currency of the payer.

MANAGING CURRENCY RISKS
A range of techniques exists that enable companies to limit their exposure to the effect of fluctuating exchange rates. The decision to protect or hedge is made after an assessment of the significance of the risk to the business of exchange rate movements. The selection of hedging technique is made for each specific situation, following a risk assessment of the impact on the business. Factors considered in the risk assessment are:
- The percentage of the company's turnover that is exposed to currency risk. The greater the proportion of sales paid in international currencies versus the home currency, the greater the risk to the business.

To Hedge or Not to Hedge

- The individual size of a single exposure. Depending on the volatility of the currency, this could be a very high risk, even threatening the continuity of the business.
- The market position of the company. This is its financial strength and consequent ability to react to competitive pressures.
- The portfolio of currencies in which the company trades, and whether there are potential offsetting transactions.
- The relationship of cost to sales within trading blocs, particularly currencies that move in lockstep with the US dollar—those of Canada, Hong Kong, Malaysia, Singapore, and Saudi Arabia.
- The ability to match the currency of sales with the currency of costs.
- The previous experience of the company in relation to currency losses, and its forecasting experience.
- The level of currency management expertise within the company.

HEDGING TECHNIQUES
Internal
Sometimes known as commercial or natural, these techniques are within the internal management control of the company.

Pricing:
- In the currency in which the majority of the costs are incurred.
- In the domestic currency of the main competitors, so that comparative prices are less affected by exchange rate variations.
- Inserting an exchange rate variation clause (always difficult commercially) to protect margins.

Matching:
- Setting up an equal and opposite commercial transaction when the original exposure is created—for example, using the currency of a receivable to buy a commodity used by the business.
- Borrow in the same currency as that needed to complete the asset purchase.

Netting:
- A partial alternative to matching—a net amount is still left exposed, but the overall risk is reduced.

Leading and lagging:
- Simply, either delaying payment, or settling early, in anticipation of falling or rising exchange rates. Safe, and simple to manage, but there is a reliance on the accuracy of a forecast.

Intercompany payment discipline:
- Intercompany payables and receivables are real exposure and should be ranked equally for settlement with external liabilities.
- There is no canceling gain or loss situation within a group. When the transaction interacts with the market there will be a gain or a loss—and it will be real.

External
When the use of internal techniques has been exhausted, external ones should be used. There are four main instruments:
- Forward contracts;
- Lending and borrowing;
- Options;
- Swaps.

Forward Contracts
A forward contract is an agreement to exchange a fixed amount of one currency for a fixed amount of another currency at an agreed date in the future. The effective exchange rate is derived from the comparative interest rates of the two currencies being exchanged. Its suitability depends on being able to forecast the currency flows confidently. If the forecast proves not to be accurate, the business has in reality created an exposure rather than protected an existing one, because the forward contract is a binding agreement to deliver a quantity of one currency and receive a quantity of another. The key features of a forward contract are:
- Certainty and simplicity—enabling good cash management;
- Off balance sheet—it does not count as borrowings that affect gearing;
- Normally sourced from a bank.

Lending and Borrowing
As an alternative to a forward contract, the currency could be exchanged immediately in the spot market, i.e. where the transaction is agreed on the "spot" and takes place immediately. The exchange rate is known as fixed, the transaction immediate (two days delivery normally), and the administration and monitoring of forward contracts are avoided. The currency is normally deposited in an interest-bearing currency account until needed.

Illustration: A forward transaction to buy yen for a capital equipment purchase has been made. Delivery will be late. A way around this problem would be to take delivery of the yen as agreed and put the amount on deposit until needed. As yen interest rates are lower than for sterling, there will be an effective interest cost. If delivery was available earlier and agreed to by the company, yen could be borrowed short term and repaid when the forward contract matured.

Approaches to Enterprise Risk Management

Options
An option is the right, but not the obligation, to exchange a fixed amount of one currency for a fixed amount of another within, or at the end of, a predetermined period. In effect, it is a forward contract that can be walked away from, where you lose only the cost of the option, which could be 3–5% of the contract value. It therefore has the advantage of limiting the downside, as the maximum cost is known at the beginning, while leaving unlimited profit potential. These options are ideally suited to translations, where the size or existence of the exposure is uncertain, for example tender-to-contract or price list exposures.

Illustration: A quantity of a commodity (or currency to pay for it) is needed in three months' time. A dealer is willing to accept US$100 per ton to supply a predetermined quantity at US$2,000 per ton. If the price of this commodity in three months' time is US$1,700 per ton, then the option would be thrown away, the product bought in the spot market, and the cost to the company would be US$1,800 per ton. The tender-to-contract or price list item would have been safeguarded, and the price could even be reduced by US$200 per ton if competitive conditions demanded. If the price of the commodity rose, the cost to the company would be contained. The option could be sold at a profit if the product was not needed, or the loss would in any event be limited to US$100 per ton.

There are two types of option:
- **Calls**—giving the right to buy a currency;
- **Puts**—giving the right to sell a currency.

Currency Options
The exchange rate (known as the strike price) and the expiry date of the option are chosen by the customer at the outset. The cost (known as the premium) of the option is calculated based on these decisions and the volatility of the currency involved. Options can be exchange-traded where they exist in standardized form, or bought over the counter, where they are written to fit a customer's particular circumstances.

There are two styles of option:
- **American option**. The buyer can exercise the option (make the exchange of currencies) at any time up to the expiry date.
- **European option**. This can be exercised on the expiry date only, and is slightly cheaper because of its lack of flexibility.

Options may have a resale value, determined by the same criteria as the original cost. When the exercise price of an option is better than the current spot exchange rate, it is called "in the money"; when it is the other way round, it is "out of the money."

Swaps
Swaps are like long-dated forward contracts. They involve the exchange of a liability now, with the exchange back at a predetermined future time, and the compensation of the other party for costs in the intervening period. Swaps are used primarily to protect an investment or portfolio of borrowings. They involve a back-to-back loan between companies with a matching but opposite need. What is "swapped" is essentially a series of cash flows.

Illustration: A UK company wishes to raise cash to invest in developing its business in the United States. It is quoted in the United Kingdom only, which means it does not have access to US capital markets and it does not have a rating, so it would be extremely difficult to borrow in the United States.

What sources of funds are available?
- Raise equity via a UK rights issue;
- Borrow sterling from a UK bank;
- Borrow in US dollars.

The first two of these options will appear on a balance sheet as sterling liabilities, but the asset will appear as a dollar asset, creating a translation exposure. The returns from the investment will be in dollars, which will create a translation exposure when they are converted to sterling income in the profit statement, and a transaction exposure when they need to be converted to pay interest or dividends in sterling.

A solution is to swap the currency flows for the duration of a loan, paying or receiving a sum of money from the other party, leaving both sides in an equivalent cash flow position but having avoided specific payments in another currency. The loan would revert to the borrowing currency on maturity.

CONCLUSION

Managing currency and related transactions is a core part of corporate risk management within the treasury function. Its importance will continue to demand boardroom time and the highest standard of corporate governance. Massive and unpredictable fluctuations in currency markets have made forecasting more difficult and the need to safeguard the value of assets, liabilities, and transactions is paramount.

To Hedge or Not to Hedge

MORE INFO

Books:

Arnold, Glen. *Corporate Financial Management*. 4th ed. Harlow, UK: FT Prentice Hall, 2008.

Boakes, Kevin. *Reading and Understanding the Financial Times*. Harlow, UK: FT Prentice Hall, 2008.

Matza, Peter (ed). *The International Treasurer's Handbook 2009*. 19th ed. London: Association of Corporate Treasurers, 2008.

Shomah, Shani Beverley. *A Foreign Exchange Primer*. 2nd ed. Chichester, UK: Wiley, 2009.

Slatyer, Will. *The Debt Delusion: Evolution and Management of Financial Risk*. Boca Raton, FL: Universal Publishers, 2008.

Websites:

DailyFX: www.dailyfx.com

Reuters Business and Finance: www.reuters.com/finance

TMI Online: www.treasury-management.com

Minimizing Credit Risk by Frank J. Fabozzi

EXECUTIVE SUMMARY
- Credit risk encompasses credit default risk, credit spread risk, and downgrade risk.
- Market participants typically gauge credit default risk in terms of the credit rating assigned by rating agencies.
- Factors that are considered in the evaluation of a corporate borrower's creditworthiness are: the quality of management; the ability of the borrower to satisfy the debt obligation; the level of seniority and the collateral available in a bankruptcy proceeding; and covenants.
- Credit risk transfer vehicles allow the redistribution of credit risk.
- Securitization is a credit risk transfer vehicle for corporations that is accomplished by selling a pool of loans or receivables to a third-party entity.
- Credit derivatives are a form of credit risk transfer vehicle.

INTRODUCTION
Financial corporations and investors face several types of risk. One major risk is credit risk. Despite the fact that market participants typically refer to "credit risk" as if it is one-dimensional, there are actually three forms of this risk: credit default risk, credit spread risk, and downgrade risk.

Credit *default risk* is the risk that the issuer will fail to satisfy the terms of the obligation with respect to the timely payment of interest and repayment of the amount borrowed. This form of credit risk covers counterparty risk in a trade or derivative transaction where the counterparty fails to satisfy its obligation. To gauge credit default risk, investors typically rely on credit ratings. A *credit rating* is a formal opinion given by a company referred to as a *rating agency* of the credit default risk faced by investing in a particular issue of debt securities. For long-term debt obligations, a credit rating is a forward-looking assessment of the probability of default and the relative magnitude of the loss should a default occur. For short-term debt obligations, a credit rating is a forward-looking assessment of the probability of default. The nationally recognized rating agencies include Moody's Investors Service, Standard & Poor's, and Fitch Ratings.

Credit *spread* risk is the loss or underperformance of an issue or issues due to an increase in the credit spread. The credit spread is the compensation sought by investors for accepting the credit default risk of an issue or issuer. The credit spread varies with market conditions and the credit rating of the issue or issuer. On the issuer side, credit spread risk is the risk that an issuer's credit spread will increase when it must come to market to offer bonds, resulting in a higher funding cost.

Downgrade risk is the risk that an issue or issuer will be downgraded, resulting in an increase in the credit spread demanded by the market. Hence, downgrade risk is related to credit spread risk. Occasionally, the ability of an issuer to make interest and principal payments diminishes seriously and unexpectedly because of an unforeseen event. This can include any number of idiosyncratic events that are specific to the corporation or to an industry, including a natural or industrial accident, a regulatory change, a takeover or corporate restructuring, or corporate fraud. This risk is referred to generically as *event risk* and will result in a downgrading of the issuer by the rating agencies.

FACTORS CONSIDERED IN ASSESSING CREDIT DEFAULT RISK
The most obvious way to protect against credit risk is to analyze the creditworthiness of the borrower. In performing such an analysis, credit analysts evaluate the factors that affect the business risk of a borrower. These factors can be classified into four general categories— the quality of the borrower; the ability of the borrower to satisfy the debt obligation; the level of seniority and the collateral available in a bankruptcy proceeding; and restrictions imposed on the borrower.

In the case of a corporation, the quality of the borrower involves assessing the firm's business strategies and management policies. More specifically, a credit analyst will study the corporation's strategic plan, accounting control systems, and financial philosophy regarding the use of debt. In assigning a credit rating, Moody's states: "Although difficult to quantify, management quality is one of the most important factors supporting an issuer's credit strength. When the unexpected occurs, it is a management's ability to react appropriately that will sustain the company's performance."[1]

Approaches to Enterprise Risk Management

The ability of the borrower to meet its obligations begins with the analysis of the borrower's financial statements. Commonly used measures of liquidity and debt coverage combined with estimates of future cash flows are calculated and investigated if there are concerns. In addition, the analysis considers industry trends, the borrower's basic operating and competitive position, sources of liquidity (backup lines of credit), and, if applicable, the regulatory environment. An investigation of industry trends aids a credit analyst in assessing the vulnerability of the firm to economic cycles, the barriers to entry, and the exposure of the company to technological changes. An investigation of the borrower's various lines of business aids the credit analyst in assessing the firm's basic operating position.

A credit analyst will look at the position as a creditor in the case of a bankruptcy. The US Bankruptcy Act comprises 15 chapters, each covering a particular type of bankruptcy. Of particular interest here are Chapter 7, which deals with the liquidation of a company, and Chapter 11, which deals with the reorganization of a company. When a company is liquidated, creditors receive distributions based on the *absolute priority rule* to the extent that assets are available. The absolute priority rule is the principle that senior creditors are paid in full before junior creditors are paid anything. For secured creditors and unsecured creditors, the absolute priority rule guarantees their seniority to equity holders. However, in the case of a reorganization, the absolute priority rule rarely holds because in practice unsecured creditors do in fact typically receive distributions for the entire amount of their claim and common stockholders may receive something, while secured creditors may receive only a portion of their claim. The reason is that a reorganization requires the approval of all the parties. Consequently, secured creditors are willing to negotiate with both unsecured creditors and stockholders in order to obtain approval of the plan of reorganization.

The restrictions imposed on the borrower (management) that are part of the terms and conditions of the lending or bond agreement are called *covenants*. Covenants deal with limitations and restrictions on the borrower's activities. Affirmative covenants call on the debtor to make promises to do certain things. Negative covenants are those that require the borrower not to take certain actions. A violation of any covenant may provide a meaningful early warning alarm, enabling lenders to take positive and corrective action before the situation deteriorates further. Covenants play an important part in minimizing risk to creditors.

CREDIT RISK TRANSFER VEHICLES

There are various ways that investors, particularly institutional investors, can reduce their exposure to credit risk. These arrangements are referred to as *credit transfer vehicles*. It should be borne in mind that an institutional investor may not necessarily want to eliminate credit risk but may want to control it or have an efficient means by which to reduce it. The increasing number of credit risk transfer vehicles has made it easier for financial institutions to reallocate large amounts of credit risk to the nonfinancial sector of the capital markets.

For a bank, the most obvious way to transfer the credit risk of a loan it has originated is to sell it to another party. The bank management's concern when it sells corporate loans is the potential impairment of its relationship with the corporate borrower. This concern is overcome with the use of *syndicated loans*, because banks in the syndicate may sell their loan shares in the secondary market by means of either an *assignment* or a *participation*. With an assignment, a syndicated loan requires the approval of the obligor; that is not the case with a participation since the payments by the borrower are merely passed through to the purchaser, and therefore the obligor need not know about the sale.

Two credit risk vehicles that have increased in importance since the 1990s are securitization and credit derivatives. It is important to note that the pricing of these credit risk transfer instruments is not an easy task. Pricing becomes even more complicated for lower-quality borrowers and for credits that are backed by a pool of lower-quality assets, as recent events in the capital markets have demonstrated.

SECURITIZATION

Securitization involves the pooling of loans and/or receivables and selling that pool of assets to a third-party, a special purpose vehicle (SPV). By doing so, the risks associated with that pool of assets, such as credit risk, are transferred to the SPV. In turn, the SPV obtains the funds to acquire the pool of assets by selling securities. When the pool of assets consists of consumer receivables or mortgage loans, the securities issued are referred to as *asset-backed securities*. When the asset pool consists of corporate loans, the securities issued are called *collateralized loan obligations*.

A major reason why a financial or nonfinancial corporation uses securitization as a fund-raising vehicle is that it may allow a lower funding cost than issuing secured debt. However, another important reason is that securitization is a risk management tool. Although the entity employing securitization retains some of the credit risk associated with the pool of loans (referred to as retained interest), the majority of the credit risk is transferred to the holders of the securities issued by the SPV.

CREDIT DERIVATIVES
A financial derivative is a contract designed to transfer some form of risk between two or more parties efficiently. When a financial derivative allows the transfer of credit exposure of an underlying asset or assets between two parties, it is referred to as a *credit derivative*. More specifically, credit derivatives allow investors either to acquire or to reduce credit risk exposure. Many institutional investors have portfolios that

counterparty risk, and this has been the major concern in recent years in view of the credit problems of large banks and dealer firms who are the counterparties.

Credit derivatives also permit banks to transfer credit risk without the need to transfer assets physically. For example, in a collateral loan obligation, a bank can sell a pool of corporate loans to a special purpose vehicle (SPV) in order to reduce its exposure to the corporate borrowers. Alternatively, it can transfer the credit risk exposure by buying credit protection for the same pool of corporate loans. In this case, the transaction is referred to as a *synthetic collateralized loan obligation*.

An understanding of credit derivatives is critical even for those who do not want to use them.

CASE STUDY
A *credit-linked note* (CLN) is a security, usually issued by an investment-grade-rated corporation, that has an interest payment and fixed maturity structure similar to a standard bond. In contrast to a standard bond, the performance of the CLN is linked to the performance of a specified underlying asset or assets as well as that of the issuing entity. There are different ways that a CLN can be credit linked, and we will describe one case here.

British Telecom issued on December 15, 2000, a CLN with a coupon rate of 8.125% maturing on December 15, 2010. The terms of this CLN stated that the coupon rate would increase by 25 basis points for each one-notch rating downgrade of British Telecom below A–/A3 suffered during the life of the CLN. The coupon rate would decrease by 25 basis points for each rating upgrade, with a minimum coupon set at 8.125%. In other words, this CLN allows investors to make a credit play based on this issuer's credit rating. In fact, in May 2003, British Telecom was downgraded by one rating notch and the coupon rate was increased to 8.375%.

---

are highly sensitive to changes in the credit spread between a default-free asset and a credit-risky asset, and credit derivatives are an efficient way to manage this exposure. Conversely, other institutional investors may use credit derivatives to target specific credit exposures as a way to enhance portfolio returns. Consequently, the ability to transfer credit risk and return provides a tool for institutional investors—the potential to improve performance. Moreover, corporate treasurers can use credit derivatives to transfer the risk associated with an increase in credit spreads (i.e., credit spread risk).

Credit derivatives include credit default swaps, asset swaps, total return swaps, credit linked notes, credit spread options, and credit spread forwards. In addition, there are index-type or basket credit products that are sponsored by banks that link the payoff to the investor to a portfolio of credits. Credit derivatives are over-the-counter instruments and are therefore not traded on an organized exchange. Hence, credit derivatives expose an investor to

As Alan Greenspan, then the Chairman of the Federal Reserve Board, in a speech on September 25, 2002, stated:

"The growing prominence of the market for credit derivatives is attributable not only to its ability to disperse risk but also to the information it contributes to enhanced risk management by banks and other financial intermediaries. Credit default swaps, for example, are priced to reflect the probability of net loss from the default of an ever broadening array of borrowers, both financial and non-financial."[2]

CONCLUSION
While market participants typically think of credit risk in terms of the failure of a borrower to make timely interest and principal payments on a debt obligation, this is only one form of credit risk: credit default risk. The other types of credit risk are credit spread risk and downgrade risk. When evaluating the credit default risk of a borrower, credit analysts look at the quality of the borrower, the ability of the borrower to satisfy

Approaches to Enterprise Risk Management

the debt obligation, the level of seniority and the collateral available in a bankruptcy proceeding, and covenants. Credit risk transfer vehicles include securitization and credit derivatives. Credit derivatives include credit default swaps, asset swaps, total return swaps, credit linked notes, credit spread options, credit spread forwards, and baskets or indexes of credits.

MAKING IT HAPPEN

Controlling credit risk requires not just an understanding of what credit risk is and the factors that affect a borrower's credit rating but other important implementation issues. These include:

- establishing the credit risk exposure that a corporation or institutional investor is willing to accept;
- quantifying the credit risk by using the latest quantitative tools in the field of credit risk modeling;
- understanding the various credit risk transfer vehicles that can be employed to control credit risk.
- evaluating the merits of different credit risk transfer vehicles to determine which are the most appropriate for altering credit risk exposure.

MORE INFO

Books:
Anson, Mark J. P., Frank J. Fabozzi, Moorad Choudhry, and Ren-Raw Chen. *Credit Derivatives: Instruments, Pricing, and Applications.* Hoboken, NJ: Wiley, 2004.
Fabozzi, Frank J., Moorad Choudhry, and Steven V. Mann. *Measuring and Controlling Interest Rate and Credit Risk.* 2nd ed. Hoboken, NJ: Wiley, 2003.

Articles:
Fabozzi, Frank J., and Moorad Choudhry. "Originating collateralized debt obligations for balance sheet management." *Journal of Structured Finance* (Fall 2003): 32–52.
Fabozzi, Frank J., Henry A. Davis, and Moorad Choudhry, "Credit-linked notes: A product primer." *Journal of Structured Finance* (Winter 2007): 67–77.
Lucas, Douglas J., Laurie S. Goodman, and Frank J. Fabozzi. "Collateralized debt obligations and credit risk transfer." *Journal of Financial Transformation* 20 (2007): 47–59.

Websites:
DefaultRisk.Com—for credit risk modeling and measurement: www.defaultrisk.com
Vinod Kothari's credit derivatives website: www.credit-deriv.com

NOTES

1 Moody's Investor Service. "Industrial Company Rating Methodology." *Global Credit Research* (July 2008): 6.

2 Speech titled "World Finance and Risk Management," at Lancaster House, London, United Kingdom.

Managing Interest Rate Risk by Will Spinney

EXECUTIVE SUMMARY
- Interest rate risk can manifest itself in several different ways.
- It is best managed within the context of the firm and a risk framework.
- Proper evaluation or measurement is key.
- Selection of a good key performance indicator is essential.
- A typical response to interest rate risk is a transfer of risk to another party.
- Many risk transfer tools are available, of which interest rate swaps are the most popular.
- The risk is usually transformed rather than eliminated.

INTRODUCTION
Almost all firms are exposed to interest rate risk, but it can manifest itself in different ways. A proper response to this risk can only come following a full understanding of the context of the firm and its strategy, along with a full evaluation of the risk. Firms should generate a well thought out key performance indicator (KPI) and then apply one or more of the many tools available in the market to transfer interest rate risk.

MAJOR WAYS THAT A FIRM CAN BE AFFECTED
Interest rate risk is the exposure of the firm to changing interest rates. It has four main dimensions:

Changing Cost of Interest Expense or Income
Companies with debt charged at variable rates (for example, based on Libor, and also called floating rates) will be exposed to increases in interest rates, whereas companies whose borrowing costs are totally or partly fixed will be exposed to falls in interest rates. The reverse is obviously true for companies with cash term deposits. This is usually the key risk that firms consider.

Impact on Business Performance by a Changing Business Environment
Changes in interest rates also affect businesses indirectly, through their effect on the overall business environment. In normal times, for example, construction firms enjoy a rise in business activity when interest rates fall, as investors build more when the cost of projects is lower. Conversely, some firms may benefit from high levels of activity that prompt a high interest rate response by central banks. So some firms may have a form of natural hedge against the other forms of interest rate risk, although for any one firm the effect may lead or lag actual changes in rates.

Impact on Pension Schemes Sponsored by the Firm
Pension schemes that carry liability and investment risk for the sponsor have interest rate risk in that liabilities act in a similar way to bonds, rising in value as interest rates fall and vice versa.

Changing Market Values of Any Debt Outstanding
Although a nonfinancial firm will usually report its bonds on issue in financial statements at substantially their face value, early redemptions must be done at the market value. This may be significantly different, as interest rates will change the value of fixed-rate debt. This risk is not commonly considered by most nonfinancial firms.

INTEREST RATE RISK IN THE CONTEXT OF THE FIRM
Investors do expect firms to take risks, especially with regard to their core business competencies. It may be that investors expect the firm to take interest rate risk. On the other hand, investors would probably not expect a firm to breach a financial covenant because of rising interest rates.

RISK MANAGEMENT FRAMEWORK
A risk management framework includes the following key stages:
- Identification and assessment of risks;
- Detailed evaluation of the highest risks;
- Creation of a response to each risk;
- Reporting and feedback on risks.

Evaluation is crucial to the management of interest rate risk and will discover exactly how a firm might be affected, thus guiding the response to the risk. Evaluation techniques include: sensitivity analysis, modeling changes in a variable

Approaches to Enterprise Risk Management

against its effect; and value at risk (VaR) analysis, based on volatilities to calculate the chances of certain outcomes.

Let us look at a simple firm with earnings before interest and tax (EBIT) of 100, borrowings of 400 (all on a floating rate), an interest rate of 6% (as a base case), and a tax rate of 30%, and apply some of these techniques.

Evaluation 1: Sensitivity Analysis
A 1% move in interest rates has an effect of 4 (1% of 400) on the annual interest charge. This is not very helpful because there is no context for the effect.

Evaluation 2: Sensitivity Analysis
A table can be constructed to show the effect on earnings and interest cover (Table 1). In the table items in bold represent the base case, whereas other columns represent the sensitivities to this base case. Earnings are earnings after interest and tax.

can construct a further table (Table 2) showing interest cover under variations in EBIT and the interest rate. Italic numerals indicate a covenant breach, and the number in bold is the base case described in Table 1.

A drop of 5 in EBIT and a rise of 0.5% in interest rates will cause a breach, a clear risk factor for the firm. If a relationship between EBIT and interest rates can be established, then further conclusions could be drawn.

Sensitivity analysis does not show the probability of these changes, but if they are available—for example from a study of market volatility—a probability distribution for a covenant breach can easily be obtained.

Evaluation 4: VaR
Suppose that investigation of the assets and liabilities in the firm's pension scheme shows that the scheme has a deficit of 50. As an illustration, VaR might tell us that, based on the volatility of the long-term interest rates used to calculate

Table 1. The effect of interest rate changes on earnings and interest cover

	Interest rate					
	4.5%	5.0%	5.5%	**6.0%**	6.5%	7.0%	7.5%
EBIT	100.0	100.0	100.0	**100.0**	100.0	100.0	100.0
Interest	(18.0)	(20.0)	(22.0)	**(24.0)**	(26.0)	(28.0)	(30.0)
Tax	(24.6)	(24.0)	(23.4)	**(22.8)**	(22.2)	(21.6)	(21.0)
Earnings	57.4	56.0	54.6	**53.2**	51.8	50.4	49.0
Interest cover	5.56	5.00	4.55	**4.17**	3.85	3.57	3.33

Table 2. Interest cover under variations in EBIT and interest rate

EBIT	Interest rate					
	4.5%	5.0%	5.5%	**6.0%**	6.5%	7.0%	7.5%
80	4.44	4.00	3.64	3.33	3.08	2.86	2.67
85	4.72	4.25	3.86	3.54	3.27	3.04	2.83
90	5.00	4.50	4.09	3.75	3.46	3.21	3.00
95	5.28	4.75	4.32	3.96	3.65	3.39	3.17
100	5.56	5.00	4.55	**4.17**	3.85	3.57	3.33
105	5.83	5.25	4.77	4.38	4.04	3.75	3.50
110	6.11	5.50	5.00	4.58	4.23	3.93	3.67
115	6.39	5.75	5.23	4.79	4.42	4.11	3.83
120	6.67	6.00	5.45	5.00	4.62	4.29	4.00

This is much more helpful, showing the effect on both earnings and interest cover. If the firm has an interest cover covenant of, say, 3.75, then the table shows a high risk of a breach, depending on how likely a rise in rates might be.

Evaluation 3: Sensitivity Analysis
Suppose now that EBIT displays volatility. We

liabilities, and taking into account that the scheme has some bond investments (in which value moves are opposite to liabilities), there is a 1 in 20 chance that the deficit will increase in the next year, because of interest rate changes alone, by 15 or more.

Interest rate risk inside a pension scheme (or other scheme for future employee benefits) often

Managing Interest Rate Risk

dwarfs interest rate risk inside the firm.
  Evaluation should reveal where a firm is sensitive to interest rates. It could be:
- Earnings, perhaps where earnings per share (EPS) is an important issue.
- Cash flow.
- Interest cover ratios, perhaps because of financial covenants.
- Other ratios, such as those used by credit rating agencies.

ESTABLISHING A KPI AND RESPONSE TO THE RISK

Evaluation should lead the firm to establish a KPI for interest rate risk. A good example of a KPI would be: Interest cover to be greater than 3.75, on a 99% confidence basis, over an 18-month period. This is better than using a simple interest cover ratio or a fixed/floating ratio as a KPI, because it speaks specifically about the risk to the firm.

The KPI should guide the response to the risk. Possible responses include:
- Avoid: It is hard to avoid interest rate risk.
- Accept: Simply accept the risk and take no further action. This may be suitable if there are no significant issues such as proximate financial covenants.
- Accept and reduce: It may be possible to reduce the risk through internal actions, such as reducing cash balances as far as possible to repay debt.
- Accept and transfer: Many market products are available that enable a firm to change the character of interest payments. This process is called hedging.

Table 3. Tools that can be used to transfer interest rate risk

Tool	Description	Comment
Forward rate agreement (FRA)	An FRA is a tool for fixing future interest rates (or unfixing them) over shorter periods, up to say 1–2 years.	A 3v6 FRA allows a firm to fix the three-month Libor (or other reference) rate in three months time. It is dealt over the counter (with banks).
Future	Futures have the same function as FRAs.	Futures are traded on an exchange, and thus have less flexibility.
Cap	A cap is an option instrument. The buyer of a cap pays a maximum interest rate over the life of the cap but enjoys lower rates as they come down. Caps have a premium.	Caps are usually dealt over the counter by firms, and the classic use is for a borrower to buy a cap that is higher than current interest rates, thus providing insurance for the borrower.
Floor	A floor is an option instrument. The buyer of a floor receives a minimum interest rate over the life of the floor but enjoys higher rates as they increase. Floors have a premium.	Floors are usually dealt over the counter by firms, and the classic use is for a depositor to buy a floor that is lower than current interest rates, thus providing insurance for the depositor.
Collar	A collar is a combination of a cap and a floor, thus providing a firm with a corridor of possible interest rates between a maximum and a minimum.	A borrower would buy a cap and sell a floor, usually over the counter, thus creating a "collar," or corridor, of rates.
Interest rate swap	An interest rate swap is probably the most widely used and popular risk transfer instrument in the field of interest rate risk. It changes the nature of a stream of interest payments from floating to fixed or vice versa.	Swaps (as they are usually called) are dealt over the counter and the market is large and (usually) deep. Terms of 5 to 7 years are common with nonfinancial firms, although terms of 30 or more years are often used by pension schemes, reflecting their different maturity horizon.
Swaption	A swaption is an instrument where the buyer of a swaption has the right to enter into an interest rate swap at a particular rate, thus protecting the buyer against adverse movements in long-term rates, while allowing them to benefit from favorable moves.	Swaptions are not very popular with nonfinancial firms but might be used near the time of bond issues, for example.

Approaches to Enterprise Risk Management

ESTABLISHING A POLICY
The factors we have seen should be formalized in a policy, as should approaches to all risks. The policy should set out:
- The overall direction of the policy.
- How the risk is to be measured.
- Who has responsibility for the risk management.
- What procedures should be in place to control the risk.
- A framework for decision-making.
- The key performance indicator.
- A reporting mechanism to view the performance of the policy.

TOOLS AVAILABLE TO TRANSFER INTEREST RATE RISK
There are a large number of tools available for the transfer of interest rate risk (Table 3).

Interest Rate Swap
This key instrument deserves a little more explanation. It is an instrument that, in its usual form, transforms one kind of interest stream into another, such as floating to fixed or fixed to floating. Each swap has two counterparties, and therefore in each swap one party pays fixed and receives floating, while the other party receives fixed and pays floating.

There are two classic uses of swaps by non-financial firms:
- A *floating-rate* borrower converts to a *fixed rate*. In this case a borrower has floating-rate bank debt and carries out a pay-fixed swap, converting the debt to a fixed rate. This is shown diagrammatically in Figure 1. The two floating-rate streams cancel each other out for the borrower, leaving it to pay only a fixed-rate stream.
- A *fixed-rate* borrower converts to a *floating rate*. In this case a borrower has fixed-rate bond debt and undertakes a receive-fixed swap, converting the debt to a floating rate (Figure 2). The two fixed-rate streams cancel each other out for the borrower, leaving it to pay only a floating-rate stream.

Figure 1. Floating-rate borrower uses swap to convert to a fixed rate

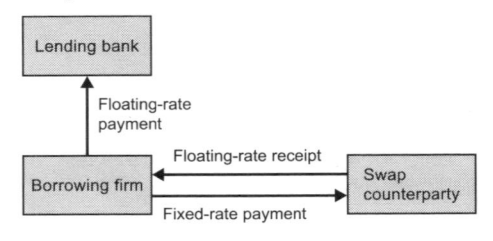

Figure 2. Fixed-rate borrower uses swap to convert to a floating rate

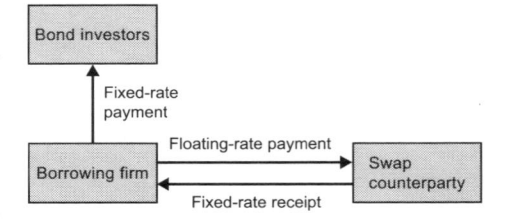

Let's suppose that our firm from above has responded to the risk of covenant breach by deciding to enter into a pay-fixed swap for 75% of its borrowing. It will pay 6% on the fixed-rate leg of the swap. The interest cover table we considered in Table 2 is now as shown in Table 4.

The italicized cells (covenant breach) now cover the width of the table but are less deep. Our firm has a lower risk of a breach from interest rates alone but has increased the risk from a falling EBIT. As interest rates are believed to be more volatile than EBIT, the overall risk to our firm has been reduced through the transfer of risk.

Table 4. Interest cover under variations in EBIT and interest rate for firm that pays fixed swap (see text for details)

EBIT	\multicolumn{7}{c}{Interest rate}
	4.5%	5.0%	5.5%	6.0%	6.5%	7.0%	7.5%
80	3.56	3.48	3.40	3.33	3.27	3.20	3.14
85	3.78	3.70	3.62	3.54	3.47	3.40	3.33
90	4.00	3.91	3.83	3.75	3.67	3.60	3.53
95	4.22	4.13	4.04	3.96	3.88	3.80	3.73
100	4.44	4.35	4.26	4.17	4.08	4.00	3.92
105	4.67	4.57	4.47	4.38	4.29	4.20	4.12
110	4.89	4.78	4.68	4.58	4.49	4.40	4.31
115	5.11	5.00	4.89	4.79	4.69	4.60	4.51
120	5.33	5.22	5.11	5.00	4.90	4.80	4.71

Managing Interest Rate Risk

MAKING IT HAPPEN
- Assess how the firm is affected by changes in interest rates.
- Evaluate the risk according to the firm's strategy, using tools such as sensitivity analysis or VaR.
- Establish a key performance indicator for the risk.
- Choose whether to avoid or to accept the risk.
- If the choice is to accept, either:
- accept and reduce; or
- accept and transfer, such as with interest rate swaps or options.
- Make frequent reports to give feedback on the risk.

FIXING PRODUCTS VERSUS OPTIONS
There is a key difference between interest-rate-fixing products (such as swaps) and options. A fixing instrument binds its user to the rate that is set when it is transacted. An option allows the buyer to walk away. So a firm taking out a pay-fixed swap, following which rates decline, is left paying the higher rates. The risk is thus transformed, rather than transferred. Exposure to rising rates has become an exposure to falling rates. Firms must be clear about this when establishing their response to risk.

Accordingly, option products may seem to be an ideal product to deal with interest rate risk, and for those prepared to pay, they can be. However, costs rise with two main factors:
- Time: The longer an option has until expiry, the higher the premium.
- Volatility: The higher the volatility in the underlying risk being hedged, the higher the premium.

Both these factors tend to deter firms from using options and, for the longer term, risk transfer-response interest rate swaps are usually the instrument of choice.

CONCLUSION
The effects of changes in interest rates on a firm can be complex, but techniques are available to evaluate and respond to any risks this presents. A clear reference back to business and financial strategy will put interest rate risk in its context, allow a suitable response, and help the firm to achieve its goals.

MORE INFO
Books:
Buckley, Adrian. *Multinational Finance*. 5th ed. Harlow, UK: Pearson Education, 2004.
Chapman, Robert J. *Simple Tools and Techniques for Enterprise Risk Management*. Chichester, UK: Wiley, 2006.

Websites:
Association for Finance Professional (AFP): www.afponline.org
Association of Corporate Treasurers (ACT): www.treasurers.org
National Association of Corporate Treasurers (NACT): www.nact.org

Managing Counterparty Credit Risk
by David C. Shimko

EXECUTIVE SUMMARY
- Counterparty risk exposure is the financial measure of performance risk in any contract.
- Many contract exposures are managed through operational or legal means; this article focuses on financial risk management.
- Counterparty credit exposure equals *current exposure* (accounts receivable minus collateral) plus an adjustment for *potential future exposure* based on possible increases in future net receivables.
- A comprehensive credit risk management policy addresses counterparty initiation and monitoring, contracting standards, credit authorities and limits, the transaction approval process, credit risk reporting, and reserving and capital policy.
- Credit risk mitigation is best handled through collateral, but there are legal and financial means to mitigate credit risk as well.
- Credit insurance can fit the exposure perfectly, but may be costly.
- Credit default swaps are linked to credit events and payments that may not correspond exactly to counterparty exposures, but may be cheaper than credit insurance.

DEFINING COUNTERPARTY RISK
Counterparty risk is the risk to each party of a contract that the counterparty will not live up to its contractual obligations; it is otherwise known as default risk.

Counterparty risk relates closely to performance risk. It arises whenever one entity depends on another to honor the terms of a contract. If a parts supplier fails to provide steering wheels to General Motors, GM will be damaged because of its inability to deliver complete cars. The resulting profit reduction is defined as the *exposure* that GM runs to its supplier. Similarly, GM runs a credit exposure to its customers who have not yet paid for their cars. This would include dealers and end customers who are financed by GMAC, GM's financing subsidiary.

Normally, performance risk is managed operationally—i.e., GM would use alternative suppliers, reserve supplies of steering wheels, and contractual nonperformance remedies to manage its performance risk. Also, to manage risk to its dealers, it may retain title to vehicles, verify insurance coverage, obtain some advance payment, and use legal means to minimize their collections risk. In addition to these counterparty risk situations, GM will experience counterparty risk from its derivative contracts.

Suppose GM wanted to purchase steering wheels on an ongoing basis from a European supplier, and protect itself from devaluation of the US dollar. It would likely enter a foreign exchange swap transaction with a bank. After entering the contract, rates would continue to change, bringing the contract in-the-money to either GM or the bank. If the dollar were to devalue, the contract would move in-the-money to GM, which would expose GM to the possible failure of the bank to honor its contract. Conversely, if the dollar were to strengthen, the bank would have an in-the-money contract with GM, and subsequently become concerned about GM's possible default risk.

MEASURING COUNTERPARTY RISK
Counterparty risk exposure can be divided into accounts receivable exposure and potential future exposure. If collateral is held as a bond for performance risk, the amount of the collateral is deducted from the gross exposure calculation. If the collateral itself is risky, such as a deposit of traded securities rather than cash, the collateral may not get full credit. Therefore, total credit exposure can be defined as follows:

Current exposure = Maximum of {Accounts receivable (A/R) − discounted collateral value} and 0

Potential future exposure = Current credit exposure + maximum likely increase in future credit exposure

The maximum likely increase in future credit exposure is defined relative to a timeframe and relative to a statistical confidence interval, typically 95%. To demonstrate this concept simply, assume a potential foreign exchange transaction

Approaches to Enterprise Risk Management

as an expected value of zero with an annual standard deviation of σ, a duration of τ, and a normally distributed risk. This is illustrated in Figure 1.

Figure 1. Exposure distribution for GM

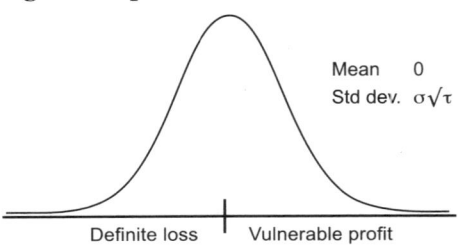

Mean 0
Std dev. σ√τ

Definite loss | Vulnerable profit

The *definite* loss shows in which cases GM will owe money to the bank, while *vulnerable profit* shows cases where the bank may owe money to GM. It is called vulnerable on account of the default risk of the bank. Although the current exposure is zero, the vulnerable profit could be as great as 1.65 standard deviations using a 95% confidence interval. This is also known as the *peak exposure*. The probability-weighted average of all the exposure figures, both zero and positive, is known as the *expected exposure*. For the normal distribution case, the expected exposure is 0.40 times the standard deviation.

To determine the expected loss conditional on default, we need to have two more pieces of information. One is the probability of default, which we will call π. The other is the *loss given default*, i.e., the percentage of the exposure that we never recover, even after settlement or bankruptcy. We call this estimate λ. Given these assumptions, we may summarize:

Peak exposure = 1.65σ√τ

Expected exposure = 0.40σ√τ

Expected loss = 0.40πλσ√τ

For example, if GM determines the euro volatility to be 15% per year, the contract to be three months in duration (0.25 years), its bank to have a default likelihood of 10%, and the loss given default to be 50%, its expected loss is (0.40 × 0.10 × 0.50 × 0.15 × √0.25) = 0.0015 times the size of the transaction—i.e., $1500 per million dollars hedged.

In the case of a swap rather than a single forward transaction, the amortization of the swap payments reduces exposure over time, so that it does not necessarily rise with the square root of time. In this case, the peak and expected exposure can be determined as in Figure 2.

The peak exposure can be used to understand how much risk is being taken with respect to the counterparty, whereas the expected exposure is an indicator of expected losses.

CREDIT RISK MANAGEMENT POLICY

Best practice credit risk management policy includes the following items:
- counterparty initiation and monitoring;
- contracting standards;
- credit authorities and limits;
- transaction approval process;
- credit risk reporting;
- a reserving and capital policy.

Counterparty initiation refers to the first time a company wishes to enter a transaction with a proposed counterparty. The credit department typically reviews available public information, credit agency reports, and counterparty financials before agreeing to trade with the counterparty. The financial status of the counterparty should be continually monitored to detect proactively situations where counterparty credit quality might deteriorate. It is also important to segregate counterparties according to legal entities; trading with a subsidiary of a triple-A company may provide little or no financial protection in the event of a default. Furthermore, one should assume in general that a benefit of trading with one legal entity *cannot* be netted against a loss to another legal entity of the same firm. For example, if a company is owed $1 million by subsidiary X, and owes $1 million to subsidiary Y of the same counterparty, and X defaults, it will still have an obligation to Y.

Contracting standards refer to the types of contracts that may be entered with an appropriately initiated counterparty. For example, in most derivative contracts, a standard contract such as the International Swaps and Derivatives Association (ISDA) contract is used. Even standard contracts require customization, however. The Credit Support Annex (CSA) of the ISDA details the unilateral or bilateral collateral posting requirements of the counterparties. It also typically contains provisions for Material Adverse Changes (MAC) in the credit quality of the counterparties,

Figure 2. Exposure of a swap

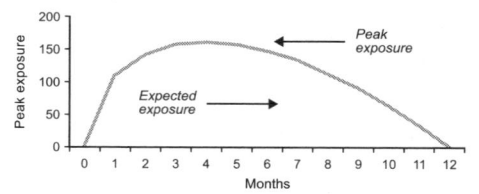

perhaps calling for more collateral when credit ratings downgrade. Finally, the CSA details rules for termination of contracts—for example, upon failure to supply collateral. ISDA Master Agreements should be established to guarantee netting across different legal entities of the same counterparty.

Credit limits refer to the amount of credit risk that may be taken to approved counterparties with approved contract forms. In most firms, credit limits are set on an aggregate basis by counterparty or credit rating—for instance, the firm is unwilling to take more than $100 million in credit risk to any one bank with a AA rating.

Credit authorities refer to the ability of any individual trader or trading desk to enter into new transactions with a counterparty, considering the possible impact on current or future credit exposure. Best practice firms use some measure of *potential future exposure* in setting their credit limits, although many focus only on *current exposure*. Some firms will also set portfolio concentration limits, for example, restricting the company's credit exposure to a particular industry. In all cases, firms must establish exception policies to deal with situations where credit limits are inadvertently or deliberately breached.

Transaction approval is a verification process to ensure that, before an individual transaction is executed, all of its requirements have been met: Counterparty initiation, contracts, collateral provisions, collateral collection if applicable, and compliance with authorities and with limits. Some firms allow slack in the process, such as transactions under a given materiality threshold with an uninitiated counterparty. These are a practical consequence of business dealings, but credit risk departments should strive to minimize these occurrences.

Credit risk reporting should address credit risk across the firm, whether risk is run in treasury, procurement, or sales. Aggregate receivables, potential future exposure, and aggregate collateral should be brought together in a comprehensive report by a non-netted legal entity. Best practice reporting includes portfolio risk measures, such as aggregate credit exposure, concentrations, and sensitivity of exposure to key economic drivers.

A *reserving policy* for expected credit losses—to be taken as a charge against earnings and reversed if losses never materialize—should be established by the office of the chief financial officer. This practice ensures that business units are held responsible for credit risk in their contracting processes. Some firms also charge business units for credit risk usage, but practices vary considerably. As a general statement, if a firm puts a price on credit risk, then business units must ensure that the profitability of their projects includes a cost factor for the credit risk being used. In general, the formula to adjust project NPV (net present value) for credit is as follows:

Project NPV = Starting NPV − Expected PV of credit losses − Cost of credit risk × PV of credit risk consumed for unexpected credit losses

In the marketing department, credit risk calculations are sometimes used as a determinant in product pricing. For example, credit card companies will factor expected collection costs and losses into its fee structure for retail clients.

CREDIT RISK MITIGATION

The most important credit risk mitigation tool is the collection of collateral and ongoing diligence with respect to enforcing collateral requirements. This may include the threat of forced terminations for failure to provide collateral. If collateral is not an option, due to contract limitations, then there are other options.

When a company determines that it has too much exposure to a single counterparty, and it is unable to collect collateral, it may undertake several actions. First, attempts may be made to close out some trading positions with the counterparty, or initiate new trading positions that have the effect of reducing the risk. Second, the company may attempt to novate a contract—i.e., reassign the contract to a different counterparty for some consideration. Third, a firm may try to "book out" a trade if it finds it has identical and offsetting trades to two different counterparties. All of these options require counterparty agreement.

Barring these operational strategies, there are two financial strategies for mitigating credit risk. One is to obtain credit insurance for the actual realized loss to a defaulting counterparty. The other is to enter a credit default swap (CDS), which is essentially a contingent payment triggered by a counterparty credit event and made by a third-party derivatives trading counterparty.

Insurance can be tailored to provide specific coverage of the actual realized loss, but because of its specificity, the insurance company margin can be seen as being excessive by some corporations. Credit default swaps can be cheaper, since they trade in broader over-the-counter (OTC) markets.

Using CDSs to manage credit risk creates three problems. First, in most trading situations, the actual exposure is variable, making it difficult

Approaches to Enterprise Risk Management

to target 100% protection. Second, in CDS markets, the payment-triggering event may not correspond exactly to a counterparty's default event. For example, when Fannie Mae and Freddie Mac were put into receivership by the US government in 2008, this was classified as a default event in CDSs and synthetic collateralized debt obligations (CDOs), which were built from those CDSs—even though there was no default. Third, as we learned in 2008, CDS spreads can become extremely high and can be subject to their own performance risk, as Lehman Brothers' counterparties discovered.

OTHER CONSIDERATIONS

Contagion. Most models of credit focus on bilateral credit arrangements, without recognizing that credit relationships are multilateral. For example, GM's supplier mentioned above may depend on other suppliers for parts. While the supplier itself may be creditworthy, its own suppliers may not be creditworthy. GM may not know how vulnerable it is to its counterparty's counterparty.

Consequences. While counterparty risk is often measured in terms of the counterparty's failure, it may be the case that default by a counterparty leads to much greater damage for a company. Many financial institutions were compromised in 2008 when the credit crisis caused a domino-like effect of systemic corporate collapse. Counterparty credit risk assessment, therefore, must include all the costs of counterparty failure, including the cost of lost reputation, lower credit rating, and, in the most extreme cases, bankruptcy.

CONCLUSION

Although a relatively young discipline, credit risk management has matured rapidly. Improved risk measurement and reporting techniques paired with comprehensive credit risk policies can provide extremely effective protection against credit risk losses. The best risk management techniques are operational and legal, with collateral providing the best financial risk mitigation. Credit insurance and credit default swaps offer financial protection against default, but each at its own cost—which must be compared to the benefits of reducing the specific risk it is intended to mitigate.

MAKING IT HAPPEN
- Set a corporate policy for credit risk management that recognizes the links to financial strategy.
- Identify corporate contracts and relationships with credit or performance risk.
- Model and quantify the organization's exposure to credit losses.
- Consider operational and financial credit risk mitigation where appropriate.

MORE INFO
Books:
Saunders, Anthony, and Linda Allen. *Credit Risk Measurement: New Approaches to Value at Risk and Other Paradigms.* 2nd ed. New York: Wiley, 2002.
Servigny, Arnaud de, and Olivier Renault. *Measuring and Managing Credit Risk.* New York: McGraw-Hill, 2004.

Measuring Country Risk by Aswath Damodaran

EXECUTIVE SUMMARY
- As companies and investors globalize and financial markets expand around the world, we are increasingly faced with estimation questions about the risk associated with this globalization.
- When investors invest in Petrobras, Gazprom, and China Power, they may be rewarded with higher returns, but they are also exposed to additional risk.
- When US and European multinationals push for growth in Asia and Latin America, they are clearly exposed to the political and economic turmoil that often characterize these markets.
- In practical terms, how, if at all, should we adjust for this additional risk? We review the discussion on country risk premiums and how to estimate them.

INTRODUCTION
Two key questions must be addressed when investing in emerging markets in Asia, Latin America, and Eastern Europe. The first relates to whether we should impose an additional risk premium when valuing equities in these markets. As we will see, the answer will depend upon whether we view markets to be open or segmented and whether we believe the risk can be diversified away. The second question relates to estimating an equity risk premium for emerging markets.

SHOULD THERE BE A COUNTRY RISK PREMIUM?
Is there more risk in investing in Malaysian or Brazilian equities than there is in investing in equities in the United States? Of course! But that does not automatically imply that there should be an additional risk premium charged when investing in those markets. Two arguments are generally used against adding an additional premium.

Country risk can be diversified away: If the additional risk of investing in Malaysia or Brazil can be diversified away, then there should be no additional risk premium charged. But for country risk to be diversifiable, two conditions must be met:
1. The marginal investors—i.e., active investors who hold large positions in the stock—have to be globally diversified. If the marginal investors are either unable or unwilling to invest globally, companies will have to diversify their operations across countries, which is a much more difficult and expensive exercise.
2. All or much of country risk should be country-specific. In other words, there should be low correlation across markets. If the returns across countries are positively correlated, country risk has a market risk component, is not diversifiable, and can command a premium. Whereas studies in the 1970s indicated low or no correlation across markets, increasing diversification on the part of both investors and companies has increased the correlation numbers. This is borne out by the speed with which troubles in one market can spread to a market with which it has little or no obvious relationship—say Brazil—and this contagion effect seems to become stronger during crises.

Given that both conditions are difficult to meet, we believe that on this basis, country risk should command a risk premium.

The expected cash flows for country risk can be adjusted: This second argument used against adjusting for country risk is that it is easier and more accurate to adjust the expected cash flows for the risk. However, adjusting the cash flows to reflect expectations about dire scenarios, such as nationalization or an economic meltdown, is not risk adjustment. Making the risk adjustment to cash flows requires the same analysis that we will employ to estimate the risk adjustment to discount rates.

ESTIMATING A COUNTRY RISK PREMIUM
If country risk is not diversifiable, either because the marginal investor is not globally diversified or because the risk is correlated across markets, we are left with the task of measuring country risk and estimating country risk premiums. In this section, we will consider two approaches that can be used to estimate country risk premiums. One approach builds on historical risk premiums and can be viewed as the *historical risk premium plus approach*. In the other approach, we estimate the equity risk premium by looking at how the market prices stocks and expected cash flows—this is the *implied premium approach*.

Approaches to Enterprise Risk Management

Historical Premium Plus

Most practitioners, when estimating risk premiums in the United States, look at the past. Consequently, we look at what we would have earned as investors by investing in equities as opposed to investing in riskless investments. With emerging markets, we will almost never have access to as much historical data as we do in the United States. If we combine this with the high volatility in stock returns in such markets, the conclusion is that historical risk premiums can be computed for these markets, but they will be useless because of the large standard errors in the estimates. Consequently, many analysts build their equity risk premium estimates for emerging markets from mature market historical risk premiums.

Equity risk premium$_{\text{Emerging market}}$ =
Equity risk premium$_{\text{Mature market}}$ + Country risk premium

To estimate the base premium for a mature equity market, we will make the argument that the US equity market is a mature market and that there is sufficient historical data in the United States to make a reasonable estimate of the risk premium. Using the historical data for the United States, we estimate the geometric average premium earned by stocks over treasury bonds of 4.79% between 1928 and 2007. To estimate the country risk premium, we can use one of three approaches:

Country Bond Default Spreads

One of the simplest and most easily accessible country risk measures is the rating assigned to a country's debt by a ratings agency (S&P, Moody's, and IBCA all rate countries). These -ratings measure default risk (rather than equity risk), but they are affected by many of the factors that drive equity risk—the stability of a country's currency, its budget and trade balances and its political stability for instance.[1] The other advantage of ratings is that they can be used to estimate default spreads over a riskless rate. For instance, Brazil was rated Ba1 in September 2008 by Moody's and the ten-year Brazilian ten-year dollar-denominated bond was priced to yield 5.95%, 2.15% more than the interest rate (3.80%) on a ten-year US treasury bond at the same time.[2] Analysts who use default spreads as measures of country risk typically add them on to the cost of both equity and debt of every company traded in that country. If we assume that the total equity risk premium for the United States and other mature equity markets is 4.79%, the risk premium for Brazil would be 6.94%.[3]

Relative Standard Deviation

There are some analysts who believe that the equity risk premiums of markets should reflect the differences in equity risk, as measured by the volatilities of equities in these markets. A conventional measure of equity risk is the standard deviation in stock prices; higher standard deviations are generally associated with more risk. If we scale the standard deviation of one market against another, we obtain a measure of relative risk.

Relative standard deviation$_{\text{Country X}}$ =
Standard deviation$_{\text{Country X}}$ ÷ Standard deviation$_{\text{US}}$

This relative standard deviation when multiplied by the premium used for US stocks should yield a measure of the total risk premium for any market.

Equity risk premium$_{\text{Country X}}$ =
Risk premium$_{\text{US}}$ × Relative standard deviation$_{\text{Country X}}$

Assume, for the moment, that we are using a mature market premium for the United States of 4.79%. The annualized standard deviation in the S&P 500 between 2006 and 2008, using weekly returns, was 15.27%, whereas the standard deviation in the Bovespa (the Brazilian equity index) over the same period was 25.83%.[4] Using these values, the estimate of a total risk premium for Brazil would be as follows:

Equity risk premium$_{\text{Brazil}}$ = 4.79% × (25.83% ÷ 15.27%)
= 8.10%

The country risk premium can be isolated as follows:

Country risk premium$_{\text{Brazil}}$ = 8.10% − 4.79% = 3.31%

While this approach has intuitive appeal, there are problems with comparing standard deviations computed in markets with widely different market structures and liquidity. There are very risky emerging markets that have low standard deviations for their equity markets because the markets are illiquid. This approach will understate the equity risk premiums in those markets.

Default Spreads and Relative Standard Deviations

The country default spreads that come with country ratings provide an important first step, but still only measure the premium for default risk. Intuitively, we would expect the country equity risk premium to be larger than the country

Measuring Country Risk

default risk spread. To address the issue of how much higher, we look at the volatility of the equity market in a country relative to the volatility of the bond market used to estimate the spread. This yields the following estimate for the country equity risk premium.

Country risk premium =
  Country default spread × (σ_{Equity} ÷ $\sigma_{Country\ bond}$)

To illustrate, consider again the case of Brazil. As noted earlier, the default spread on the Brazilian dollar-denominated bond in September 2008 was 2.15%, and the annualized standard deviation in the Brazilian equity index over the previous year was 25.83%. Using two years of weekly returns, the annualized standard deviation in the Brazilian dollar-denominated ten-year bond was 12.55%.[5] The resulting country equity risk premium for Brazil is as follows:

Additional equity risk premium$_{Brazil}$ =
  2.15% × (25.83% ÷ 12.55%) = 4.43%

Unlike the equity standard deviation approach, this premium is in addition to a mature market equity risk premium. Note that this country risk premium will increase if the country rating drops or if the relative volatility of the equity market increases. It is also in addition to the equity risk premium for a mature market. Thus, the total equity risk premium for Brazil using this approach and a 4.79% premium for the United States would be 9.22%.

Both this approach and the previous one use the standard deviation in equity of a market to make a judgment about country risk premium, but they measure it relative to different bases. This approach uses the country bond as a base, whereas the previous one uses the standard deviation in the US market. It also assumes that investors are more likely to choose between Brazilian government bonds and Brazilian equity, whereas the previous approach assumes that the choice is across equity markets.

Implied Equity Premiums

There is an alternative approach to estimating risk premiums that does not require historical data or corrections for country risk but does assume that the market, overall, is correctly priced. Consider, for instance, a very simple valuation model for stocks:

Value = Expected dividends next period
  ÷ (Required return on equity − Expected growth rate)

This is essentially the present value of dividends growing at a constant rate. Three of the four inputs in this model can be obtained externally—the current level of the market (value), the expected dividends next period, and the expected growth rate in earnings and dividends in the long term. The only "unknown" is then the required return on equity; when we solve for it, we get an implied expected return on stocks. Subtracting out the risk-free rate will yield an implied equity risk premium. We can extend the model to allow for dividends to grow at high rates, at least for short periods.

The advantage of the implied premium approach is that it is market-driven and current, and it does not require any historical data. Thus, it can be used to estimate implied equity premiums in any market. For instance, the equity risk premium for the Brazilian equity market on September 9, 2008, was estimated from the following inputs. The index (Bovespa) was at 48,345 and the current cash flow yield on the index was 5.41%. Earnings in companies in the index are expected to grow 9% (in US dollar terms) over the next five years, and 3.8% thereafter. These inputs yield a required return on equity of 10.78%, which when compared to the treasury bond rate of 3.80% on that day results in an implied equity premium of 6.98%. For simplicity, we have used nominal dollar expected growth rates[6] and treasury bond rates, but this analysis could have been done entirely in the local currency. We can decompose this number into a mature market equity risk premium and a country-specific equity risk premium by comparing it to the implied equity risk premium for a mature equity market (the United States, for instance).

- Implied equity premium for Brazil (see above) = 6.98%.
- Implied equity premium for the United States in September 2008 = 4.54%.
- Country specific equity risk premium for Brazil = 2.44%.

This approach can yield numbers very different from the other approaches, because they reflect market prices (and views) today.

CONCLUSION

As companies expand operations into emerging markets and investors search for investment opportunities in Asia and Latin America, they are also increasingly exposed to additional risk in these countries. While it is true that globally diversified investors can eliminate some country risk by diversifying across equities in many countries, the increasing correlation across

Approaches to Enterprise Risk Management

markets suggests that country risk cannot be entirely diversified away. To estimate the country risk premium, we considered three measures: the default spread on a government bond issued by that country, a premium obtained by scaling up the equity risk premium in the United States by the volatility of the country equity market relative to the US equity market, and a melded premium where the default spread on the country bond is adjusted for the higher volatility of the equity market. We also estimated an implied equity premium from stock prices and expected cash flows.

MORE INFO

Book:
Falaschetti, Dominic, and Michael Annin Ibbotson (eds). *Stocks, Bonds, Bills and Inflation*. Chicago, IL: Ibbotson Associates, 1999.

Articles:
Booth, Laurence. "Estimating the equity risk premium and equity costs: New ways of looking at old data." *Journal of Applied Corporate Finance* 12:1 (1999): 100–112.
Chan, K. C., G. A. Karolyi, and R. M. Stulz. "Global financial markets and the risk premium on US equity." *Journal of Financial Economics* 32:2 (1992): 137–167.
Indro, D. C., and W. Y. Lee, "Biases in arithmetic and geometric averages as estimates of long-run expected returns and risk premium." *Financial Management* 26 (1997): 81–90.

Report:
Damodaran, A. "Equity risk premiums: Determinants, estimation and implications." Working Paper, SSRN.com, 2008. Online at: pages.stern.nyu.edu/~adamodar/pdfiles/papers/ERPfull.pdf

NOTES

1 The process by which country ratings are obtained is explained on the S&P website at www2.standardandpoors.com/aboutcreditratings
2 These yields were as of January 1, 2008. While this is a market rate and reflects current expectations, country bond spreads are extremely volatile and can shift significantly from day to day. To counter this volatility, the default spread can be normalized by averaging the spread over time or by using the average default spread for all countries with the same rating as Brazil in early 2008.
3 If a country has a sovereign rating and no dollar-denominated bonds, we can use a typical spread based upon the rating as the default spread for the country. These numbers are available on my website at www.damodaran.com
4 If the dependence on historical volatility is troubling, the options market can be used to get implied volatilities for both the US market (about 20%) and for the Bovespa (about 38%).
5 Both standard deviations are computed on returns: returns on the equity index and returns on the ten-year bond.
6 The input that is most difficult to estimate for emerging markets is a long-term expected growth rate. For Brazilian stocks, I used the average consensus estimate of growth in earnings for the largest Brazilian companies which have ADRs listed on them. This estimate may be biased as a consequence.

Measuring Company Exposure to Country Risk
by Aswath Damodaran

EXECUTIVE SUMMARY
- Following the piece on "Measuring Country Risk" (pp. 125–128), we focus on a related question: Once we have estimated a country risk premium, how do we evaluate a company's exposure to country risk?
- In the process, we will argue that a company's exposure to country risk should not be determined by where it is incorporated and traded.
- By that measure, neither Coca-Cola nor Nestlé are exposed to country risk. Exposure to country risk should come from a company's operations, making country risk a critical component of the valuation of almost every large multinational corporation.

INTRODUCTION
If we accept the proposition of country risk, the next question that we have to address relates to the exposure of individual companies to country risk. Should all companies in a country with substantial country risk be equally exposed to country risk? While intuition suggests that they should not, we will begin by looking at standard approaches that assume that they are. We will follow up by scaling country risk exposure to established risk parameters such as betas (β), and complete the discussion with an argument that individual companies should be evaluated for exposure to country risk.

THE BLUDGEON APPROACH
The simplest assumption to make when dealing with country risk, and the one that is most often made, is that all companies in a market are equally exposed to country risk. The cost of equity for a firm in a market with country risk can then be written as:

Cost of equity = Risk-free rate +
    β(Mature market premium) + Country risk premium

Thus, for Brazil, where we have estimated a country risk premium of 4.43% from the melded approach, each company in the market will have an additional country risk premium of 4.43% added to its expected returns. For instance, the costs of equity for Embraer, an aerospace company listed in Brazil, with a beta[1] of 1.07 and Embratel, a Brazilian telecommunications company, with a beta of 0.80, in US dollar terms would be:

Cost of equity for Embraer =
    3.80% + 1.07(4.79%) + 4.43% = 13.35%

Cost of equity for Embratel =
    3.80% + 0.80(4.79%) + 4.43% = 12.06%

Note that the risk-free rate that we use is the US treasury bond rate (3.80%), and that the 4.79% figure is the equity risk premium for a mature equity market (estimated from historical data in the US market). It is also worth noting that analysts estimating the cost of equity for Brazilian companies, in US dollar terms, often use the Brazilian ten-year dollar-denominated rate as the risk-free rate. This is dangerous, since it is often also accompanied with a higher risk premium, and ends up double counting risk.

THE BETA APPROACH
For those investors who are uncomfortable with the notion that all companies in a market are equally exposed to country risk, a fairly simple alternative is to assume that a company's exposure to country risk is proportional to its exposure to all other market risk, which is measured by the beta. Thus, the cost of equity for a firm in an emerging market can be written as follows:

Cost of equity = Risk-free rate +
    β(Mature market premium + Country risk premium)

In practical terms, scaling the country risk premium to the beta of a stock implies that stocks with betas above 1.00 will be more exposed to country risk than stocks with a beta below 1.00. For Embraer, with a beta of 1.07, this would lead to a dollar cost of equity estimate of:

Cost of equity for Embraer =
    3.80% + 1.07(4.79% + 4.43%) = 13.67%

For Embratel, with its lower beta of 0.80, the cost of equity is:

Cost of equity for Embratel =
    3.80% + 0.80(4.79% + 4.43%) = 11.18%

Approaches to Enterprise Risk Management

The advantage of using betas is that they are easily available for most firms. The disadvantage is that while betas measure overall exposure to macroeconomic risk, they may not be good measures of country risk.

THE LAMBDA APPROACH

The most general, and our preferred, approach is to allow for each company to have an exposure to country risk that is different from its exposure to all other market risk. For lack of a better term, let us term the measure of a company's exposure to country risk to be lambda (λ). Like a beta, a lambda will be scaled around 1.00, with a lambda of 1.00 indicating a company with average exposure to country risk and a lambda above or below 1.00 indicating above or below average exposure to country risk. The cost of equity for a firm in an emerging market can then be written as:

Expected return = R_f + β(Mature market equity risk premium) + λ(Country risk premium)

Note that this approach essentially converts our expected return model to a two-factor model, with the second factor being country risk, with λ measuring exposure to country risk.

Determinants of Lambda

Most investors would accept the general proposition that different companies in a market should have different exposures to country risk. But what are the determinants of this exposure? We would expect at least three factors (and perhaps more) to play a role.

1. *Revenue source*: The first and most obvious determinant is how much of the revenues a firm derives from the country in question. A company that derives 30% of its revenues from Brazil should be less exposed to Brazilian country risk than a company that derives 70% of its revenues from Brazil. Note, though, that this then opens up the possibility that a company can be exposed to the risk in many countries. Thus, the company that derives only 30% of its revenues from Brazil may derive its remaining revenues from Argentina and Venezuela, exposing it to country risk in those countries. Extending this argument to multinationals, we would argue that companies like Coca-Cola and Nestlé can have substantial exposure to country risk because so much of their revenues comes from emerging markets.
2. *Production facilities*: A company can be exposed to country risk, even if it derives no revenues from that country, if its production facilities are in that country. After all, political and economic turmoil in the country can throw off production schedules and affect the company's profits. Companies that can move their production facilities elsewhere can spread their risk across several countries, but the problem is exaggerated for those companies that cannot move their production facilities. Consider the case of mining companies. An African gold mining company may export all of its production but it will face substantial country risk exposure because its mines are not movable.
3. *Risk management products*: Companies that would otherwise be exposed to substantial country risk may be able to reduce this exposure by buying insurance against specific (unpleasant) contingencies and by using derivatives. A company that uses risk management products should have a lower exposure to country risk—a lower lambda—than an otherwise similar company that does not use these products.

Ideally, we would like companies to be forthcoming about all three of these factors in their financial statements.

Measuring Lambda

The simplest measure of lambda is based entirely on revenues. In the last section, we argued that a company that derives a smaller proportion of its revenues from a market should be less exposed to country risk. Given the constraint that the average lambda across all stocks has to be 1.0 (someone has to bear the country risk!), we cannot use the percentage of revenues that a company gets from a market as lambda. We can, however, scale this measure by dividing it by the percentage of revenues that the average company in the market gets from the country to derive a lambda.

λ_j = % of revenue in country$_{Company}$ ÷ % of revenue in country$_{Average\ company\ in\ market}$

Consider the two large and widely followed Brazilian companies—Embraer, an aerospace company that manufactures and sells aircraft to many of the world's leading airlines, and Embratel, the Brazilian telecommunications giant. In 2002, Embraer generated only 3% of its revenues in Brazil, whereas the average company in the market obtained 85% of its revenues in Brazil.[2] Using the measure suggested above, the lambda for Embraer would be:

Measuring Company Exposure to Country Risk

$\lambda_{Embraer} = 3\% \div 85\% = 0.04$

In contrast, Embratel generated 95% of its revenues from Brazil, giving it a lambda of

$\lambda_{Embratel} = 95\% \div 85\% = 1.12$

Following up, Embratel is far more exposed to country risk than Embraer and will have a much higher cost of equity.

The second measure draws on the stock prices of a company and how they move in relation to movements in country risk. Bonds issued by countries offer a simple and updated measure of country risk; as investor assessments of country risk become more optimistic, bonds issued by that country go up in price, just as they go down when investors become more pessimistic. A regression of the returns on a stock against the returns on a country bond should therefore yield a measure of lambda in the slope coefficient. Applying this approach to Embraer and Embratel, we regressed monthly stock returns on the two stocks against monthly returns on the ten-year dollar-denominated Brazilian government bond and arrived at the following results:

$Return_{Embraer} = 0.0195 + 0.2681\ Return_{Brazil\ dollar-bond}$

$Return_{Embratel} = -0.0308 + 2.0030\ Return_{Brazil\ dollar-bond}$

Based upon these regressions, Embraer has a lambda of 0.27 and Embratel has a lambda of 2.00. The resulting dollar costs of equity for the two firms, using a mature market equity risk premium of 4.79% and a country equity risk premium of 4.43% for Brazil are:

Cost of equity for Embraer =
  3.80% + 1.07(4.79%) + 0.27(4.43%) = 10.12%

Cost of equity for Embratel =
  3.80% + 0.80(4.79%) + 2.00(4.43%) = 16.49%

What are the limitations of this approach? The lambdas estimated from these regressions are likely to have large standard errors; the standard error in the lambda estimate of Embratel is 0.35. It also requires that the country have bonds that are liquid and widely traded, preferably in a more stable currency (dollar or euro).

RISK EXPOSURE IN MANY COUNTRIES

The discussion of lambdas in the last section should highlight a fact that is often lost in valuation. The exposure to country risk, whether it is measured in revenues, earnings, or stock prices, does not come from where a company is incorporated but from its operations. There are US companies that are more exposed to Brazilian country risk than is Embraer. In fact, companies like Nestlé, Coca-Cola, and Gillette have built much of their success on expansion into emerging markets. While this expansion has provided them with growth opportunities, it has also left them exposed to country risk in multiple countries.

In practical terms, what does this imply? When estimating the costs of equity and capital for these companies and others like them, we will need to incorporate an extra premium for country risk. Thus, the net effect on value from their growth strategies will depend upon whether the growth effect (from expanding into emerging markets) exceeds the risk effect. We can adapt the measures suggested above to estimate the risk exposure to different countries for an individual company.

We can break down a company's revenue by country and use the percentage of revenues that the company gets from each emerging market as a basis for estimating lambda in that market. While the percentage of revenues itself can be used as a lambda, a more precise estimate would scale this to the percentage of revenues that the average company in that market gets in the country.

If companies break earnings down by country, these numbers can be used to estimate lambdas. The peril with this approach is that the reported earnings often reflect accounting allocation decisions and differences in tax rates across countries.

If a company is exposed to only a few emerging markets on a large scale, we can regress the company's stock price against the country bond returns from those markets to get country-specific lambdas.

CONCLUSION

A key issue, when estimating costs of equity and capital for emerging market companies relates to how this country risk premium should be reflected in the costs of equities of individual companies in that country. While the standard approaches add the country risk premium as a constant to the cost of equity of every company in that market, we argue for a more nuanced approach where a company's exposure to country risk is measured with a lambda. This lambda can be estimated either by looking at how much of a company's revenues or earnings come from the country—the greater the percentage, the greater the lambda—or by regressing a

Approaches to Enterprise Risk Management

company's stock returns against country bond returns—the greater the sensitivity, the higher the lambda. If we accept this view of the world, the costs of equity for multinationals that have significant operations in emerging markets will have to be adjusted to reflect their exposure to risk in these markets.

MORE INFO

Book:
Falaschetti, Dominic, and Michael Annin Ibbotson (eds). *Stocks, Bonds, Bills and Inflation*. Chicago, IL: Ibbotson Associates, 1999.

Articles:
Booth, Laurence. "Estimating the equity risk premium and equity costs: New ways of looking at old data." *Journal of Applied Corporate Finance* 12:1 (1999): 100–112.
Chan, K. C., G. A. Karolyi, and R. M. Stulz. "Global financial markets and the risk premium on US equity." *Journal of Financial Economics* 32:2 (1992): 137–167.
Damodaran, A., "Country risk and company exposure." *Journal of Applied Finance* 13:2 (2003): 64–78.
Godfrey, S., and R. Espinosa. "A practical approach to calculating the cost of equity for investments in emerging markets." *Journal of Applied Corporate Finance* 9:3 (1996): 80–90.
Indro, D. C., and W. Y. Lee, "Biases in arithmetic and geometric averages as estimates of long-run expected returns and risk premium." *Financial Management* 26 (1997): 81–90.
Stulz, R. M. "Globalization, corporate finance, and the cost of capital." *Journal of Applied Corporate Finance* 12:3 (1999): 8–25.

Report:
Damodaran, A. "Measuring Company Risk Exposure to Country Risk." Working Paper, SSRN.com, 2008. Online at: pages.stern.nyu.edu/~adamodar/pdfiles/papers/ERPfull.pdf

NOTES

1 We used a bottom-up beta for Embraer, based upon an unlevered beta of 0.95 (estimated using aerospace companies listed globally) and Embraer's debt-to-equity ratio of 19.01%. For more on the rationale for bottom-up betas, read the companion paper on estimating risk parameters, "Measuring Country Risk" (pp. 125–128).

2 To use this approach, we need to estimate the percentage of revenues both for the firm in question and for the average firm in the market. While the former may be simple to obtain, estimating the latter can be a time-consuming exercise. One simple solution is to use data that are publicly available on how much of a country's gross domestic product comes from exports. According to the World Bank data in this table, Brazil got 23.2% of its GDP from exports in 2008. If we assume that this is an approximation of export revenues for the average firm, the average firm can be assumed to generate 76.8% of its revenues domestically. Using this value would yield slightly higher betas for both Embraer and Embratel.

Pension Schemes: A Unique and Unintended Basket of Risks on the Balance Sheet
by Amarendra Swarup

EXECUTIVE SUMMARY
- Pension schemes are often the most overlooked part of a company's balance sheet, despite the large hidden and complex risks they can pose. Some of the unique risks within pension schemes are exposure to interest rates, inflation, market risk, and longevity.
- The problem is particularly acute for defined-benefit pension schemes—common in many developed countries—where the benefits are predetermined, are often index-linked, and can be passed on to dependents. The present cost of bearing these risks has risen sharply in recent decades, and many companies have closed their pension schemes to new members.
- In the short term, changing economic, financial, and demographic perceptions can materially alter the valuation of a pension scheme's assets and liabilities from one day to the next, potentially leaving many finance directors with an uncontrolled liability on otherwise well-managed balance sheets.
- The waters can be muddied further by another fundamental problem: for most schemes, liabilities are calculated infrequently using ad hoc or out-of-date assumptions, which can often present a less than prudent valuation of the true costs.
- Options to manage and even reduce these uncertainties are now appearing. The key is to have a proactive and realistic approach to the risks that are being carried on the balance sheet.

INTRODUCTION
The only function of economic forecasting, the late American economist J. K. Galbraith once noted, was to make astrology look respectable. And, knowingly or not, it's a belief that's endemic in the corporate world.

The overriding concern is to find the hidden value in companies—whether in their balance sheet or in their intellectual property—and extract it in the most efficient way possible. Every financial and operational risk is carefully studied and, where possible, mitigated. Lines of credit are negotiated at known terms to suit the company's horizon. Capital structures are continually redrawn to maximize efficiency. Balance sheets are scrutinized line by line and operations are streamlined.

There is no obsession with predicting GDP, or agonizing over the evolution of the labor market over the next decade, for example. No, these are all nebulous questions for economic forecasters to ponder. For the seasoned financial director, the wider economy only matters insofar as it affects that all important cash flow.

Yet, hidden in that otherwise well-managed balance sheet might be a host of unconstrained liabilities that threaten to undo the most meticulous business plan and expose companies to a whole host of unknown risks—all housed within an often overlooked pension plan.

The problem is particularly acute for defined benefit schemes—occupational schemes where the pension benefits are fixed in advance and are often calculated as a proportion of an employee's final salary. Many include provision for dependents such as widows, and can even be indexed to inflation. These proved to be enormously popular in the aftermath of the Second World War, when many companies saw them as an effective way to defer compensation for workers to future years. However, these schemes placed a host of unintended and poorly understood risks with the sponsoring employer, such as exposure to longevity, to future interest rates, and to the capricious whims of financial markets.

In recent decades, as companies found themselves confronted with declining employment and a growing retiree problem, the present cost of bearing these risks has escalated sharply, and many have closed their pension schemes to new members. Furthermore, pension schemes and, in some jurisdictions, their associated healthcare liabilities, are increasingly a growing factor in corporate finance transactions.

A potentially attractive merger or acquisition may become unstuck because of the pension fund, or, worse still, an existing company may hit difficulties as the full cost of the pension obligation becomes known. The abortive takeover of Sainsbury's in the United Kingdom and

Approaches to Enterprise Risk Management

the well-publicized troubles at General Motors in the United States are but the most visible tip of the proverbial iceberg, and are indicative of a problem that can consign businesses to a slow decline.

But more than just eroding stockholder value in the present, defined benefit schemes are also a danger to a company's long-term survival in an increasingly competitive global economy. Many management teams now face the problem of maintaining a set of financial commitments made in another era, when assumptions and expectations were vastly different. These commitments are difficult to measure—let alone anticipate—and they are tied to the health of the corporate sponsor of the pension fund, which is legally required to underwrite any deficit. If the company does go under, the responsibility of meeting at least part of these liabilities may then be transferred to governments and taxpayers. This may create additional problems, as pension scheme members will likely receive reduced benefits, and the addition of significant numbers of liabilities to the government balance sheet is eventually likely to become politically unpalatable.

A GROWING PROBLEM

Anyone who doubts the potential scale of the problem only has to look at the case of the American Civil War veterans' pension fund—one of the earliest defined benefit schemes. Originally set up during the war to pay pensions to disabled veterans, the scheme was gradually extended to include all veterans and their dependants, making its final payment only in 2004—nearly 140 years after the war ended. By then, the scheme had cost the US government hundreds of billions in today's dollars, and at its peak in the early 1890s, it had even constituted over 40% of the annual federal budget.

It's a stark warning for many pension schemes and their corporate sponsors today.

Any views on interest rates over the next decade? Your debt financing may have excellent terms, and it may seem a moot point, but the pension fund's liabilities and their associated accounting costs will swing violently over the next few decades with movements in the prevailing interest rates. By some estimates, the drop in long-term interest rates from 1999 to 2002 increased the value of pension liabilities by 30–40%.

How about inflation—any thoughts on how it might evolve over the next half century? Many scheme members, particularly in the United Kingdom, have index-linked pensions, and the burden of payments can quickly become onerous. Figures from the UK Office for National Statistics show that from 1970 to 2007, annual employer contributions to pension schemes went up a factor of 53, and they trebled over the last seven years alone of that period (Figure 1). Wage inflation too can rapidly push up costs.

And what about people living longer? For individuals and society, increased longevity is desirable, but living longer can often also create large unanticipated costs. Ever since German Chancellor Otto von Bismarck thought he'd pulled off a politically brilliant move back in 1889, by promising pensions at 70 when the average German lived to less than 50 years of age, the

Figure 1. Annual contributions to UK pension schemes by employers and employees 1970–2007. (*Source*: Office for National Statistics)

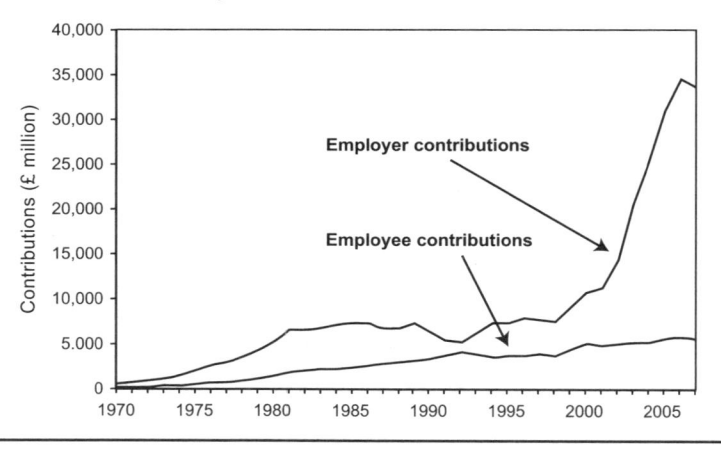

Pension Schemes: A Unique and Unintended Basket of Risks

continual improvements in life expectancies have rapidly unraveled the best-laid pension plans. Even more troubling, the current upward trend shows little sign of leveling off, and it is increasingly clear that this is the most significant risk to the finances of pension schemes and their sponsors. The rising life expectancies for males and females in the United Kingdom are shown in Figure 2.

scheme from one day to the next. It's a headache for many finance directors, who are left with an uncontrolled liability on otherwise well-managed balance sheets.

It becomes extremely difficult under these circumstances to determine the ability of a defined benefit pension scheme to pay its annuities 40 years down the track. Throw in the increasingly common belief that the economic environment

Figure 2. Increasing life expectancy in the United Kingdom for 65-year-olds. (*Source*: Office for National Statistics)

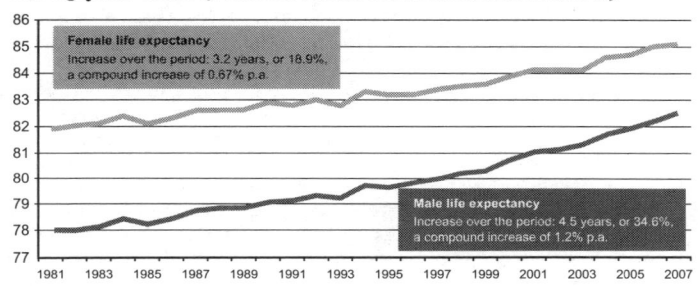

[Chart showing female life expectancy: Increase over the period: 3.2 years, or 18.9%, a compound increase of 0.67% p.a. Male life expectancy: Increase over the period: 4.5 years, or 34.6%, a compound increase of 1.2% p.a. Years from 1981 to 2007, values from 77 to 86.]

In a field typified by extremes, the case of Jeanne Calment is a situation that's humorlessly reminiscent of reality for many pension schemes. When Madame Calment's lawyer agreed in 1965 to pay her an annual income worth one-tenth of the value of her flat on the understanding that he would inherit the property on her death, it seemed like a shrewd bargain. Madame Calment was then 90 years old, and it seemed unlikely that she had much longer to go on this particular journey. Unfortunately, bearing testament to perhaps one of the most misjudged investment decisions ever, Jeanne went on to live to the ripe old age of 122. Along the way, she also became the oldest rap artist ever, releasing an album at 121, but that is unlikely to have provided much consolation to her poor aforementioned lawyer. By then, he was long dead and his widow was still making the payments.

THE DANGERS OF VOLATILE MARKETS

It's a complex basket of risks and, in the short term, changing economic and demographic perceptions can materially alter the valuation of a pension scheme's liabilities from one day to the next. Even the assets are not immune, as many pension schemes have more than half their assets in equities—a consequence of their long-term perspective, adherents argue. In the short term, however, volatility in the markets can materially alter the valuation of a pension

in the coming years is likely to be far less favorable than in recent years, and increased volatility seems inevitable.

In early 2008, for example, Aon Consulting estimated that sharp falls in the FTSE caused UK pension schemes to lose $60 billion in just a single week, wiping out all the gains made in 2007. More worryingly for companies, equity markets have declined significantly since their highs in mid-2007. Given that these companies are often older, and therefore have a much greater role as pension sponsors than the percentage of market capitalization that they represent, sponsor risk is also an increasingly major concern across the board.

It's a growing headache for many firms, for whom such risks often lie far from familiar territory and who are charged with looking after a broad church of stakeholders, not just pensioners. Though the increased pension fund liabilities are often longer term than most corporate horizons, they must be carried on the company's balance sheet, reducing net asset value and increasing financial leverage. As the corporate sponsor, they generally also have an obligation to fund at least part of these unexpected costs, giving them an uncertain command over their own cash flow and reducing future distributions to investors. The impact can go far beyond the immediate cash flow hit—filtering through to the P & L, lowering profits, hurting competitiveness, and, ultimately, even impacting the share price.

Approaches to Enterprise Risk Management

In the case of General Motors, for example, net obligations are estimated to be about $170 billion across all of GM's US operations, dwarfing its current market cap of $3 billion. To meet its soaring obligations, the company contributed an astonishing $30 billion to its US pension plans in 2003 and 2004, but the accounts are still tens of billions of dollars in deficit. Now, pension and healthcare costs make up more of the average GM vehicle's price tag than the steel used to build it. Consequently, the company is inexorably losing ground to a wave of foreign competitors with lower cost bases and less debt on their balance sheets—resulting in a catastrophic decline in stock price for investors, from $55 in January 2004 to under $10 today.

MUDDY WATERS
The waters are muddied further by another fundamental problem. For most schemes, liabilities are calculated infrequently, using out-of-date longevity assumptions and ad hoc discount rates, and often presenting a less than prudent valuation of the true costs of delivering pensioners full financial security. As people live longer—15 minutes more for every passing hour by some estimates—and accounting standards move more toward valuing balance sheets on a mark-to-market basis, the immediately calculable costs can rise dramatically as outdated assumptions are revised.

Many pension schemes value their liabilities by using a discount rate that is implicitly linked to the assumed return on their assets. The problem is that they are effectively banking on an uncertain set of future gains to pay off their obligations to millions of current and future pensioners. Even worse, the discount rates vary from scheme to scheme. Some may choose a point in time and a single discount rate for all their liabilities, while others may choose to be more sophisticated and look at evolving discount rates over time. Regardless, most discount rates are ultimately linked to AA-rated corporate bond yields—the result of an implicit belief that returns of this order can be harvested without difficulty.

This is not to say that corporate bonds are not good investments. They are an investment staple with good reason and can provide low-risk returns. However, they are not risk-free, and any prudent investor needs to be cognizant of the default, credit, and liquidity risks that go with the asset class. In recent months, the problem has been highlighted by the credit crunch, which has seen prices of AA corporate bonds collapse and their yields soar. No wonder many schemes were feeling pleasantly flush and in surplus over the last couple of years—their liabilities dramatically lessened over the same time period!

It's a false optimism. The downturn in prices reflects the increasing fear that some of these corporate bonds might default. Even if one claimed that investing everything in AA corporate bonds today could still provide these returns at low risk, there simply aren't enough around. Taking the United Kingdom as an example, the total value of AA corporate bonds floating around the UK financial markets at last count was just over $142 billion—a fraction of the some $1,200 billion of liabilities they are supposed to underpin.

It's a troubling mismatch problem. Although there is a tradition of pension schemes and insurers "booking" some potential asset gains in advance, it is important for companies not to bank on future gains to work out their liabilities. An unembellished picture of the liabilities, stripped of any assumed risk premiums, can often be a good guide when setting investment targets and managing the risk on your balance sheet.

The area is also coming under increased regulatory scrutiny, with more stringent accounting standards being imposed. For example, the pensions regulator in the United Kingdom is now pushing schemes to adopt more realistic mortality assumptions that reflect the latest scientific evidence—a change that could equate to an additional cost of $40 billion for the UK defined benefit industry with every added year of life expectancy. This also presents additional shorter-term risks for sponsors, as they may have to divert extra cash into the scheme to meet these future liabilities via a contribution notice.

SOLUTIONS ON THE HORIZON
Company finance directors must feel victimized. Constrained by ever-growing liabilities on the balance sheet and a volatile pension asset portfolio, they often find themselves on the wrong side of the window when it comes to securing their retirees' benefits. Changing interest rates, rising inflation, and ever-increasing allowances for longevity mean that the liabilities are often a fast-moving target. Throw in a worsening economic environment, and keeping apace is complicated by potentially thorny negotiations with trustees and retirees for additional injections.

So how are trustees and sponsors to manage these new, troubling risks? It's hard enough to judge market returns over the next few years, without crystal ball gazing to estimate the lifespan of all the scheme members under your responsibility—past, present, and future.

Pension Schemes: A Unique and Unintended Basket of Risks

The answer today is that it is largely a dark art. The current trend is unlikely to be your friend here; longevity improvements have repeatedly defied the hopeful shackles of successive actuarial models, despite the most Orwellian filtering of data by job, medical history, and even postcode. The latest models—even if true—give scant comfort. For example, by 2050 a 65-year-old UK male might live to be between 86 and 97 years old, up from 83 today.

However, there are options. Like any other risk, these uncertainties can be managed, and even reduced, once understood. The key is to have a proactive and realistic approach to the risks that are being carried on the balance sheet. Sponsors need to engage actively with trustees and walk a fine line between investors' expectations and the funding needs for the pension scheme.

Unique solutions are now appearing in the market. A whole industry has now sprung up in the United Kingdom offering full insurance buyouts, where the pension liabilities are transferred away to dedicated specialists. This can often improve the situation for pension scheme members, as these specialist insurers are tightly regulated, operate within strict investment and asset/liability guidelines, and have to hold capital against any extreme losses.

It also helps troubled sponsors: Securing pension liabilities away from balance sheets improves their ability to raise finance, and removes the situation where, in a falling equity market with a commensurate fall in the valuation of a scheme's assets, a sponsor looking to invest in the business might also find trustees coming cap in hand. Above all, it enables management to get on with running the business, free from the peripheral distractions of administering a pension scheme.

However, insurance buyout valuations use more cautious longevity assumptions and paint a truer picture of the hidden arrears, increasing the liabilities and the premiums required significantly. Like customers outside a Ferrari showroom peering in through the window, it is simply unaffordable for many companies and not available in many countries.

But there are alternatives to help transfer risk. Schemes can execute partial buyouts for some of their liabilities, such as current pensioners. If that overshoots the budget and the deficit is still too large, or the options are not available in your jurisdiction, there are now innovative corporate solutions to help transfer risk, ranging from taking on the entire scheme and its myriad liabilities, to specific solutions for specific risks.

For example, trustees and sponsors can implement bond or swap-based hedging strategies to nullify the impact of interest rates and inflation on their liabilities, and thereby on the balance sheet. There is even a growing market in longevity swaps, allowing people also to hedge this idiosyncratic risk. Although they introduce new risks in lieu, such as the health of the counterparties on the other side of the swap, these steps are cost-effective and can ensure that the larger part of a scheme's risk—its volatile liabilities—is better constrained, while precious assets are freed up to invest in assets with higher returns.

Another alternative is to delegate the holistic management of all the scheme's assets and liabilities to a third-party fiduciary manager, who will manage them on a real-time basis within tight guidelines agreed with the trustees. These specialists will typically hedge all the liabilities where possible and diversify the assets among a range of best of breed providers. This ensures that the funding position is improved, and its ultimate targets, such as a full buyout, are reached in an efficient and structured manner. The asset/liability management approach has proved popular in countries such as The Netherlands, where it has significantly improved funding positions.

It's a rapidly evolving environment, and, with new solutions appearing fast, corporate sponsors can be hopeful of finding innovative ways of managing these new risks on their horizon. Most importantly, they can go back to finding and building businesses—not reading horoscopes.

Approaches to Enterprise Risk Management

MORE INFO

Reports:

Eich, Frank, and Amarendra Swarup. "Pensions tomorrow: A white paper." London School of Economics, 2008. Online at: www.lse.ac.uk/collections/management/PDFs/Pensions_Tomorrow_White_Paper.pdf

Eich, Frank, and Amarendra Swarup. "Longevity: Trends, uncertainty and the implications for pension systems." London School of Economics, 2009. Online at: www.lse.ac.uk/collections/management/PDFs/Pensions_Tomorrow_Longevity_paper.pdf

Website:

London School of Economics—Pensions Tomorrow, an initiative launched by the LSE to stimulate debate on how to take pension systems forward: www.lse.ac.uk/collections/management/pensionsTomorrow

Essentials for Export Success: Understanding How Risks and Relationships Lead to Rewards
by Paul Beretz

EXECUTIVE SUMMARY
- The global business environment can present opportunities for rewards for the exporter if international risk attributes can be determined and mitigated.
- Exporters who want to succeed should be able to identify and evaluate their "IQ" (international qualities).
- The risk elements of country, currency, and culture can significantly impact global business transactions.
- Relationship-building and the ability to sustain those relationships are necessary qualities for reaping rewards.

INTRODUCTION
More and more, companies located throughout the world are recognizing that the way to sustain long-term growth is not by continuing to emphasize local, in-country markets. Whether it be for better or worse, global business is a factor that can provide businesses with the opportunity to consider new and challenging markets. In 2008, we saw that severe credit and financial issues could spread quickly, and that no part of the world was immune. Therefore, an understanding of the key risk factors that can lead to rewards is essential.

How should a business assess world markets? One initial approach for exporters is to determine their "IQ," or international qualities, before either entering or expanding their overseas markets.

RATING YOUR COMPANY'S "IQ"
The "IQ" test shown in Figure 1 will address your company's readiness to compete in the global marketplace. For each question, give your company a letter grade (A–F, or U for "Unknown") and state the reason(s) for your grade. Grade A = 90–100%, B = 80–89%, and so on.

Figure 1. The "IQ" test

"IQ" question	Grade	Reason
What percentage of your revenues do you expect from the country or countries you will be exporting to?		
What do you expect as your market share and industry ranking in that country (or countries)?		
Will you establish direct sales relationships with your major customers?		
Will you ever expect to be considered a company that is "part" of the country you are exporting to?		
Have you analyzed all the cultural, currency, and country issues you will encounter in exporting to a particular country?		
What is your knowledge of the market for your product in a given country?		
What is your knowledge of the economic structure and the current state of the economy in a new country?		
Have you analyzed the legal system in a new country for the legality of your contracts or relationships? Can you cancel a relationship with a distributor or an agent if necessary? Is your documentation of sale legally binding?		
Once the sale is made, and payment is not forthcoming, what are your options in achieving payment? Practically, culturally, and legally, what are the norms?		

Approaches to Enterprise Risk Management

RISKS FACING THE EXPORTER
An exporter will face many risks once the decision to sell in overseas markets is made. Key risk areas, in particular, are known as the "three Cs"—country, currency, and culture.

Country Risk
Figure 2 outlines the dimensions of country risk when goods or services are sold globally. Exporters may wish to use the chart to classify the major risk issues and attributes of each risk by country.

investment abroad, will there be access to the invested capital and will earnings be able to be repatriated? This could impact cash flow and the ability to meet its trade obligations.

Currency Risk
Exporters have to consider selling in foreign currencies to offshore customers. In this competitive environment, an exporter needs flexibility in determining the currency that is billed to the customer. In a volatile global economy, however, billing a buyer in a currency that differs from the

Figure 2. Dimensions of country risk

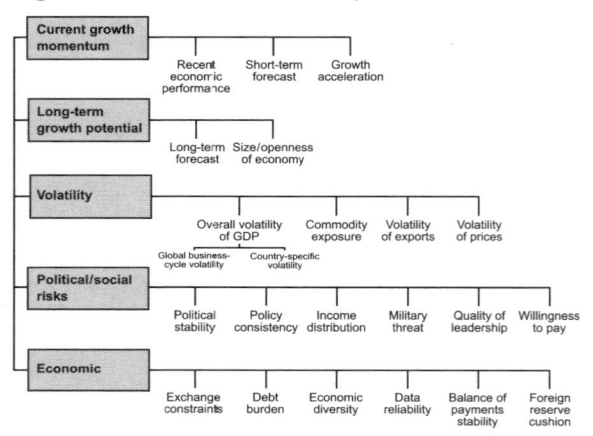

```
Current growth momentum
    ├── Recent economic performance
    ├── Short-term forecast
    └── Growth acceleration
Long-term growth potential
    ├── Long-term forecast
    └── Size/openness of economy
Volatility
    ├── Overall volatility of GDP
    │   ├── Global business-cycle volatility
    │   └── Country-specific volatility
    ├── Commodity exposure
    ├── Volatility of exports
    └── Volatility of prices
Political/social risks
    ├── Political stability
    ├── Policy consistency
    ├── Income distribution
    ├── Military threat
    ├── Quality of leadership
    └── Willingness to pay
Economic
    ├── Exchange constraints
    ├── Debt burden
    ├── Economic diversity
    ├── Data reliability
    ├── Balance of payments stability
    └── Foreign reserve cushion
```

These are the questions to ask when determining the dimensions of country risk:

- What currency will you be selling in? Is the decision a competitive one? Are you equipped internally to deal in multicurrencies?
- Do you know the laws in specific countries? (For example, a joint venture in China must balance imports with exports, or else it could be barred by the government from obtaining hard currency.)
- What is the recent political history (that could influence the availability of funds or internal stability)? This will include government takeover of properties, whether with or without compensation, operational restrictions, or damage to property or personnel.
- What is the current economic environment in the country? Have there been local currency devaluations recently?
- Have there been border disputes that could escalate military readiness and therefore impact the availability of hard currency, both within the country's borders and as funds leaving the country? If the exporter's customer base is expanding through direct

seller's own currency can be fraught with risk: When payment is due, has the value of the currency fallen in value against the seller's currency?

One approach for the exporter is to deal in the foreign exchange (FX) market, which is an enormous, sophisticated, and efficient global communications system operating around the clock to enable international transactions. Large commercial banks are the dominant players in the FX market, serving as intermediaries between supply and demand; corporations are the principal end-users. FX transactions are speculative by nature and thus can be volatile, thereby increasing risk.

Three basic transactions for managing FX risk are *spot transactions, forward transactions* and *options*. Spot transactions are purchases or sales of foreign currency for "immediate" delivery. *Forward transactions* carry a specified price and stipulated future value date for the exchange of currencies. They are used most often to cover future foreign currency payables and anticipated receipts. *Options* are a more suitable tool for "hedging" risk when a foreign customer's commitment is not firm. Buyers pay a premium for

Essentials for Export Success

CASE STUDIES

Country Risk
A large forest products company based in the United States had solid business relations with five distributors located in a Latin American country. These distributors, in total, owed US$10 million to the exporter, all within payment terms. When the central bank of the country froze all payments leaving the country, the government bank instructed all vendors selling into the country that they would have to wait five years for any repayment of debt. The country manager of the forest products company, who had developed excellent relations with several key executives at the central bank over the years, was able to discount the US$10 million debt with a global bank located outside the country. The result? The exporter was paid 95 cents on the dollar within 60 days. In addition, future sales were paid through an escrow account with the same bank. What is the moral of the story? Even though the five customers were well financed and deemed extremely creditworthy, a country calamity impacted their ability to process business normally. Without the relationship the forest products country manager had developed, the exporter would have had to wait five years for payment.

Currency Risk
Tyco International, Ltd., based in Bermuda, with headquarter operations in Princeton, NJ, US, is a maker of safety, industrial, and construction products. According to a *Wall Street Journal* article of November 12, 2008 ("Tyco warns currencies, costs will hit earnings"), the company said that in September and October 2008, it saw about a 20% devaluation in currencies of foreign countries where the company did business. The chief executive estimated that these exchange rate fluctuations could reduce fiscal revenue in 2009 by about $2 billion and reduce annual earnings by about 38 cents a share. Tyco generates about 50% of its revenue abroad.

Culture Risk
A large chemical company had been negotiating a licensing agreement with a Middle-Eastern country for close to a year. As the final meeting was drawing to a close, a junior member of the exporter's team asked the customer's executives present at the meeting if everything was "OK" and, at the same time, made the standard Western gesture meaning the same thing.
In the customer's culture this hand signal was an insulting and vulgar sign, so the customer took offense and walked out of the meeting. It took numerous apologies from the exporter and another six months to restore the relationship before the transaction was eventually consummated.

---

the option to exchange foreign currency at a predetermined rate ("strike price"). Options are bought and sold on the "exchange-traded" (less flexible, less expensive) and "over the counter" (more flexible, more expensive) markets, and they allow buyers to take advantage of favorable changes in currency rates while guarding against adverse changes.

The prudent financial manager recognizes that currency risk is a major factor in the export decision.

Culture Risk
The proactive, truly globally oriented exporter living in today's competitive marketplace understands that business decision making is a form of art as much as a science. All the evaluation tools available cannot take the place of experience. It is essential to possess a fundamental, analytical approach to the export selling process. The "art" form of today's global business process includes an understanding of how the cultures and negotiation processes of different countries become part of the arsenal of tools in making an intelligent decision. How the culture of each country or region impacts the risk is material to the ultimate business decision.

A lack of awareness—whether it be intentional or not—can impact the business relationship, impede the negotiations, and end the opportunity to complete the business transaction. Does the exporter understand customs and practices regarding whether or not to shake hands and what clothes to wear? Does the exporter know about presenting business cards (in different languages)—and not writing on the card? Mistakes that involve eating and drinking have been known to end a business opportunity; many Westerners do not know that in certain Chinese provinces the act of putting chopsticks in a rice bowl means "death" to the person on the other side of the table. In many world cultures, the customer expects the eldest representative of the exporter to be involved in negotiations (such elders are known as the "gray-haired gods"), even if this person is not the most astute.

Approaches to Enterprise Risk Management

HOW RELATIONSHIPS CAN LEAD TO REWARDS FOR THE EXPORTER
Awareness, attitude, and anticipation are crucial. In the global business environment, the observant exporter should know how to watch and listen, rather than expect the transaction to happen "now." Relationship building is not only critical with offshore customers, but also imperative with a company's own "internal" customer—the branch office or agent in that country of business. Many exporters demonstrate hubris in their belief that how they do business in their own country is how it is best to do business in the country of the potential importer.

The proactive, successful exporter desiring to succeed in other lands will study behavior, learn about verbal and nonverbal differences that exist, and often will use a "go-between" in order to create the desired relationship. The person who is the intermediary may be one's own country manager; or it could be a banker, business owner, or government employee in a key position in the country who understands how to help achieve the connection between the two parties. Any person-to-person relationship, especially in the business world, has a better chance of succeeding when trust is both understood and established. This need for relationship means that a feeling of complete trust and confidence must exist, not only that the other party will not take advantage of them, but also that they can presume upon the indulgence of the other.

Trust, as part of relationship-building, is paramount in much of the negotiating process. In China, *guanxi* literally means "relationships" and is understood as the network of relationships among various parties that cooperate together and support one another. In Japan, *shokaijo* can mean a letter of introduction, indicating that the status of the exporter is confirmed with the Japanese customer or contact, as opposed to a "cold" call. It provides more of a "guarantee" that the exporter is connected to the business process in Japan. *Jeito* (in Brazil) is the way a businessperson, though local contacts and experiences, is given the chance to succeed.

CONCLUSION
The exporter needs to evaluate their "IQ." Once that process is completed, the exporter should identify the critical risk factors of country, currency, and culture with the business transaction. Woven into these risk factors are the attributes of relationships. By carefully evaluating the risks and ensuing relationships, an exporter can reap rewards.

MAKING IT HAPPEN
To understand how to navigate both the risks and the relationships to reap the rewards, the exporter should:
- Be proactive in determining the ("IQ") international qualities of their own organization.
- Evaluate the risk dimensions of the particular country (or countries) where they want to do business.
- Know enough about how to assess currency risks to know when to call the experts.
- Study, study, and study some more the cultural mores of the countries in which they do business.
- Observe, listen, and learn from their mistakes.

MORE INFO
Books:
Coface Handbook of Country Risk 2009–2010. 11th ed. London: GMB Publishing, 2009.
Morrison, Terri, Wayne A. Conaway, and Joseph J. Douress. *Dun & Bradstreet's Guide to Doing Business Around the World.* Paramus, NJ: Prentice Hall, 2000.

Websites:
Country risk—Investopedia: www.investopedia.com/terms/c/countryrisk.asp
Culture risk—Wise GEEK: www.wisegeek.com/what-is-a-faux-pas.htm
Currency risk—Investopedia: www.investopedia.com/terms/c/currencyrisk.asp
FCIB (an association of executives in finance, credit and international business): www.fcibglobal.com
International Education Systems: www.marybosrock.com/faux_pas.html

How to Manage Emerging Market Risks with Third Party Insurance
by Rod Morris

EXECUTIVE SUMMARY
- Emerging markets present significant noncommercial political risks.
- Political risks can be mitigated through insurance products known as political risk insurance (PRI).
- PRI is a vehicle designed to help both equity investors and financial institutions to mitigate the losses that can result from a foreign government's substantive violation of the terms and conditions that originally attracted the foreign investment.
- More than 40 insurers, both private and public sector, offer such coverage.
- This article gives a comparative overview of the features of the public and private sector approaches.

INTRODUCTION
There are numerous issues that investors and companies must consider when contemplating an investment in a foreign country. Take for example cultural differences, the tax regime, foreign currency exchange restrictions, the regulatory and legal environment, the judicial system, and security requirements for both assets and employees. For emerging markets in particular, each of these factors can be further complicated by the potential for politically motivated interference, or changes in the government's attitude to foreign investment.

Foreign governments, especially those without an effective system of checks and balances, can create a favorable investment climate and then reverse or alter it quickly and dramatically. The results can be devastating to a foreign investor's ability to survive. A government's abrogation or unilateral alteration of an investor's licenses or agreements, new and onerous regulations or taxes, confiscation of property, and so on can happen, do happen, and will continue to happen, even if an investor hires an entire team of international and local lawyers and does everything right. None of that will matter when the local political environment takes an abrupt turn, which can happen for any number of reasons, including financial crisis, coup, or regime change. Nor will it be much use if terrorists or organized crime factions create an untenable atmosphere of insecurity.

There is also a growing trend known as "resource nationalism," in which governments have tried to grab a bigger share of the control and profits derived from diminishing supplies of, or increasing demand for (and therefore increasing prices of), their country's commodities such as tin, gold, and oil. Some governments are forcing unilateral restructuring of contracts and concessions, or even forcing a change in ownership that flips the foreign investor from a majority to minority position. The trend is particularly notable in Russia, Latin America, and Africa. Even if an investment is experiencing no problems with the sovereign government, there is no guarantee that it will be safe from interference from increasingly militant local governments, local judges interpreting local laws, or activist community organizations, which can frustrate or destroy a project just as effectively as an outright confiscation.

It is therefore essential that any potential investor makes a study of the current and likely economic and political risks of a country. Countries with developing or struggling economies and immature or undemocratic political structures can offer significant opportunities but at the same time pose significant risk. Much of that risk can be described as political, and many of these political risks can be mitigated through insurance products, known generically as PRI (political risk insurance). Assessing these risks may require some outside assistance, and there are a number of organizations that can help (see the More Info section).

WHAT IS PRI?
Political risk insurance is a broad term that includes a variety of coverage options for losses that have as their cause some kind of political motivation—whether by those in government or by others acting against it. PRI is designed to help both equity investors and financial institutions

Approaches to Enterprise Risk Management

to mitigate the kinds of losses that can result from a host government's substantive violation of the terms and conditions which attracted the original investment. For equity investors, PRI can indemnify them for losses of their assets and/or interruption of their business income resulting not only from politically inspired violence, but also from the type of governmental actions that go beyond the normal, prudent, reasonable, and responsible exercise of governmental authority. For financial institutions, PRI provides the aforementioned coverage, as well as additional benefits such as the ability to increase capacity for international loans; the ability to offer clients more attractive financial terms; risk management of country, region, or sector concentrations; and protection against payment defaults by a governmental entity.

PRI products insure a wide range of risks or causes of loss, but, for the sake of simplicity, the coverage options generally fall within three broad categories: expropriation, inconvertibility, and political violence.

Expropriation (CEN)
Expropriation is the most commonly purchased political risk coverage. It is also referred to as confiscation, expropriation, and nationalization (CEN) coverage. Essentially, it insures against wrongful interference by a foreign government that deprives investors of their fundamental rights to proceeds or ownership. Such actions can include not only outright confiscation or nationalization, but also breach of contracts, abrogation of licenses, changes that result in unfairly discriminatory treatment in regulation, taxes, tariffs, and/or impairment of the ability to pass costs through to consumers. Coverage can apply to a single discrete action, such as the seizure of assets, plants, or equipment by the government, or a series of actions that ultimately make the investment no longer economically viable—usually referred to as "creeping expropriation."

Although it does not fit well within the category of expropriation, there is a related product that is referred to as "nonhonoring of a sovereign guarantee." Briefly, this protects financial institutions and exporters against a payment default guaranteed by a sovereign, sub-sovereign, or in some cases a sovereign-owned enterprise.

Inconvertibility (T&C)
Also known as transfer and convertibility (T&C) insurance, inconvertibility coverage insures earnings, return of capital, principal and interest payments, and technical assistance fees against the imposition of new currency restrictions or controls that prevent conversion from local currency to hard currency and/or the transfer and repatriation of funds. It does not protect against currency fluctuation, devaluation, or any pre-existing restrictions on conversion or transfer.

Political Violence
This coverage protects against a loss of assets or income due to events such as terrorism, sabotage, revolution, insurrection, war, civil war—essentially, any politically motivated act of violence. This coverage is a much broader protection than is normally afforded under property and casualty insurance policies, which typically exclude perils such as war, or offer very limited protection against terrorism and sabotage. *No one can afford to assume that they are immune from potential loss due to terrorism and violence.* The number of terror attacks worldwide continues to rise, and emerging markets are at greater risk than Western Europe or the United States. According to the regional breakdown shown in Table 1, there are almost 15,000 terrorist attacks per year. It is unlikely that the world will see a sudden reversal of this trend. Far from it.

PRI INSURERS
A web search will produce a number of hits for both insurers and intermediaries (brokers and consultants) offering PRI products. Such a search, however, provides no clear evidence of the competence, capabilities, or financial strength of these companies. There is, nevertheless, an association of over 40 of the most reputable PRI carriers in the world, both private and public, known as the Berne Union. You can access a list of its members at www.berneunion.org.uk and be confident that you will find a responsible insurer. Although Lloyd's syndicates are not members, they are equally excellent.

Table 1. Terror attacks 2005–07. (*Source*: US National Counterterrorism Center)

Year	Africa	East Asia	Europe and Eurasia	Middle East	South Asia	Western Hemisphere	Total
2005	256	1,005	780	4,222	4,022	868	11,153
2006	422	1,036	659	7,755	3,654	826	14,352
2007	835	1,429	606	7,540	3,607	482	14,449

Manage Emerging Market Risks with Third Party Insurance

PRI insurers fall into two categories: government-sponsored (public) and private. Government-sponsored programs are offered by many developed countries to encourage trade and investment in emerging markets. Such programs would include not only those sponsored by single governments (for example, EFIC of Australia, NEXI of Japan, OPIC of the United States, Sinosure of China), but also multilateral organizations (for example, ADB, the Asian Development Bank; ICIEC, of the Islamic Development Bank; and MIGA of the World Bank) that are funded and supported by multiple countries.

In general, private-market insurers such as Lloyd's, AIG, Chubb, and Zurich are unwilling to assume as much risk or offer terms, limits, or policy periods that are as expansive as the public insurers such as OPIC and MIGA. This can present significant practical problems not only for investors, but also for intermediaries such as brokers, as evidenced by the case study below.

COMPARISON OF PRI FROM PUBLIC AND PRIVATE INSURERS

A detailed comparison of the differences between individual programs is not possible here, but some general comments on some of the more significant considerations as between the private and public markets may be informative. Generalities are never quite fair, but they can provide some basic insight into what to expect when seeking cover. For government-sponsored programs, the references below are to OPIC and MIGA since they are the largest and most experienced. When referring to private insurers, the commonalities of programs from companies such as AIG, Zurich, and Lloyd's are used.

Capacity: The private market offers less per project/investment than government-sponsored programs. The capacity of private insurers has increased over the years, but it is still considerably less than MIGA's $200 million and OPIC's $250 million policy maximum, with the ability to exceed even this ceiling under extremely unusual circumstances.[2]

CASE STUDY
Sempra Energy: A Cautionary Tale

Sempra Energy, a Fortune 500 energy services holding company, successfully bid to participate in the privatization of the Argentine gas sector in the 1990s. Sempra then became interested in purchasing PRI for its investment, and hired Marsh USA Inc. to act as its broker in finding an appropriate product. Argentina's spotty and inconsistent handling of foreign investment justified the company's concern, and it believed that Marsh would survey the market and identify the best choice. Marsh chose a policy from National Union, an AIG affiliate. In January 2002, the government of Argentina was in the midst of a financial crisis that resulted in the enactment of, *inter alia*, the Emergency System Act, which converted and froze public utility tariffs in pesos rather than the agreed US dollar amounts.

Sempra filed a claim with National Union, but compensation was denied. Sempra took the denial to arbitration and lost because, in fact, National Union's contract was not sufficiently broad to provide coverage under the particularly confusing chain of facts. In its arbitral opinion, however, the panel pointed out that an OPIC policy would, in fact, have provided coverage. Considering that Marsh had selected the National Union policy over the OPIC policy, Sempra then filed suit[1] in July of 2007 in the Los Angeles Superior Court alleging that Marsh had failed "to obtain an insurance policy that provided the coverage it promised to procure for Sempra." It accused Marsh of negligence, breach of oral and written contracts, breach of fiduciary duty, and negligent misrepresentation. Sempra was awarded US$48.5 million in damages.

This case illustrates a number of lessons but, suffice to say, investors should review carefully their approach to emerging market investments: Analyze the country risk, and make an informed decision about mitigating the risk through insurance or some other approach; carefully evaluate any intermediaries; vet the reasons and justifications for PRI recommendations; and carefully evaluate the recommended product to be certain that it is sufficiently broad to cover the types of claims or problems that might arise.

Notwithstanding the events in the case study, it has to be said that private insurers can often be more flexible in terms and conditions and quicker to execute contracts, and they are not encumbered by statutes or covenants that restrict eligibility or require a lot of information. Additionally, public carriers do not like to be seen as competing with the private market. Their preference is that investors only approach them when the private market is inadequate or unavailable.

Approaches to Enterprise Risk Management

MAKING IT HAPPEN

The always quotable American baseball player, Yogi Berra, said: "If you don't know where you're going, chances are you'll wind up someplace else." Without a clear perspective on the political, judicial, regulatory, and social climate for foreign investment, one can easily make a mistake. Even with full knowledge of current conditions, the climate for investment can change very quickly. It is always prudent to consider options in mitigating the substantial risks that can arise and overtake you.

- Consider the use of firms that provide expert analysis of emerging market risks.
- Compare and contrast the advantages of the private and public PRI carriers for the needs of your specific investment.
- There are many advantages to using an insurance broker but, especially for the public PRI carriers, they are not required.
- Insist that the insurance broker thoroughly explains all your options and the reasons for their recommendations to satisfy yourself that the recommendations fulfill your needs rather than theirs.
- Pick an insurer that is financially strong with a proven track record.

Term: Private insurers usually cover contracts for no longer than 15 years, whereas MIGA offers 15–20 years, and OPIC has offered 20-year contracts for a very long time.

Eligibility: Private insurers are basically unrestricted, while MIGA is restricted to insuring investors from member countries, and OPIC is restricted to investors with significant US ownership.

Rates: Private insurers price for profit, while the public market prices to be self-sustaining. Low-risk situations favor the private market, but, as risk increases, any such advantage tends to disappear. Also, much more than government-sponsored insurers, private insurers increase price based on demand and their own country concentrations. OPIC's rates are based only on risk and are guaranteed for the full term of the contract.

Appetite: OPIC and MIGA are designed to be markets of last resort (i.e. an investor is expected to try the private market first), yet they may very well be the only viable or affordable market in high-risk situations—for example, Afghanistan, Pakistan, and much of Africa.

Small business: Private insurers find it difficult to make money on policies for small amounts. Government-sponsored carriers, on the other hand, assist small investors as a matter of public policy.

Financial strength: Certainly Lloyd's and all of the Berne Union insurers are A-rated or equivalent. Because it is a US government agency, OPIC is not rated, but a rating is unnecessary as it is backed by the full faith and credit of the US government.

Coverage: OPIC has a history and reputation of being a product innovator but is sometimes constrained by its authorizing statute. With respect to political violence, however, only OPIC covers losses resulting from chemical, nuclear, and biological events. In today's world, that is not an insignificant difference. OPIC is the only carrier in the world that has been offering such broad coverage, and they have been doing it for decades.

Loss avoidance: Government-sponsored insurers have the ability to bring considerable pressure to bear on foreign governments when there is advance indication of a potential problem.

Claim payment histories: For many reasons, private insurers reveal almost no information about the number, type, or amounts of paid claims, denied claims, or claim determinations that are in dispute or arbitration. The same is not true of OPIC, which is the only carrier in the world whose records are open to the public both with respect to individual claim determinations and to aggregate numbers, which convey some interesting stories and patterns.

Ease of doing business: Without question, it is easier to do business with private market insurers. Public carriers require more information, both at the time of application and throughout the term of the contract. They need additional information in order to report to their governing bodies that they are fulfilling their missions, by supporting investments which help both the country of investment as well as its people by protecting worker and human rights and the environment, while doing no harm to the US economy or jobs.

CONCLUSION

Investment in emerging markets is replete with risk. A thorough vetting should be done not only

Manage Emerging Market Risks with Third Party Insurance

of the risk factors, but also of the tools that can be used to mitigate those risks. Political risk insurance is one of the best tools for mitigating these risks and it is available from a growing and capable population of insurers, both private and public.

MORE INFO
Brokers:
Aon: www.aon.com/uk/en/risk_management/political-risk
Lloyd's: www.pri-center.com/directories/partner_specific.cfm?pgid=5&orgnum=34313
Marsh: global.marsh.com/risk/politicalRisk
Willis: www.willis.com/Client_Solutions/Services/Political_Risk

Sovereign Ratings and Other Info:
Fitch Ratings: www.fitchratings.com
IMF: www.imf.org/external/country
Moody's (registration required): www.moodys.com
S&P—Find "Sovereigns" from the home page: www.standardandpoors.com

Other Sources:
Berne Union: www.berneunion.org.uk
CountryRisk.com guide to country research on the internet: www.countryrisk.com
Economist Intelligence Unit: www.eiu.com
Eurasia Group: www.eurasiagroup.net
Global Insight: www.globalinsight.com
Oxford Analytica global strategic analysis: www.oxan.com

NOTES
1 Sempra Energy v Marsh USA Inc. et al., case no. cv07-5431 in US District Court, Central District of California.
2 Having greater limits available from one carrier is always an advantage when the alternative is to piece cover together from a number of different carriers with the potential for gaps in cover or tenor that may require yet another contract to cover the "Difference in Conditions" (DIC).

Political Risk: Countering the Impact on Your Business by Ian Bremmer

EXECUTIVE SUMMARY
- Business decision-makers must understand the political dynamics within the emerging market countries in which they operate.
- We can measure a state's stability—the ability of its government to implement policy and enforce laws despite a shock to the system.
- Essential to managing any type of risk is the development of a detailed and effective hedging strategy.
- Companies should not accept too much risk exposure within any one country or region.
- Rules of the game can change quickly in developing countries, and the cultivation of "friends in high places" isn't always a strong enough hedge.
- Operating in some developing countries comes with reputational risks at home.
- Too many companies have historically relied for insight into local politics and culture on employees who have lived in a particular country for only a short time—or have even merely traveled there.
- Those doing business in developing states need to have credible emergency response plans in place when events outside their control shut down supply chains, prevent local workers from coming to work, or otherwise disrupt operations.
- Developing strategies to recruit and train local managers serves several useful purposes.
- Devoting a share of profits to investment in local schools and universities, infrastructure, and charities can generate stores of goodwill, which is sometimes essential for cooperation with local workers and government officials.
- In some countries, foreign companies should be wary of transferring proprietary information to local partners or developing it inside the country.
- A foreign firm must look beyond what its local competitors are capable of producing today. It must anticipate how those capabilities are likely to develop over time.
- Conditions sometimes force companies to cut their losses and head for the exit. Ensuring that process is as painless and inexpensive as possible forms a crucial part of any sound risk mitigation strategy.
- Political risk can be managed. It should not be avoided altogether.

INTRODUCTION
Over the past several years, and across a broad range of companies, corporate decision-makers seeking opportunities overseas have learned that it is not enough to have a knowledge of a foreign country's economic fundamentals. They also have to understand the forces and dynamics that shape these countries' politics. This is especially true for emerging markets, where politics matters at least as much as economic factors for market outcomes. Of course, understanding that political risk matters is one thing. Knowing how to use it is another.

STABILITY
Starting with the basics, when committing a company to risk exposure in an emerging market country, it's essential to understand how political risk impacts the underlying strength of its government. There are two key elements to consider: stability and shock. Shocks are especially tough to forecast, because there are so many different kinds and because shocks are, by definition, unpredictable. We can't know when an earthquake will strike Pakistan, an elected leader will fall gravely ill in Nigeria, or a previously unknown group will carry out a successful terrorist attack in Indonesia.

But we can take the measure of a state's stability, which is defined as a government's ability to implement policy and enforce laws despite a shock to the system. The global financial crisis, a potent shock, has inflicted heavy losses on Russia's stock market. But Prime Minister Vladimir Putin has amassed plenty of political capital over the past several years, and President Dmitry Medvedev, his handpicked successor, basks in Putin's reflected glow. Neither need fear that large numbers of Russian citizens will turn on them anytime soon. In addition, a half-decade of

Approaches to Enterprise Risk Management

windfall energy profits has generated more than $500 billion in reserves, ready cash that can be used to bail out stock markets, banks, and, if necessary, an unpopular government. That's why, for the near-term, Russia will remain stable.

Pakistan is a different story. The country's newly elected government has a range of rivals and enemies. Inflation, power shortages, and a wave of suicide attacks have undermined the ruling Pakistan Peoples Party's domestic popularity. The financial crisis leaves the country at risk of debt default, forcing the government to negotiate a loan package with the International Monetary Fund that could impose austerity measures—the kind that helped topple civilian governments in Pakistan in the 1990s. The country is less stable than Russia, because it is much more vulnerable to the worst effects of shock.

President Luiz Inácio Lula da Silva has bolstered Brazil's stability over the past several years by quelling fears of left-wing populism with responsible (and predictable) macroeconomic policies. The Chinese Communist Party's ability to generate prosperity at home via three decades of successful economic liberalization has helped its leadership to build durable near-term stability.

But Nigeria's future stability remains at the mercy of President Umaru Yar' Adua's failing health, as historical tensions between northern Muslims and southern Christians combine with ongoing security challenges in the oil-rich Niger Delta region to prevent his government from building a national reputation for competence, vision, and strength. Iran's theocrats and firebrand president Mahmoud Ahmadinejad have effectively used the international conflict over the country's nuclear program to shore up support for the government in the face of high inflation and gasoline rationing. Underlying political factors in all these countries have a substantial impact on stability—and, therefore, on the country's business climate.

DIVERSIFY

Yet it is not sufficient to possess broad insights into state stability. If corporate decision-makers are to design a credible business strategy that mitigates political risk and maximizes profit opportunities, they have to look deeper at the vulnerabilities that are peculiar to each country, each province, each community. Essential to managing any type of risk is the development of a detailed and effective diversification strategy. Given the political volatility within many developing world states—countries that will generate a large share of global growth over the next several decades—this kind of strategy is especially important. Even within a country as relatively stable as China, a closer look at internal political dynamics can identify various kinds of risk.

Two years ago, US officials worried publicly over a spike in sales of Russian arms to China. Dire predictions of a developing Russian–Chinese military axis became commonplace. But in 2007, sales of Russian arms to China fell by some 62%. Was it because the two governments had some sort of behind-the-scenes falling out? Did the Chinese leadership suddenly doubt the quality of Russian-made products? In reality, the arms sales slowed because China had mastered the design of many of the weapons, and Chinese companies began to produce them in sufficient quantities that demand for foreign-made weaponry fell sharply.

This is a cautionary tale, one that reminds us that any company betting heavily on long-term access to Chinese consumers (or to customers in many other developing countries) may be making a big mistake. There is plenty of money to be made in China for the next several years, but putting too many eggs in a single basket remains as risky as ever. For businesses with supply chains in China and other developing states, it's also important to build redundancies that are not overly exposed within any one region within these countries.

There are other, less obvious, components of a solid diversification strategy. Multinational companies should use all the leverage that their home governments and international institutions can provide to ensure that the governments of the countries in which they accept risk exposure protect their intellectual property rights, enforce all local laws intended to safeguard their commercial interests, and maintain open markets. Rules of the game can change quickly in developing countries, and the cultivation of "friends in high places" isn't always by itself an effective plan.

KNOW THE COUNTRY

Gaining insight into a country's political, economic, social, and cultural traditions is essential for a successful risk-mitigation strategy. Where should this insight come from? Too many companies have historically relied on employees who have lived in a particular country for only a short time—or may even have done no more than travel there. Turning to the guy who backpacked through country X during college for useful information about its politics and culture—not as rare a phenomenon as you might think—is no substitute for the knowledge that can be gained from local workers themselves and from trained political risk analysts.

Political Risk: Countering the Impact on Your Business

DESIGN AN EMERGENCY RESPONSE
Generally speaking, emerging market countries are more vulnerable than rich world states to large-scale civil unrest, public health crises, and environmental disasters. Those doing business in developing states need credible emergency response plans in place when events outside their control shut down supply chains, prevent local workers from coming to work, or otherwise disrupt operations. Some businesses have designed technology plans that allow workers to work from home. In cases when circumstances force foreign workers to leave the country, locals should have the necessary training and skills to assume their responsibilities for an extended period. The added expense and time for training are well worth the cost. In some countries, they're essential.

INVEST IN LOCAL WORKERS
Developing strategies to recruit and train local managers serves several useful purposes. First, it gives the host country government an investment in the success of a foreign-owned business. Every job created by a foreign firm is one that local government doesn't have to create. All governments want to keep unemployment at a minimum. Second, it gives local citizens a stake in the foreign company's success and helps to build solid relationships within the community. Some multinational firms have formed mutually profitable partnerships with local colleges and universities that give companies a fertile recruiting ground and ambitious students opportunities for work.

INVEST IN THEIR COMMUNITIES
Devoting a share of profits to investment in local schools and universities, infrastructure, and charities can generate stores of goodwill, which is sometimes essential for cooperation with local workers and government officials. Yet, sensitivity to the local culture matters too. In many developing states, suspicions that Western (especially American) companies have a political or ideological agenda can undermine efforts to promote trust. Contributions to local quality of life should be seen to come without strings attached.

PROTECT INTELLECTUAL PROPERTY
In some countries, foreign companies should be wary of transferring proprietary information to local partners or developing it inside the country. Forging alliances with local partners in joint ventures often serves as an effective risk mitigation strategy, but today's partner can become tomorrow's competitor, and a foreign firm can't always count on local courts or officials to safeguard its assets. Ironically, some foreign multinationals with long-term plans to remain inside a particular emerging market country have invested in local innovation. In the process, they have given locals an incentive to press their own government for stronger legal protections for intellectual property rights. Others have pooled their lobbying efforts with both local businesses and other foreign firms. When lobbying a government, strength in numbers can make a difference.

KNOW THE LOCAL COMPETITION
Successful firms understand their comparative advantages. But a foreign company must look beyond what its local competitors are capable of producing today. It must anticipate how those capabilities are likely to develop over time. Identifying the markets in which a firm's core competencies are likely to deliver profits for the foreseeable future is essential for long-term risk-mitigation strategies.

In many emerging market countries, local companies are often better at large-scale efficient manufacturing than at designing products, marketing them, and delivering them to the customer. Knowing how quickly the local competition can climb the value chain helps with the design of an intelligent, long-term business strategy.

KNOW WHERE TO FIND THE EXITS
Many companies have made lots of money in emerging markets. But as Wall Street veterans like to say, "Don't confuse brilliance with a bull market." Some companies have gotten away with ignoring the need for solid risk-management strategies and have simply ridden the wave produced by the inevitable rise of emerging market economies.

Yet, as skepticism of globalization grows in some developing countries, as their governments respond to domestic political pressure by rewriting rules to favor local companies at the expense of their foreign competitors, and as the challenges facing multinational companies operating inside these countries become more complex, it's important to have an exit strategy. There are plenty of developing states that are now open for business and investment. They have different strengths and vulnerabilities. Too much risk exposure in any one of them can create unnecessary risks. Conditions sometimes force companies to cut their losses and head for the door. Ensuring that this process is as painless and inexpensive as possible forms a crucial part of any sound risk-mitigation strategy.

Approaches to Enterprise Risk Management

DON'T FORGET THE POWER OF PERCEPTION

Operating in some developing countries comes with reputational risks at home. Several US companies have faced tough domestic criticism for doing business with governments that are accused of violating international labor, environmental, and human-rights standards. For a company's leadership, clearly communicating what the company will and won't do to gain market access in certain countries—and strict adherence to these standards of conduct—can help to minimize this risk.

POLITICAL RISK INSURANCE

As a last resort, a firm can purchase political risk insurance from providers like the Multilateral Investment Guarantee Agency, an arm of the World Bank, or the US government's Overseas Private Investment Corporation. But this should be a last resort strategy, because high premiums, substantial transaction and opportunity costs, and the complexities of establishing a valid claim have taught many companies that it is far more cost-effective to prevent or pre-empt bad outcomes than to rely heavily on plans to cope with their aftermath.

A LITTLE TOLERANCE IS A GOOD THING

It's useful to remember that having a good exit strategy does not require you to use it. Doing business in developing states comes with risk. But refusing to enter these markets or pulling out at the first sign of trouble comes with a high cost to opportunity. Foreign companies will be earning solid profits within emerging market states for many years to come. Political risk can be managed. It should not be avoided altogether.

MORE INFO

Books:
Bracken, Paul, Ian Bremmer, and David Gordon (eds). *Managing Strategic Surprise: Lessons from Risk Management and Risk Assessment.* New York: Cambridge University Press, 2008.
Howell, Llewellyn D. (ed.). *Handbook of Country and Political Risk Analysis.* 3rd ed. East Syracuse, NY: Political Risk Services Group, 2002.
Moran, Theodore H. (ed.). *Managing International Political Risk.* London: Blackwell Publishing, 1999.
Moran, Theodore H., Gerald T. West, and Keith Martin (eds). *International Political Risk Management: Meeting the Needs of the Present, Anticipating the Challenges of the Future.* Washington, DC: World Bank Publications, 2007.
Wilkin, Sam (ed.). *Country and Political Risk: Practical Insights for Global Finance.* London: Risk Books, 2004.

Articles:
Bremmer, Ian, and Fareed Zakaria. "Hedging political risk in China." *Harvard Business Review* 84:11 (2006): 22–25.
Henisz, Witold J., and Bennet A. Zelner. "Political risk management: A strategic perspective." Online at: www.management.wharton.upenn.edu/henisz/papers/hz_prm.pdf
"Insuring against political risk." *The Economist* (April 4, 2007). Online at: www.economist.com/finance/displaystory.cfm?story_id=8967224.
"Integrating political risk into enterprise risk management." Online at: www.pwc.com/extweb/pwcpublications.nsf/docid/EAB01AC994713716852570FF006868B6
Stanislav, Markus. "Corporate governance as political insurance: Firm-level institutional creation in emerging markets and beyond." *Socio-Economic Review* 6:1 (2008): 69–98.

Websites:
Eurasia Group, global political risk advisery and consulting firm: www.eurasiagroup.net
Multilateral Investment Guarantee Agency (MIGA)'s Political Risk Insurance Center: www.pri-center.com
PricewaterhouseCoopers: www.pwc.com. Enter "political risk" in search box to find articles and resources.

Identifying and Minimizing the Strategic Risks from M&A by Peter Howson

EXECUTIVE SUMMARY
- The high failure rate of acquisitions can be mitigated considerably by dealing with the strategic risks that are present at every stage of the acquisition process.
- It is best to start with a well-developed business strategy, a clear idea of the place of mergers and acquisitions (M&A) in this strategy, and an acquisition target that furthers strategic aims.
- Before embarking on negotiations, acquirers should avoid the risk of overpaying by setting a price above which they will not go.
- Before negotiating the final details, due diligence should be used as a final confirmation of the strategy and the target's fit.
- The most important thing is to make sure that the post acquisition plan is put together early and in as much detail as possible. Acquirers need to add value, and they can only do this if they are clearly focused on the sources of extra value and how to realize them right from the very start.

INTRODUCTION
M&A is extremely risky. Studies carried out over the last 30 years suggest that the failure rate is above 50% and probably close to 75%. However, by identifying and acting to minimize the strategic risks early on in the process, the rewards can be spectacular.

There are four stages in the M&A process:
- acquisition strategy
- due diligence
- negotiation
- post-acquisition integration.

Strategic risks are present in each.

Acquisition Strategy
M&A is glamorous. Market analysts see M&A as a sign of a dynamic management and mark up share prices accordingly. For management, M&A can be a means of bolstering short-term performance and/or masking underlying problems. It is hardly surprising that the failure rate is so high when the mystique of M&A encourages acquirers to rush into acquisitions.

M&A Is a Strategic Tool
This brings us to the first strategic risk—a failure to recognize that M&A is a strategic weapon. Strategy is all about giving customers what they want, and to do it better or more cheaply than anyone else. It is about competitive advantage gained through superior capabilities and resources. M&A should fit into this framework.

Given the high risk of failure, acquirers should ask themselves if acquisition is the best means of achieving aims. There will generally be a tradeoff between risk and time. Acquisition is the highest-risk route to corporate development, but it is often the quickest. Acquisition should be examined alongside all the other options—organic development, joint venture, merger, etc.

Is the Timing Right?
Implementation is the key to successful strategy and this is the clue to the next strategic risk—is this the right time to be acquiring? Getting the transaction done and integrating it afterwards will take up a disproportionate amount of time, resource, and expertise. This means making sure that there is:
- a strong base business (if existing operations are struggling, acquisitions will only add to the problems);
- the resources to add value (where there are insufficient resources to manage an acquisition, the chances of adding value are slim).

Select the Right Target
The next risk may sound obvious, but one of the biggest ever M&A disasters stemmed in part from selecting the wrong target. In 1991 AT&T, the US telecommunications company, bought NCR for $7.48 billion. AT&T was implementing a so called "3Cs strategy" where communications, computers, and consumer electronics were expected to coalesce into a new market. It bought NCR to provide a capability in computers. But NCR was not a computer company. Its core business was in retail transaction processing and banking systems, and it happened also to manufacture a range of "me too" personal computers. While this may be an extreme example, it is not uncommon for buyers to misunderstand the target company's capabilities.

Approaches to Enterprise Risk Management

Due Diligence
The strategic risks in due diligence all stem from making the focus of due diligence too narrow.

The success of any acquisition depends on buyers creating value. Due diligence presents a potential buyer with the access and information it needs to confirm that a transaction can be a long-term success. This means using due diligence not just as an input to the sale and purchase agreement but, more importantly, also to confirm both the robustness of synergy assumptions and their deliverability. As people will deliver the extra value, buyers should also make sure that due diligence covers cultural and people issues.

Negotiation
In negotiation, the strategic risk is overpaying. Buyers are almost certainly going to have to pay a premium for the control of a company. The challenge is to make sure that the synergies are big enough to cover both the premium and the deal costs. Work out a price in advance and, as it is all too easy to get carried away, always set a maximum walk-away price before negotiations begin.

Post-Acquisition Integration
The major cause of acquisition failure is poor integration. Integration is poorly carried out because it gets forgotten. Doing the deal may

CASE STUDY

In 1996, Federal-Mogul, a US auto parts company, appointed a new Chairman and Chief Executive, Dick Snell, whose view was that in the automotive industry, a firm must be big.

Automobile makers were focusing on assembly, branding, and marketing, and were encouraging parts manufacturers to play a bigger role in the design and development of components. They were also encouraging the larger suppliers to supply modules and systems rather than components.

Federal-Mogul's "growth by acquisition" strategy had the simple aim of increasing sales from $2 billion to $10 billion in six years. The company already made gaskets and seals, but not enough to market a full engine or transmission-sealing package. Federal-Mogul also made engine bearings, but did not have the ability to market the bearings as a system complete with pistons, piston rings, connecting rods, and cylinder liners.

Federal-Mogul first bought T&N Plc (in 1997), a supplier of engine and transmission products and Europe's leading supplier of gaskets. With sales of $3 billion, T&N was bigger than Federal-Mogul itself. Soon after (in 1998), Federal-Mogul paid $720 million for privately held Fel-Pro Inc., of Skokie, IL. Fel-Pro was a leading brand of replacement sealing products. Following these two acquisitions, Federal-Mogul had a $1 billion global sealing business and the basis for providing an integrated engine package. Later that year, Federal-Mogul went on to buy Cooper Automotive for $1.9 billion. Cooper added three completely new product areas (see Table 1).

In July 1998, Federal-Mogul's share price was $72. By September 2001 it was $1. On October 1, 2001, the company filed under Chapter 11 of the US Bankruptcy Code. What went wrong?

Table 1. Federal-Mogul's acquisitions

	Existing operations (as of 1996)	1997: T&N acquisition	1998: Fel-Pro acquisition	1998: Cooper Automotive acquisition
Engine and transmission				
Engine Bearings	X	X		
Pistons and piston rings		X		
Seals	X	X	X	
Camshafts	X	X		
Other				
Lighting	X			
Fuel pumps	X			
Friction (brake and clutch pads)		X		
Powdered metals		X		
Ignition				X
Chassis				X
Wiper blades				X

Identifying and Minimizing the Strategic Risks from M&A

be sexy, but integration is where the real money is made or lost. The strategic risks stem from not starting work on the integration plan early enough in the process. As integration is central to valuation, the integration plan must be put together well before negotiations begin, and the other golden rules of acquisition integration also demand an early plan:

- Integrate quickly to minimize uncertainty. In particular, integration changes related to personnel need to be made as soon as possible; early communication is paramount; and there should be early victories to demonstrate progress.
- Do not neglect the soft issues. The culture of a company is the set of assumptions, beliefs, and accepted rules of conduct that define the way things are done. These are never written down, and most people in an organization would be hard pressed to articulate them. However, they can substantially increase post-acquisition costs or hold back performance
- Manage properly. Buyers should appoint an integration manager. Like any other big project, acquisitions need one person to be accountable for the project's success.

Overambitious Strategy
Following the Fel-Pro acquisition, the logical thing would have been to continue building the engine and transmissions business. Instead, Federal-Mogul kept its electrical businesses and the friction businesses acquired with T&N, and went on to add three entirely new product ranges. Focusing only on revenue and growth rarely, if ever, produces a strong organization and financial results over the long term.

Problems Picked Up in Due Diligence Not Acted On
T&N had at one time manufactured building products containing asbestos, and for years it paid out an increasing number of compensation claims for asbestos-related diseases. Following the takeover, the number of asbestos claims against T&N and its former subsidiaries exploded. In October 2001 there were 365,000 asbestos claims pending. By the end of 2001, Federal Mogul had paid out $1 billion in claims.

While Federal-Mogul was aware of the asbestos issue, Federal-Mogul leaders did minimal due diligence, failed to appreciate just how serious it was, and believed that, because it operated in the United States, it would be able to manage the litigation better.

Poor Integration
Federal-Mogul paid a high price for T&N and the other big acquisitions, promised too much, and failed to deliver. Federal-Mogul leadership repeatedly promised the market that integration would bring tens of millions of dollars worth of synergies. In fact, according to a stockholder class action, the company's integration activities destroyed the acquired businesses. The class action claimed that, "After an acquisition, the Company would slash sales staff at the acquired company, close manufacturing and warehouse facilities, reduce investment in research and development, reduce customer service and implement aggressive sales practices."

Federal-Mogul's management lacked an understanding of how international businesses operate. It was obsessed with the Detroit Big Three and dismissive of the other vehicle assemblers, yet the strategic logic of acquiring parts manufacturers should be to broaden geographic reach and bring closer relationships with vehicle assemblers.

Federal-Mogul management also failed to appreciate that the rest of the world was not like the United States and, in particular, that Europe was not like a group of US states. Federal-Mogul centralized all its operations, including customer service. When Federal-Mogul moved aftermarket operations to the United States, it was surprised that its telecom ordering system did not recognize overseas telephone numbers. In contrast, T&N had given a great deal of autonomy to its regions.

Finally, Federal-Mogul lost key staff by insisting that anyone who stayed had to move to Detroit. Most former T&N leaders opted to take the money. While it is not impossible to buy a company larger than yourself, it is difficult to manage something the size of T&N without retaining most of the management team—and T&N was actually quite good at managing asbestos claims.

Federal-Mogul emerged from Chapter 11 bankruptcy on December 27, 2007 after a financial reorganization designed to protect it from asbestos claims.

Approaches to Enterprise Risk Management

MAKING IT HAPPEN
- Think of M&A as a means to gain competitive advantage rather than short-term improvements in financials.
- M&A is the most risky form of corporate development, so be sure to consider alternatives such as organic growth or joint ventures.
- M&A will divert resources from the existing business, so make sure it is strong before embarking on acquisitions.
- Be sure to understand the target company—what it does, how it operates, how it makes money—and be able to articulate why it fits the strategy.
- Do not neglect soft issues like management and culture. Do not assume that "they are just like us," because they won't be.
- Prepare a detailed integration plan in advance.
- Keep the due diligence scope wide. Always use it to confirm the sources of added value identified and quantified in the integration plan.
- Never be lured into overpaying. Set a clear walk-away price and do not exceed it.
- Once the deal is done, communicate immediately, clearly, consistently, and abundantly to everyone concerned. Do not forget external parties, above all customers.
- Implement changes quickly and smoothly and do not underestimate the size of the task.

MORE INFO

Books:
Camp, J. *Start with NO: The Negotiating Tools that the Pros Don't Want You to Know*. New York: Crown Business, 2002.
Carey, Dennis, et al. *Harvard Business Review on Mergers & Acquisitions*. Boston, MA: Harvard Business School, 2001.
Cleary, P. J. *The Negotiation Handbook*. Armonk, NY: M. E. Sharpe, 2001.
Freund, James C. *Smart Negotiating: How to Make Good Deals in the Real World*. New York: Fireside, 1993.
Howson, Peter. *Due Diligence: The Critical Stage in Acquisitions and Mergers*. Aldershot, UK: Gower Publishing, 2003.
Howson, Peter. *Commercial Due Diligence: The Key to Understanding Value in an Acquisition*. Aldershot, UK: Gower Publishing, 2006.
Howson, Peter. *Checklists for Due Diligence*. Aldershot, UK: Gower Publishing, 2008.
Howson, Peter, with Denzil Rankine. *Acquisition Essentials*. London: Pearson Education., 2005.
Hubbard, Nancy. Acquisition: *Strategy and Implementation*. Basingstoke, UK: Palgrave Macmillan, 1999.
Hunt, J. W., S. Lees, J. J. Grumbar, and P. D. Vivian. *Acquisitions: The Human Factor*. London: London Business School and Egon Zehnder International, 1987.
Lajoux, Alexandra Reed, and Charles Elson. *The Art of M&A Due Diligence: Navigating Critical Steps and Uncovering Crucial Data*. New York: McGraw-Hill, 2000.
Rankine, Denzil. *Why Acquisitions Fail: Practical Advice for Making Acquisitions Succeed*. London: Pearson Education, 2001.

Article:
Davy, A. J., et al. "After the merger: Dealing with people's uncertainty." *Training and Development Journal* 42 (November 1988): 57–61.

Report:
KPMG. "Unlocking shareholder value: Keys to success." London: KPMG, 1999. Online at: www.imaa-institute.org/docs/m&a/kpmg_01_Unlocking%20Shareholder%20Value%20-%20The%20Keys%20to%20Success.pdf

Websites:
Commercial due diligence—AMR International: www.amrinternational.com
Financial due diligence—BDO Stoy Hayward: www.bdo.co.uk

Due Diligence Requirements in Financial Transactions by Scott Moeller

EXECUTIVE SUMMARY
- There is an urgency for companies to conduct intensive due diligence in financial deals, both before announcement (when it should be easy to call off the deal) and after.
- Traditional due diligence merely verifies the history of the target and projects the future based on that history; correctly applied due diligence digs much deeper and provides insight into the future value of the target across a wide variety of factors.
- Although due diligence does enable prospective acquirers to find potential black holes, the aim of due diligence should be this and more, including looking for opportunities to realize future prospects for the enlarged corporation through leveraging of the acquiring and the acquired firms' resources and capabilities, identification of synergistic benefits, and post-merger integration planning.
- Due diligence should start from the inception of a deal.
- Areas to probe include finance, management, employees, IT, legal, risk management systems, culture, innovation, and even ethics.
- Critical to the success of the due diligence process is the identification of the necessary information required, where it can best be sourced, and who is best qualified to review and interpret the data.
- Requesting too much information is just as dangerous as requesting too little. Having the wrong people looking at the data is also hazardous.

INTRODUCTION
This is not your father's due diligence.

Due diligence is one of the two most critical elements in the success of a mergers and acquisitions (M&A) transaction (the other being the proper execution of the integration process), according to a survey conducted in 2006 by the Economist Intelligence Unit (EIU) and Accenture. Due diligence was considered to be of greater importance than target selection, negotiation, pricing the deal, and the development of the company's overall M&A strategy.

But not even a decade ago, when due diligence was conducted in financial transactions, the focus was almost always limited to financial factors, pending law suits, and information technology (IT) systems. Today, those areas remain important, but they must be supplemented during the due diligence process by attention to the assessment of other factors: management and employees (and not just their contracts, but how good they actually are in their jobs), commercial operations (products, marketing, strategy, and competition—both existing and potential), and corporate culture (can the companies actually work together when they're merged?). But even these areas are now mainstream when due diligence is conducted. Newer areas of due diligence are developing rapidly: risk management, innovation, and ethical (including corporate social responsibility) due diligence.

The 2006 EIU/Accenture survey also found that although due diligence is considered as a top challenge by 23% of CEOs in making domestic acquisitions, this rises to 41% in the much more complex cross-border transactions, which make up the majority of financial transactions, even in today's depressed markets.

ORGANIZING FOR DUE DILIGENCE
It's a two-way street: Buyers must understand what they are buying; and targets must understand who's pursuing them and whether they should accept an offer.

To be successfully conducted, due diligence must have senior management involvement and control, often assisted by outside experts such as management consulting firms, accountants, investment banks, and maybe even specialist investigation firms.

To quote from a PricewaterhouseCoopers report issued in late 2002: "We always have to make decisions based on imperfect information. But the more information you have and the more you transform that into what we call knowledge, the more likely you are to be successful."

That said, there is only a certain amount that can be handled by the number of people involved,

Approaches to Enterprise Risk Management

the time restrictions under which they are working, and the quality and variety of resources available to them. Moreover, there is the danger of being overloaded by too much information if those involved do not have good management and analytical methods they can deploy.

By and large, it is not the quantity of information that matters so much as its quality and how it is used. Although diligence may not be cheap (as a result of fees charged for often highly complex work by professional services firms), the alternative of litigation or the destruction of stockholder value (as a consequence of having been "penny wise and pound foolish" in the execution of the due diligence process) may prove far more costly in the long run.

THE DUE DILIGENCE PROCESS

Although due diligence may be only one part of an acquisition or investment exercise, in many ways it is by far the most significant aspect of the M&A process. Done properly, acquirers should be better able to control the risks inherent in any deal, while simultaneously contributing to the ultimate effective management of the target and the realization of the goals of the acquisition.

As an instrument through which to reveal and remedy potential sources of risk, due diligence—by confirming the expectations of the buyer and the understanding of the seller—enables firms to formulate remedies and solutions to enable a deal to proceed. In many ways, due diligence lends comfort to an acquirer's senior management, the board, and ultimately the stockholders, who should all insist on a rigorous due diligence process, which provides them with relative (though not absolute) assurance that the deal is sensible, and that they have uncovered any problems pertaining to it that may derail matters in the future.

Ideally, due diligence should start during the conception phase of the deal, and initially it can use publicly available information. It should then continue throughout the merger process as further proprietary information becomes available. Full use of the due diligence information collected would mean that it is not just used to make a go/no-go decision about whether the acquisition should proceed and to determine the terms of the deal, but that the findings from due diligence should also be incorporated in the planning for the post-merger integration.

Clearly it is easier to obtain high-quality data if the deal is friendly; in unfriendly deals due diligence may never progress further than publicly available data. This lack of access to internal information has scuppered many a deal—for example, the takeover attempt by Sir Philip Green of Marks & Spencer in 2004.

THE SCOPE OF DUE DILIGENCE[1]

Before undertaking due diligence—given the typical time, cost, and data constraints—it is important to focus on areas that are likely to have the most impact on value. Thus, due diligence should be tailored to:

- the type of transaction
- the motivation for doing the deal
- plans for the target once acquired
- the impact on the existing operations of the acquirer.

Some basic questions to ask include:

- Is the acquirer a strategic or a financial buyer?
- How fully integrated will the target be once acquired, and in what time frame?
- Is the whole company being acquired?
- Does the target represent new product lines, marketing channels, or geographic territories, or is there overlap with the acquirer's existing operations?
- Will certain functional operations of the target be eliminated?
- Will the IT systems of the target be retained?
- How will the rating agencies respond to the transaction?

TYPES OF DUE DILIGENCE INFORMATION

Each industry has its own special due diligence requirements. For example, an insurance company will need a review of major policies, actuarial assumptions, and sales practices, whereas the purchase of a bank would require a review of its marking policies and risk management systems.

As noted above, one starts with external sources. Although these rarely provide a sufficient overview of an organization at the level required to obtain a proper understanding, secondary sources do equip management with valuable information, allowing them to strategize and develop honed, and more focused, questions for their further internal due diligence on the prospective acquisition.

In spite of the centrality of financial, legal, cultural, and other areas of due diligence, examples abound of transactions that were completed without effective due diligence being done through lack of time, or because management was overconfident in its ability to understand the target, resulting in devastating losses of stockholder value.

Due Diligence Requirements in Financial Transactions

Financial Due Diligence
Financial due diligence enables companies to obtain a view of an organization's historical profits, which can then be used as a canvas on which to paint a picture of the company's financial future. Developed around an array of building blocks—including auditing and verifying financial results on which an offer is based, identifying deal breakers, reviewing forecasts and budgets, pinpointing areas where warranties or indemnities may be needed, and providing confidence in the underlying performance, and therefore future profits, of a company—financial due diligence allows the bidder to make the proper offer for the target, or perhaps uncover reasons for not proceeding with the deal.

Legal Due Diligence
As companies expand into hitherto commercially less experienced parts of the world in search of new markets and products (such as China, Vietnam, or certain countries in the Middle East and Africa), the requirement to conduct effective and sufficient legal due diligence work can prove more trying, and in certain cases near impossible. Nevertheless, the need to check title over assets that are being sold, and to ensure that the entity being acquired is legitimate and free of any contractual or legal obstacles which might derail the M&A process, will undoubtedly remain pivotal to the due diligence process no matter where the target resides. Governmental regulatory concerns, such as monopolies, employment law, taxes, etc., will also be investigated as part of the legal due diligence.

Commercial Due Diligence
Given that companies are bought not for their past performance but for their ability to generate profits in the future, acquirers must use commercial due diligence to obtain an objective view of a company's markets, prospects, and competitive position. As noted by Towers Perrin in a discussion of operational due diligence, there is a "need to look at all the relevant sources of value to avoid unpleasant surprises."[2] This means a deeper query into certain operations that heavily determine a target's ultimate value to the acquirer—i.e. growth opportunities and resulting future income.

Whether obtained to reduce risk associated with the transaction, to help with the company valuation, or to plan for post-merger integration, commercial due diligence enables acquirers to examine a target's markets and performance—identifying strengths, weaknesses, opportunities, and threats. Focused on the likely strategic position of the combined entity, commercial due diligence, by reviewing the drivers that underpin forecasts and business plans, concentrates on the ability of the target's businesses to achieve the projected sales and profitability growth post acquisition.

CASE STUDY

Failure in Due Diligence: VeriSign's Purchase of Jamba

In June 2004, VeriSign acquired privately held Berlin-based Jamba for US$273 million. VeriSign was an internet infrastructure services company which provided the services that enabled over 3,000 enterprises and 500,000 websites to operate. Through its domain name registry it managed over 50 million digital identities in more than 350 languages. Revenues exceeded US$1 billion dollars in the previous year. VeriSign had extensive experience with acquisitions, having made 17 acquisitions prior to Jamba, including four that were valued at more than this particular purchase.

Jamba had millions of subscribers and was the leading provider of mobile content delivery services in Europe. It was best known for the Crazy Frog character used in the most successful ring tone of all time.

But, beneath the surface, trouble was brewing that could easily have been uncovered by even the most rudimentary due diligence: complaints to regulators had noted that Jamster, the UK and US rebranding of Jamba, was targeting children, despite the fact that Jamster's mobile content services were intended for adult customers only. Perhaps more disturbingly, only days before the acquisition VeriSign discovered that a significant portion of Jamba's profits came from the distribution of adult content in Germany—despite a VeriSign policy of not supporting adult or pornographic companies. There were backlashes in Germany over other issues and Jamba was forced to make a declaration of discontinuance regarding many of its contracts. Other legal actions were pending in Germany and the United States.

Unsurprisingly, Jamba's revenues peaked early the following year.

Approaches to Enterprise Risk Management

CASE STUDY
No Cultural Fit for Sony in the Movie Industry
In 1988, Sony (a Japanese electronics manufacturer) acquired Columbia Pictures (an American moviemaker) for US$3.4 billion. With cultures that could scarcely have been more different, the acquisition—which involved little consideration of cultural fit between the two entities—failed to live up to commercial expectations, with Sony famously writing down US$2.7 billion on the deal by 1994.

Despite the seemingly obvious pivotal benefits that commercial due diligence can bring to acquiring organizations, *Competitive Intelligence Magazine* reported in 2003 that "only 10% of respondents to an Accenture survey of M&A practitioners said that their due diligence process included four or more sources from outside the company."

Innovation Due Diligence
Linked closely to commercial risk but meriting special attention is the due diligence of the research and development (R&D) process. This is more than just an analysis of intellectual property rights. Many nonindustrial companies may not have explicit R&D groups, but still remain dependent on the development of intellectual property to maintain their business growth. It must be understood how this is encouraged.

Management Due Diligence
Naturally, acquirers need to perform discrete investigations in order to evaluate both the competence of the target's management and the quality of their past performances, and to ensure that the management of the target and acquirer are compatible. One would think that this would be recognized by any acquirer today, but one acquisition team recently told us that their senior management felt confident enough in their own ability to conduct their management due diligence that they could do this "over a cup of tea," basically, by eyeing the management team from across the table. Nevertheless, in the rush to do deals in the peak merger year of 2007, many of the largest deals properly included extensive management surveys, including 360 degree appraisals, psychometrics, and even investigative reporting.

Cultural Due Diligence
Since one of the more difficult areas for integrating two companies concerns combining their corporate cultures, due care needs to be applied to ensure cultural fit. Indeed, cultural fit is so important that 85% of underperforming acquisitions blame different management attitudes and culture for the poor performance of the combined entities, as reported at a conference in 2006 by Towers Perrin and Cass Business School. Thus, by assessing soft factors such as a company's leadership style, corporate behavior, and even dress code, an acquirer may be able to build an accurate picture of a target's values, attitudes, and beliefs, and so determine if there will be a good cultural fit within their own organizational structure.

Ethical Due Diligence
There is an emerging area, best described as ethical due diligence, that overlaps in many ways

MAKING IT HAPPEN
Key factors in conducting informative and timely due diligence are:
- Identifying the critical areas to probe: financial, legal, business, cultural, management, ethical, risk management, etc.
- Identifying the most important information to collect in those areas, as there is never enough time to look at everything in as much detail as one might want.
- Identifying the right sources for the desired information.
- Identifying the right people to review the data: this should include those who know most about that area and also those who will be managing the business post acquisition.

Due diligence should not be a mere confirmation of the facts. Bridging the strategic review and completion phases of any merger or acquisition exercise, the due diligence process allows prospective acquirers to understand as much as possible about the target company, and to make sure that what it believes is being purchased is actually what is being purchased. The due diligence process digs deeper before the point of no return in consummating a deal.

Due Diligence Requirements in Financial Transactions

with management and cultural due diligence but is not to be confused with legal due diligence. The most obvious requirement of ethical due diligence is to determine whether management have engaged in unethical professional acts (as defined, usually, by the ethical standards of the acquiring company), but it also necessarily includes assessment of the corporate social responsibility activities of the company.

Risk Management Due Diligence

It is critical to understand how the target reports and monitors its inherent business risks. The events in financial and real estate markets in the past several years highlight the need to check carefully not just all risk management systems, but also the *culture* of risk in a company.

CONCLUSION

According to the EIU/Accenture survey, only 18% of executives were highly confident that their company had carried out satisfactory due diligence. This is probably due to the lack of attention given to this critical aspect of a deal, or to the view that it is merely a box-ticking exercise conducted by outside advisers.

In short, the probing of a wide variety of due diligence areas should provide a counterbalance to the short-termism of traditionally limited financial and legal due diligence, helping acquirers to understand how markets and competitive environments will affect their purchase, and confirming that the opportunity is a sensible one to undertake from a commercial and strategic perspective, especially in cross-border deals.

MORE INFO

Books:
Howson, Peter. *Due Diligence: The Critical Stage in Mergers and Acquisitions*. Aldershot, UK: Gower Publishing, 2003.
Moeller, Scott, and Chris Brady. *Intelligent M&A: Navigating the Mergers and Acquisitions Minefield*. Chichester, UK: Wiley, 2007.
Sudarsanam, Sudi. *Creating Value from Mergers and Acquisition: The Challenges*. Harlow, UK: Pearson Education, 2003.

NOTES

1 Adapted from Fell, Bruce D. "Operational due diligence for value." *Emphasis* no. 3 (2006): 6–9. Online at: tinyurl.com/d7w36t
2 *Ibid.*

Checklists
Policies and Processes

Balancing Hedging Objectives with Accounting Rules (FAS 133)

DEFINITION
FAS 133 was published in 1998 and introduced in 2001 to establish accounting and reporting standards for stand-alone derivatives and those embedded in other contracts. The aim was to provide greater transparency by requiring companies to record derivative contracts as assets or liabilities on their balance sheets.

Gains and losses on derivatives can be deferred until they mature, but only if the company proves that they are being used to manage risk rather than for market speculation. Companies have to provide evidence that the timing and the amount of the derivative matches the commodity against which it is being hedged.

The reporting requirements are extremely onerous. Hedges have to be documented before or as soon as they are implemented, and companies have to explain why the transaction is being undertaken. Every three months derivatives have to be marked to market to prove that the underlying exposure is being hedged effectively.

Although FAS 133 offers detailed direction on how derivatives can qualify for hedge accounting, critics say that the rules manage to be both overly complex and vague. Indeed, the Financial Accounting Standards Board (FASB) is in the process of trying to simplify the standard.

Currently, three categories of hedge are allowed by the standard:
- fair-value hedges for recognized assets;
- cash flow hedges for recognized assets or forecast transactions;
- hedges for foreign currency exposure.

If a hedge is "highly effective," it will not affect reported earnings. According to the standard, a hedge is defined as "highly effective" if changes in the fair value or cash flow of the hedged item and the hedging derivative offset each other to a significant extent.

At the moment the rules are complex, and because of the quarterly reporting requirement some derivatives will fail to meet the "highly effective" definition throughout their lifespan.

A number of companies have also had to restate their accounts because of their failure to satisfy the complex reporting documentation required by FAS 133. Hotel and casino operator Wynn had to restate its earnings for 2003, 2004, and part of 2005. Sunglasses manufacturer Oakley had to restate its reports for the five years up to 2005. And at the beginning of 2007 General Electric said its restatement would reduce earnings by a total of $343 million. Earnings were to be cut for 2001 and 2002, and increased for 2003, 2004, and 2005.

ADVANTAGES
- FAS 133 introduced more transparent accounting standards following substantial hedging losses in the mid-1990s arising from the use of derivatives.
- FAS 133 seeks to give both existing and potential investors more information on companies' risk management practices and the kind of derivative exposure they take on.
- The standards can result in better hedging practices by highlighting the distinction between the genuine hedging of risk and speculative activity.

DISADVANTAGES
- FAS 133 is one of the most complex accounting standards ever introduced, running to over 200 pages. This has led to some major companies being forced to restate their earnings over a number of years.
- Initially there was concern that the non-applicability of hedge accounting in some circumstances could lead to unnecessary volatility in corporate earnings. This now seems to be less of a concern as companies have come to grips with the measures.
- Critics argue that FAS 133 fails to provide a meaningful snapshot of a company's performance and can even represent an unwelcome temporary distraction from the true direction of a company's results.

DOS AND DON'TS
DO
- To help ensure full compliance with FAS 133, companies should assess the ways that they document underlying exposures, including how cash flows are measured for hedging related to exposure carrying nonspecific timing horizons.
- Companies should also seek to analyze how effective past hedging has been using techniques such as regression analysis.
- Consider the value of costing and recording of the time value of hedges for every measurement period.

Approaches to Enterprise Risk Management

DON'T
- When seeking to hedge exposure to cash flows with uncertain timing, don't simply assume that the key terms of the exposure and the option used for the hedge are perfectly matched.
- Similarly, when using an option for a hedge, do not expense the option premium only at the option's expiry. Rather assess the decay value continuously prior to the option's expiration.

MORE INFO

Book:
Green, James F., and the Accounting Research Manager Group. *2007 CCH Accounting for Derivatives And Hedging*. Chicago, IL: CCH, 2006.

Articles:
Osterland, Andrew. "Life under FAS 133." *CFO* (July 2001). Online at: www.cfo.com/article.cfm/2997729/1/c_3046507
Park, Jongchan. "The economic consequences of FAS-133 for bank holding companies." *Bank Accounting & Finance* (October 2005).

Websites:
The Financial Accounting Standards Board official website: www.fasb.org
iTreasurer.com focus on FAS 133: www.fas133.com

The Chief Audit Executive's (CAE) Roles and Responsibilities

DEFINITION
The CAE has an in-depth knowledge of the business and is concerned principally with its systems for internal control and efficiency of operations, the reliability of its financial reporting, and its observance of relevant laws and regulations.

Corporate accounting scandals and the resultant outcry for transparency and honesty in reporting have led to a progressively more important role for the CAE. A CAE has two important and sometimes conflicting functions within an organization. The first is to examine and evaluate the organization's systems of internal control, as part of the requirement for stricter corporate governance. The second is to be fully cognizant of the risks, goals, policies, and processes of the organization while maintaining autonomy from management direction and control.

The CAE normally reports directly to the management and audit committee and is responsible for producing an annual assessment of the effectiveness of the organization's risk management and processes for control and governance, as set out by the board or management. Risk management deals with the way an organization sets goals, then recognizes, interprets, and reacts to risks that could affect its ability to realize those goals. Processes for control and governance deal with the effectiveness and efficiency of operations, the reliability of financial reports and conformity with appropriate rules and laws.

ADVANTAGES
- CAEs improve business organization and risk management by providing reassurance on the effectiveness and efficiency of operations, the reliability of financial reporting, and compliance with applicable laws and regulations.
- CAEs provide management with an in-depth and unbiased understanding of the risks that the organization may be facing, allowing for pre-emptive planning.
- CAEs give company officers and directors forewarning of ethical and legal issues that the organization may be facing.

DISADVANTAGES
- Although CAEs are meant to be independent and impartial, they are paid by the company and are an integral part of the company's management. This can lead to conflicts of interest.
- CAEs' judgments, estimates, and interpretations are not always objective because of their close relationships with the organizations for which they work.
- A CAE's relationship with the management of a company is generally informal and the CAE's position does not carry the power to change processes.
- Although there are international bodies such as the Institute of Internal Auditors (IIA), CAEs as a profession are unregulated.

ACTION CHECKLIST
✓ Has the CAE previously worked in related business fields? If so, for how long and what did they achieve?

✓ How good is the CAE's track record on risk assessment and planning for contingencies?

✓ In assessing business processes, how up-to-date is the CAE with information audit technology controls?

✓ To which internationally recognized standards-setting body, such as the IIA, does the CAE belong?

DOS AND DON'TS
DO
- Allow CAEs unrestricted access to information to enable them to evaluate risks, management activities, and personnel better.
- Take into account that CAEs are not responsible for carrying out company activities; their role is solely advisory.
- Consult with the CAE if there are any implications where ethical or legal issues may be involved.

DON'T
- Don't involve CAEs in decisions that might compromise their autonomy as independent internal auditors.

Approaches to Enterprise Risk Management

MORE INFO
Websites:
Institute of Internal Auditors: www.theiia.org
Knowledge Leader: www.knowledgeleader.com

Creating a Risk Register

DEFINITION
A risk register, also sometimes called a "risk log," is usually used when planning for the future. Future plans may include project plans, organizational plans, or financial plans. Risk registers are used in the area of risk management.

Risk management is a method of managing risks or uncertainty relating to a perceived threat. Risk management will usually involve having strategies in place to deal with risks, whether by avoiding the risk, transferring it elsewhere, reducing its effect, or dealing with the consequences. Financial risk management deals with risks that can be managed using traded financial instruments.

Risk management uses risk registers to identify, analyze, and manage risks in a clear, concise way. A risk register usually takes the form of a table—however long or wide that may end up being.

A risk is an event that, if it occurred, would have an adverse (or positive) impact on a project, investment, or similar. The risk register contains information on each risk that is identified. One of the main skills in risk management is to successfully identify all possible risks. The risk register should contain, in summarized form, the planned response in the event that a risk materializes, as well as a summary of what actions should be taken beforehand to reduce a particular risk. Much financial legislation, such as Basel II, also impels organizations to take steps to reduce risk. Risks are often ranked in order of likelihood, or of their impact. The risk register lists the analysis and evaluation of the risks that have been identified.

ADVANTAGES
- A risk register can identify and make provision for dealing with risks, enabling an organization to save millions if things go wrong.
- Should a risk materialize, there is already a set list of actions to run through immediately to start minimizing the consequences.
- An organization can have the confidence to press on with a project or investment knowing that procedures to deal with any risks arising have been put in place.

DISADVANTAGES
- Much time, effort, and money can be spent on creating risk registers to deal with events that will never occur.

ACTION CHECKLIST
✓ Establish a risk management team. The team should meet regularly to discuss the risks associated with each project, investment, etc., to review procedures, and to ensure that the risk register is kept up to date. Appoint a team member to keep abreast of any legislative requirements that may affect the risk register.

✓ Identify and list all potential risks, and decide on the likelihood of their occurrence. Determine the expected impact if they do occur. Identify any interdependencies with other risks and what knock-on effects there may be.

✓ Decide who will bear the risk.

✓ Identify countermeasures to mitigate the risk before it occurs.

✓ Keep track on the risk register of the current status of any risk that has occurred and what action is being taken.

DOS AND DON'TS
DO
- Create a risk register for each new project or investment.
- List each risk as a separate entry in the register's table.
- Identify an "owner" for each risk, i.e. a person who will be in charge of resolving the risk.
- Follow up on actions and status for each risk identified.
- Revisit the risk register regularly to evaluate any changes to the likelihood of a risk and its potential impact. Changes to projects and investments should also be evaluated for their effect on previously assessed risks or new risks that may arise.

DON'T
- Don't ignore the possibility of risks becoming a reality.
- Don't lose track of the risk register.

Approaches to Enterprise Risk Management

MORE INFO

Books:
Ackermann, Fran. *Systemic Risk Assessment: A Case Study*. Management Science Theory Method and Practice Series. Glasgow, UK: Department of Management Science, University of Strathclyde, 2003.
Bateman, Mike. *Tolley's Practical Risk Assessment Handbook*. 5th ed. Boston, MA: Elsevier, 2006.
Brinded, Malcolm. *Perception vs Analysis: How to Handle Risk*. Eighth Annual Royal Academy of Engineering Lloyd's Register Lecture. London: Royal Academy of Engineering, 2000.

Journal:
Risk Management. Published quarterly by Palgrave Macmillan. Online at: www.palgrave-journals.com/rm

Website:
The Institute of Risk Management (UK): www.theirm.org

Establishing a Framework for Assessing Risk

DEFINITION
Instituting a framework for identifying risks (or opportunities), assessing their probability and impact, and determining which controls should be in place can be critical to achieving the company's business objectives. Identifying and proactively addressing risks and opportunities helps businesses to defend themselves. Debt rating agencies and regulators are also increasingly stipulating that companies institute risk-identifying frameworks.

Enterprise Risk Management (ERM) is a name given to the structures, methods, and procedures used by organizations to identify and combat risk. The setting up and monitoring of ERM is typically performed by management as part of its internal control activities, such as appraisals of analytical reports or management committee meetings with relevant experts to make sure that the risk-response strategy is working and that the objectives are being achieved.

Once the risks have been identified and assessed, management chooses a risk-response approach. This may include:
- Avoidance: Leave risky activities.
- Reduction: Lessen their probability or impact.
- Share or insure: Diminish risk by transferring or sharing.
- Accept: In response to a cost–benefit analysis, take no action.

The most widely used ERM frameworks are COSO (from an organization that prepares audit-related reports) and RIMS (The Risk and Insurance Management Society). Both use methods for identifying, analyzing, responding to, and scrutinizing risks or opportunities within the internal and external settings of the business.

ADVANTAGES
- ERM allows an enterprise to identify and prioritize the risks that might be facing the organization.
- An improved understanding of the risks—both systemic and non-systemic—facing businesses can help in contingency planning for when the unexpected happens.
- Robust identification of risks can protect businesses from events that might otherwise threaten the viability of the entity.

DISADVANTAGES
- Protracted risk-framework evaluation could be counterproductive if the fruitless pursuit of perfection leaves the company exposed to the very risks it hoped to avoid.
- Evaluating risks depends on judgments, estimates, and interpretation. Risks are often intangible issues that might be highly relevant but cannot be easily measured.

ACTION CHECKLIST
✓ Overcome resistance to the introduction or upgrading of risk frameworks by ensuring that the board and managers are conscious of the fact that it is in everyone's interest to be aware of business risks.

✓ Encourage an open environment when establishing a risk framework. Some risks are obvious, but stakeholders or managers of individual business sectors may sometimes know more about hidden risks.

✓ Engage key business stakeholders and managers in the evaluation of risks and when seeking the best resolutions for those risks.

DOS AND DON'TS
DO
- Regularly update risk-assessment frameworks, as these can help to keep management informed of the constantly changing business environment and its risks.
- Spell out in clear terms the risks that the organization may be facing, their probability, and their potential impact.

DON'T
- Don't take risks for granted; just because a risk has been the same in the past, there is no guarantee that it will be the same in the future. Only by fully understanding the risks and updating risk frameworks can you counteract the dangers.
- Don't get bogged down by risk frameworks. Risk is sometimes a natural and acceptable part of doing business.

Approaches to Enterprise Risk Management

MORE INFO
Websites:
American Accounting Association: www.aaa-edu.org
The Society of Actuaries: www.soa.org

Key Components of a Corporate Risk Register

DEFINITION
Most large enterprises have a procedure for managing corporate risks. The procedure is intended to identify, record, and communicate risks in terms of their comparative importance to the company. The corporate risk register also forms the basis for reporting risk issues in the annual report. The information is usually stored in a central register, catalog, or inventory of risks. This should contain information suitably sorted, standardized, and merged for relevance to the appropriate level of management. Its key function is to provide management, the board, and key stakeholders with significant information on the main risks faced by the business. Every risk in the register should have the following features: opening date, title, short description, probability, and importance. A risk might also have a dedicated manager responsible for its resolution.

A risk register should help management to:
- understand the nature of the risks the business faces;
- be aware of the extent of those risks;
- identify the level of risk that they are willing to accept;
- recognize its ability to control and reduce risk.

However, a risk register is often out of date, incomplete, or inconsistent when selecting the appropriate controls and countermeasures for each risk. Many companies, therefore, use outside risk consultants. These consultants, working in conjunction with company staff, are better able to take an objective view of risks, assess their relative importance, and assign priorities.

ADVANTAGES
- A corporate risk register provides management and the board with important information on the main risks faced by the business.
- The register allows management to identify and prioritize risks, ensuring that risks with the greatest probability or the greatest potential loss are handled first.

DISADVANTAGES
- If risks are improperly assessed and prioritized, they can divert resources that could be used more profitably.
- Unless it is competently maintained and updated, the risk register may not be comprehensive or consistent, leading to unrecognized risks.
- The risk information may not be presented in a logical and unbiased form and, as such, can unintentionally mislead.

ACTION CHECKLIST
✓ Thoroughly check the risk register against any potential business risk you might foresee and compare similar companies' risk registers.

✓ Research your market and make sure that you have analyzed the consequences of any risks upon your own business.

✓ Encourage an atmosphere of openness about the kinds of risks facing the organization. Some risks are obvious, but managers of individual business units may sometimes know more about hidden risks. Only by fully understanding risks can you attempt to counteract them.

DOS AND DON'TS
DO
- Seek the advice of specialist strategic risk advisers. Risk management is very complex. Experts from specialist risk management companies can help devise customized risk registers to protect against potential problems.
- Keep in mind the distinction between risk and uncertainty. Risk can be measured by using the formula: Impact multiplied by Probability.
- Quantify and differentiate between risks that are merely the cost of doing business and those that might have an impact on objectives.

DON'T
- Don't make the error of failing to check the risk register thoroughly for inconsistencies.
- Don't believe that you can totally cover every risk your business could face.
- Don't rely on single controls and countermeasures for each risk.

Approaches to Enterprise Risk Management

MORE INFO
Websites:
American Institute of Certified Public Accountants: www.aicpa.org
Knowledge Leader: www.knowledgeleader.com

Managing and Auditing the Risk of Business Interruption

DEFINITION
The key to managing disruptions to business processes successfully is a business continuity plan (BCP) that brings together the company's documented approach to dealing with incidents.

CONSIDER INSURANCE
Developing a continuity plan will also reveal events that will lead to business interruptions which cannot be dealt with internally. In these cases it may be necessary to consider the use of insurance to cover potential losses.

There are a vast number of policies that are designed to cover the cost of recovering from an event. It should be noted, however, that although these offer some protection, they will not restore a business to the position in its markets that it occupied prior to an interruption.

As the policies are intended to cover financial losses, the insured company needs to ensure that its documentation takes into account all income and losses that could result from an interruption. These may include items such as penalty payments for failing to complete contracts as well as lost sales.

ACTION CHECKLIST
There are five key stages in this risk management process.

✓ 1. Establish the context
The first stage for an organization that is developing a business continuity plan is to identify its business processes, the interdependencies between these processes, and their priority in relation to the organization's key objectives. These interdependencies should then be mapped.

✓ 2. Identify and assess the risks
Once the organization has identified the key processes, it can undertake a business impact analysis to assess the effect of the loss of one of those processes. It should identify the maximum acceptable outage times for those processes within the context of overall business continuity.

Risks can be rated according to their significance in terms of business interruption—for instance, by measuring their likely duration. High-rated risks will cause an interruption that is longer than the maximum acceptable outage.

Some risks may be tolerated because they are relatively minor in their impact on the whole business process and toleration is the most cost-effective approach. Other risks can be treated either by a preventive approach, which reduces the risk of the interruption happening, or by corrective controls that are intended to respond to an event and ameliorate its consequences.

✓ 3. Implement treatments
The company should then identify potential plans and controls that are designed to minimize the effect of business interruptions. The most effective mixture of preventative and reactive controls and plans should be selected on the basis of the organization's priorities and objectives. Documentation should include names of responsible parties, the plan's budget allocation, and the timetable for both the implementation of the plan and the frequency of its review.

✓ 4. Monitor and review
Sufficient documentation needs to be provided to enable periodic revision and auditing of the effectiveness of the plan and controls. Some companies integrate risk assessment into their overall annual business planning process to ensure its periodic review.

✓ 5. Test the plan
Although it might be impractical and unnecessarily disruptive to test the whole plan, recovery processes and procedures can be trialed in a variety of ways. For instance, scenarios can be created and teams can be challenged to find weaknesses in a plan. They may spot, for example, that the recovery of one process is dependent on the completed function of another, or that they do not know where to find vital sources of information.

Approaches to Enterprise Risk Management

MORE INFO

Books:
Barnes, James C. *A Guide to Business Continuity Planning*. Chichester, UK: Wiley, 2001.
Hiles, Andrew (ed). *The Definitive Handbook of Business Continuity Management*. 2nd ed. Chichester, UK: Wiley, 2007.

Website:
BS 25999 Business continuity: www.bsi-global.com/en/Assessment-and-certification-services/management-systems/Standards-and-Schemes/BS-25999

Managing Your Credit Risk

DEFINITION
Credit risk is the risk of loss caused by a debtor defaulting on a loan or other line of credit, whether the principal, the interest, or both. The sound management of credit risk involves reining in all exposure to financial risk to within acceptable limits. A company's rate of return should always be risk-adjusted to take account of credit risk and other risks.

Good control of credit risk involves managing not only the risk associated with individual deals or transactions, but also that of an entire portfolio (i.e. ensuring that risk is both minimized and evenly spread). Banks in particular need to have a comprehensive policy in place for managing all kinds of risk—credit risk forms the most important part of any such policy. The collapse of Barings Bank in 1995 is a textbook example of what can happen when an organization lacks safeguards for managing credit risk. Loans tend to be the main source of credit risk for many banks. They are, however, exposed to other sources of credit risk, such as in the trading book, or on and off the balance sheet. For all kinds of companies credit risk also exists in other financial instruments, such as interbank or currency transactions, trade financing, equities, and derivatives.

Exposure to credit risk remains a key problem on a global basis. Companies need to learn lessons from high-profile cases such as Barings and Northern Rock. The Basel Committee drew up a set of principles to be used when evaluating a credit risk management system. Although the principles are aimed at financial institutions, they apply equally to all organizations. How a company approaches the issue will vary according to factors such as the supervisory techniques they use, whether they employ external auditors, and the size of the institution. Smaller businesses, in particular, need to ensure they have an adequate risk–return policy in place.

Firms are exposed to credit risk when, for example, they do not insist on advance payment for products or services. By billing after delivery, the company takes the risk that the customer may default on payment, leaving it out of pocket. Many companies quote payment terms of 30 days as standard, and it only takes one large defaulted payment to expose the firm to cash flow problems and possible bankruptcy.

Many firms operate a credit risk department whose role is to assess the financial health of their customers and decide whether to extend credit or not. They may use software to analyze such risks and assess how to avoid, reduce, or transfer any credit risk. Credit rating companies such as Standard & Poor's, Moody's, and Dun and Bradstreet also sell financial intelligence to firms needing external assistance in managing credit risk with their clients.

Companies can lessen their credit risk by, for example, cutting their payment terms to 15 days, limiting the amount of goods or services available on credit per transaction, or even insisting on payment up-front. Strategies such as these cut exposure to risk, but the downside is that they can affect the volume of sales and subsequent cash flow.

ADVANTAGES
- A keen awareness of credit risk that includes processes to identify, measure, monitor, and control credit risk should protect all but the smallest organizations from major problems.

DISADVANTAGES
- Small firms that have only a very few customers find it difficult to manage credit risk due to their vulnerability should a customer turn out to be a late-payer or even default on payment entirely.

ACTION CHECKLIST
Specific credit risk management practices vary among organizations according to the type and complexity of their credit activities. A comprehensive policy for managing credit risk should address the following points:

✓ Create an appropriate credit risk environment.

✓ Implement a policy that ensures the credit-granting process is sound.

✓ Assess the quality of your assets and determine that you have adequate provisions and reserves.

✓ Maintain quality procedures for credit administration, measurement, and monitoring processes.

✓ Ensure that you have adequate controls in place.

Approaches to Enterprise Risk Management

MORE INFO
Books:
Bluhm, Christian, Ludger Overbeck, and Christoph Wagner. *An Introduction to Credit Risk Modeling.* Financial Mathematics Series. Boca Raton, FL: Chapman & Hall/CRC, 2002.
de Servigny, Arnaud, and Olivier Renault. *The Standard & Poor's Guide to Measuring and Managing Credit Risk.* New York: McGraw-Hill, 2004.
Duffie, Darrell, and Kenneth J. Singleton. *Credit Risk: Pricing, Measurement, and Management.* Princeton Series in Finance. Princeton, NJ: Princeton University Press, 2003.

Setting Up a Key Risk Indicator (KRI) System

DEFINITION
Key risk indicators (KRI) are measurements that are used by management to show how risky an activity is—a project or an investment, for example. They are called key because they warn of the most obvious areas where problems may arise. KRI help to flag up warnings of a possible adverse impact arising from an activity in the future.

In the United States the Risk Management Association (RMA) manages an initiative that is designed for financial services companies interested in improving their risk management. Going by the name of the KRI Library and Services, its aim is to achieve a degree of consistency and standardization to enable KRI to be compared, analyzed, and reported at the corporate level. The RMA's intention is that the library initiative will lead to distinct improvements in the effective use and benchmarking of KRI with peer groups.

Most companies find the development of effective KRI to be a key challenge. In financial institutions there are plenty of credit risk and market risk indicators, many with frameworks set out within existing financial legislation. However, pulling these data together and developing operational risk indicators is not easy. Conversely, nonfinancial institutions may be in possession of a mass of business and quality information gained from balanced scorecard and quality initiatives. However, their difficulty lies in developing KRI for financial risk or technology risk.

All companies have the awkward task of developing KRI that can provide effective early warning of potential future problems.

It is in the area of forecasting losses that KRI are most likely to gain their stripes, but the majority of companies have yet to master the techniques of setting up effective KRI systems that can do this.

ADVANTAGES
- KRI can provide early warning of future losses or other problems.
- They are useful in supporting management decisions and actions.
- They can be benchmarked both internally and externally.

DISADVANTAGES
- Mastering KRI has proven difficult to date.
- The company has to believe in them, even though past history may not fully support their value.

ACTION CHECKLIST
Some of the following resources can be useful in helping create your own KRI list.

✓ Policies and regulations, particularly those that are aimed at regulating the business activities of the company. Such KRI may include risk exposures relating to compliance with regulatory requirements and standards.

✓ Strategies and objectives. Corporate and business strategies, as established by senior management, are a good source.

✓ Previous losses and incidents. Databases containing historical losses and incidents can provide useful input on what processes or events can cause losses.

DOS AND DON'TS
DO
- Make your KRI quantifiable.
- Base KRI on consistent methodologies and standards.
- Track them along a timeline against standards or limits.
- Link KRI to objectives, risk owners, and standard risk categories.
- Run regular overviews to check that your formulae are still relevant and accurate in assessing risk.

DON'T
- Don't complicate risk.
- Don't be too simplistic.
- Don't put 100% faith in your initial KRI.

Approaches to Enterprise Risk Management

MORE INFO
Books:
Alexander, Carol. *Mastering Risk, Volume 2: Applications. Your Single-Source Guide to Becoming a Master of Risk*. Mastering Series. Upper Saddle River, NJ: FT Prentice Hall, 2001.
PricewaterhouseCoopers for Committee of the Sponsoring Organizations of the Treadway Commission (COSO). *Enterprise Risk Management—Integrated Framework*. New York: AICPA, 2004. Hard copies (two volumes) can be ordered from COSO (www.coso.org) or from the Institute of Internal Auditors (www.iia.org.uk)

Websites:
KRI Library Services (US): www.kriex.org
The Institute of Risk Management (UK): www.theirm.org
The Risk Management Association (US): www.rmahq.org/RMA

What Is Forensic Auditing?

DEFINITION
Forensic auditing is a blend of traditional accounting, auditing, and financial detective work. Technology has an increasingly important role to play, with complex data analysis techniques employed to help flag areas that warrant further investigation.

Forensic auditing offers a toolset that company managers can use to help detect and investigate various forms of white-collar financial impropriety and inappropriate or inefficient use of resources. As company structures and controls become ever more complex, so too does the scope for employees with specialized knowledge of the way control systems work to bypass them. In the past, various forms of auditing have been employed after a major control breach has come to light, but executives are now increasingly looking at forensic auditing to help identify vulnerabilities in financial control.

ADVANTAGES
- Forensic auditing strengthens control mechanisms, with the objective of protecting the business against financial crimes, be they potentially catastrophic one-off events that could threaten the viability of the business, or smaller-scale but repetitive misappropriations of company assets over a number of years.
- Forensic auditing can play an important role for companies under review by regulatory authorities and can also be invaluable to ensure regulatory compliance. For example, forensic auditing can be useful in helping companies to ensure that their anti-money laundering procedures are both effective and robust.
- Forensic auditing can help protect organizations from the long-term damage to reputation caused by the publicity associated with insider crimes. A forensic audit also provides a sound base of factual information that can be used to help resolve disputes, and can be used in court should the victim seek legal redress.
- Forensic auditing can improve efficiency by identifying areas of waste.
- Forensic auditing can help with the detection and recording of potential conflicts of interest for executives by improving transparency and probity in the way resources are used, in both private and public entities.

DISADVANTAGES
- A poorly managed forensic audit could consume excessive amounts of management time and could become an unwelcome distraction for the business.
- Forensic audits can have wide-ranging scope across the business. Under certain circumstances, the scope of the audit may need to be extended, with a corresponding increase in the budget.
- Some employees can interpret a proactive forensic audit as a slight on their integrity, rather than as a means to improve control procedures for the benefit of the business.

ACTION CHECKLIST
✓ Understand your risks, routes to their potential exploitation, and the tools available to detect abuses, fraud, or wastage.

✓ Analyze numerical data, comparing actual costs against expected costs.

✓ Investigate possible reasons for inconsistencies.

✓ Consider whether covert detection techniques might be more appropriate when investigating cases of possible fraud. Higher-profile full forensic audits can deter future fraud but could also reduce the likelihood of witnessing the culprit carrying out a fraudulent act.

✓ External auditing specialists with extensive experience of complex forensic audits can offer industry-specific experience, auditing management expertise, and advanced interviewing techniques. A combination of these external specialists and companies' internal accountants/auditors can achieve shorter audit timescales and lower levels of disruption to the business.

DOS AND DON'TS
DO
- Remember that well-resourced forensic auditing processes can help to identify misreporting at many levels of an organization.
- Bear in mind that regular proactive forensic audits can help businesses to ensure that their processes stay robust.

(Continued overleaf)

Approaches to Enterprise Risk Management

DO (cont.)
- Be prepared to widen the scope of a forensic audit to ensure maximum effectiveness.
- See forensic auditing as a continuous process, rather than a one-off event. On completing one audit, restarting the process could uncover something relevant that was previously overlooked.
- Be prepared to share the findings of the forensic audit with other areas of your company, and take into account industry best practice to improve efficiency and combat fraud.

DON'T
- Don't lose sight of the objective of a forensic audit. The cost of a forensic audit can be high, but the potential cost of not undertaking an audit and implementing its findings can be even higher.
- Don't fall into the trap of overlooking the importance of the "forensic" element of the audit. With the results of such a process deemed suitable for inclusion in legal proceedings, the high potential costs of the forensic audit process could easily be recovered from dispute resolution or higher levels of loss recovery.

MORE INFO

Book:
Cardwell, Harvey. *Principles of Audit Surveillance*. Reprise Edition. Philadelphia, PA: R.T. Edwards, 2005.

Articles:
Brannen, Laurie. "Is a forensic audit in your future?" *Business Finance* (June 2007).
Roberts, Marta. "Fraud fight in the Wild West." *Security Management* 48:11 (2004).

Websites:
American Institute of Certified Public Accountants: www.aicpa.org
Institute of Chartered Accountants in England and Wales: www.icaew.com
Institute of Forensic Accounting & Investigative Audit: www.ifaia.org

Checklists
Risk Measurement and Management

Applying Stress-Testing to Business Continuity Management

DEFINITION
Business continuity management (BCM) is an important component of the risk management framework for regulated institutions. It increases the resilience to business disruption that may arise from internal or external events and should reduce any adverse impact on business operations, as well as profitability and reputation.

Business operations have become increasingly complex over the years, increasing their vulnerability to disruption by outside events. BCM has thus become an essential part of a company's risk management framework. A whole industry has sprung up devoted to supporting companies on BCM issues.

Although major disruptions to business are rare, few have forgotten the events of 9/11, which resulted in massive disruption to business. External threats from terrorism, computer crime, and viruses are unlikely to go away. Businesses need to put in place continuity plans that are consistent with the scale of their operations.

Stress-testing is crucial to an organization's BCM and its planning for risk management. Stress-testing and scenario analysis both provide management with the information it needs to assess and adjust risks to the organization and to mitigate them effectively. They enable firms to understand how they should deal with certain threats, pick up on any shortfalls, and implement actions to improve their processes for BCM.

Wider use of BCM, stress-testing, and scenario analysis would have a beneficial effect on the robustness of the world's financial systems. There is, however, no simple formula for a company to follow for its own stress-testing and scenario analysis. Depending on its size and global reach, each organization must formulate its own strategies and plans for testing its BCM processes.

ADVANTAGES
Stress-testing of business continuity management should:
- reduce the impact of disruptions to business operations in the event of a problem;
- increase protection to stakeholders and beneficiaries;
- promote confidence in the organization and the whole financial system.

DISADVANTAGES
- The cost of planning and actions.
- The time spent on the whole process.

ACTION CHECKLIST
✓ Put a BCM strategy in place.

✓ Set up methods and routines for stress-testing and scenario analysis.

✓ Carry out regular tests.

✓ Determine follow-up points.

✓ Carry out any necessary actions to improve the BCM plan.

DOS AND DON'TS
DO
- Review your BCM plans and processes regularly.
- Identify actions to update your BCM as appropriate.
- Follow up these actions.

DON'T
- Don't leave your BCM proposals unmonitored once you have put them in place.
- Don't restrict stress-testing to specific threats.

Approaches to Enterprise Risk Management

MORE INFO

Books:
Hiles, Andrew (ed). *The Definitive Handbook of Business Continuity Management.* 2nd ed. Chichester, UK: Wiley, 2007.
Osborne, Andy. *Practical Business Continuity Management: Top Tips for Effective, Real-World Business Continuity Management.* Evesham, UK: Word4Word, 2007.

Journal:
Journal of Business Continuity & Emergency Planning. Online at: www.henrystewart.com/jbcep

Websites:
Continuity Central for business continuity news, information, and resources: www.continuitycentral.com
UK Resilience, a British government news and information service for emergency practitioners, has this page on business continuity: www.ukresilience.gov.uk/preparedness/businesscontinuity.aspx

Applying Stress-Testing to Operational Risk Exposure

DEFINITION
As global financial markets have become more diversified and complex, many more "new" economies have entered the markets. With the greater number of players and the increased funds available, it has become imperative that all parties with a vested interest in markets and risk exposure—from investment banks to private investors—are properly prepared to assess exposure and able to quantify risk. Stress-testing refers to the various ways that financial and other entities estimate their vulnerability to an exceptional event of plausibility.

The use and practice of stress-testing have increased over the past decade following the occurrence of several notable events in the financial markets: the 1997 Asian crisis, the Enron scandal of 2001, and the collapse of Barings Bank in 1995. As the markets turned bearish in late 2007, it has become standard practice for an institution to acquire the ability to stress-test itself accurately.

Many major institutions stress-test their portfolios on a monthly basis to assess their risk profile and gauge the possible effects of various scenarios on their profit and loss accounts. Stress-testing requires that employees are trained to understand the mathematics and theory behind the process to ensure that the information garnered is both accurate and comprehensive.

Stress-testing can be divided into two distinct categories: simple sensitivity tests (SST), and scenario analysis.

The SST explores changes to a portfolio's value following a change in one risk factor, for example interest rates. It is a very simple yet effective way of flagging major deficiencies and weaknesses in a portfolio. The SST is frequently used by smaller banks and institutions as well as private investors. The drawback of this technique is that it is not plausible that just one variable should change—a massive increase in US interest rates, for example, would have a massive effect on exchange rates and equities.

This is why larger and more complex organizations use scenario analysis, which takes into account a wide range of possible variables such as exchange rates, equity prices, and interest rates and extrapolates possible outcomes and their probabilities. The process is not dissimilar to forecasting the weather—like the weather, a financial forecast is susceptible to change and must be repeated regularly.

Stress-testing is only as accurate as the information fed into it. Thus, practitioners must have a thorough understanding of economic theory and the effects on the institution's portfolio. It is an exceptionally flexible tool that can be applied to virtually any aspect of an institution's operations that have substantial exposure to risk—country risk, illiquidity exposure, etc. It is not an end-product as stress-testing treats variables separately; companies are currently trying to develop a testing procedure that is more holistic and accumulative in scope.

ADVANTAGES
A properly conducted stress-test program can help insure against otherwise unnoticed risks and flag problematic investment strategies. If the scenarios and metrics of the system are set clearly, a great deal of benefit can be gained, both for long-term strategy and for day-to-day management. Taking a risk is fine, but it must be accurately gauged, and a properly conducted stress-testing procedure can greatly reduce the potential for error in exposure calculations.

DISADVANTAGES
If conducted improperly, stress-testing can create a false sense of security. Any stress-test that scored exposure to risk too low would be exceptionally dangerous to an institution. It can be time-consuming and expensive to train employees to use stress-testing, and it must be applied in continually changing environments.

ACTION CHECKLIST
✓ Ensure that the users of the system and the institution's managers understand the limitations, intent, and scope of the process.

✓ Ensure that the results are produced in a comprehensible format.

✓ Ensure that the stress-test is company-wide.

Approaches to Enterprise Risk Management

DOS AND DON'TS

DO
- Introduce stress-testing; but
- Make the reports comprehensible and comprehensive.

DON'T
- Don't be deluded into believing that stress-testing is an end in itself. Like all tools, it will only be of benefit if used properly.
- Don't assume that just because a stress-test has been conducted the process is complete.

MORE INFO

Book:
Engelmann, Bernd, and Robert Rauhmeier (eds). *The Basel II Risk Parameters: Estimation, Validation, and Stress Testing*. Berlin: Springer-Verlag, 2006.

Articles:
Sorge, Marco. "Stress-testing financial systems: An overview of current methodologies." BIS working paper no. 165. Basel: Bank for International Settlements, 2004.

Sorge, Marco, and Kimmo Virolainen. "A comparative analysis of macro stress-testing methodologies with application to Finland." *Journal of Financial Stability* 2:2 (June 2006): 113–151.

Tan, Kok-Hui, and Inn-Leng Chan. "Stress testing using VaR approach—a case for Asian currencies." *Journal of International Financial Markets, Institutions and Money* 13:1 (February 2003): 39–55.

Assessing Cash Flow and Bank Lending Requirements

DEFINITION
Lack of cash flow is a major cause of a business failing as, even though it may be turning a profit, if the money does not flow in on time the business will not be able to settle its debts. Cash flow is basically the measure of a company's financial health, showing the amount of cash generated and used by a company in any given period. Cash flow is essential to ensure solvency, as having enough cash ensures that creditors and employees can be paid on time. Banks require companies to show the difference between sales and costs within a specified period, which acts as an indicator of the performance of a business better than the profit margins. Sales and costs and, therefore, profits do not necessarily coincide with their associated cash inflows and outflows. Even though a sale has been secured and goods delivered, payment may be deferred as a result of credit to the customer, yet suppliers and staff still have to be paid and cash invested in rebuilding depleted stocks. The net result is that although profits may be reported, the business may experience a short-term cash shortfall.

The main sources of cash flow into a business are receipts from sales, increases in bank loans, proceeds of share issues and asset disposals, and other income, such as interest earned. Cash outflows include payments to suppliers and staff, capital and interest repayments for loans, dividends, taxation, and capital expenditure. Cash flow planning entails forecasting and tabulating all significant cash inflows and analyzing in detail the timing of expected payments, which include suppliers, wages, other expenses, capital expenditure, loan repayments, dividends, tax, and interest payments.

A computerized cash flow model can be used to compile forecasts, assess possible funding requirements, and explore the financial consequences of other strategies. Computerized models can help prevent major planning errors, anticipate problems, and identify opportunities to improve cash flow and negotiate loans.

Banks must ensure that a business is viable, which entails asking pertinent questions. Lenders will insist on up-to-date information on the type of industry, management capabilities and experience, business plans and daily operations, key competition, and PR and marketing plans. They have to know that the business makes sense and can repay a loan, and what security is available in case of insolvency. Companies have to keep within their cash limits regardless of anticipated business. Business factoring is an alternative to bank loans—a factoring company buys your credit invoices and provides you with immediate cash in exchange for a small fee ranging between 1.5% and 5.0%. Factoring is more flexible than a bank loan.

ADVANTAGES
Ensuring good cash flow through a company helps to:
- increase sales;
- reduce direct and indirect costs and overhead expenses;
- raise additional equity;
- gain the confidence of banks and potentially secure more loans.

DISADVANTAGES
- If your profit margins are already low, you might not be able to afford bank fees.
- The banks have a tendency to up fees and charge for late payments.

ACTION CHECKLIST
It is essential to keep track of your cash and not allow any surplus to sit idle. Accounts must be carefully monitored and cash invested to maximize returns. There are many ways to increase cash flow:

✓ reducing credit terms for historically slow payers;

✓ reviewing customer payment performance;

✓ becoming more selective when granting credit;

✓ seeking other ways to pay rather than all in one installment, such as deposits or staggered payments;

✓ reducing the amount of time of the credit terms;

✓ invoicing immediately the work has been done;

✓ improving collection systems for billing;

✓ adding late payment charges.

Approaches to Enterprise Risk Management

DOS AND DON'TS

DO
Do understand the way your company works, using a detailed analysis of banking procedure and taking into consideration:
- overdraft facilities and investment accounts;
- the number of monthly transactions;
- the number of written monthly checks;
- how customers pay you;
- the suitability of electronic banking for your business;
- cash access facilities;
- interest income;
- overall expenses and fees.

DON'T
- Don't overestimate sales forecasts.
- Don't underestimate costs.
- Don't underestimate delays in payments.
- Don't forget to check your debtors' credit history carefully.

MORE INFO
Books:
Fight, Andrew. *Cash Flow Forecasting*. Oxford: Butterworth-Heinemann, 2006.
Mulford, Charles W., and Eugene E. Comiskey. *Creative Cash Flow Reporting and Analysis: Uncovering Sustainable Financial Performance*. Hoboken, NJ: Wiley, 2005.
Reider, Rob, and Peter B. Heyler. *Managing Cash Flow: An Operational Focus*. Hoboken, NJ: Wiley, 2003.

Building a Forex Plan

DEFINITION
Forex, which is short for "foreign exchange," is the largest trading market in the world, turning over as much as US$1.5 trillion every day. There is no central marketplace for currency exchange, which is done over the counter. Currencies are traded on a global basis 24 hours a day, five days a week. Financial transactions involve one party purchasing a quantity of one currency in exchange for selling a quantity of another. Trading commonly occurs between large and central banks, currency speculators, corporations, governments, and other institutions. Currency prices depend on many factors, but ultimately the price depends upon supply and demand.

Forex markets react to trade levels and trends. Trade and investment flows indicate the demand for goods and services, in turn indicating demand for a country's currency to conduct trade. Trade deficits can have a negative impact on a nation's currency. A currency loses value when a country experiences rising inflation, which erodes demand for that particular currency. As a generalization, the healthier a country's economy, the better its currency will perform. Factors to look out for include economic factors, political conditions, and market psychology.

An effective and proven plan can help a company to exploit the forex currency trading system to its best potential. Customizing a forex plan in line with specific issues and needs can help to manage foreign exchange in the most cost-effective and efficient way. It is customary—and wise—to begin with a simulated forex trading account, which does not need any investment upfront but is used to train beginners in the strategies and fundamentals of forex trading.

A well-considered forex plan needs to take into account various elements. Decide whether you will hedge recorded or future assets and liabilities and how. Choose a trustworthy and competitive forex supplier. Plan the scope of activity taking into account objectives and time frames in which to achieve set goals. Make sure you schedule regular assessments of your forex business and revise any activities as needed. A forex plan should be sustainable, so aim to negotiate transactions at the most favorable prices. Keep track of your forex exposure by implementing methods for data capture. A good plan also has internal controls—consider your business processes and documentation requirements, ensure that you have strict authorization limits, and keep tasks segregated where necessary. Finally, stay familiar with accounting and reporting requirements.

A forex plan should be reviewed at every stage, from the first planning phase and throughout implementation. Senior management should sign off all decisions to ensure that risks are minimized. If the forex plan is of limited duration (for example for a specific project), then a post-implementation review is wise as it can identify areas for improvement and efficiency gains if you decide to enter the forex markets in the future.

ADVANTAGES
- When a company needs to use forex (for example, if it conducts business abroad), a strong forex plan can boost profits if transactions are conducted with care and insight. A good understanding of how to use forex transactions to advantage can also give an edge over business competitors.

DISADVANTAGES
- There is always a risk of losing money and thus profit, especially if you ignore advice and are overconfident about market conditions.

ACTION CHECKLIST
✓ Be as informed as you can on how the forex currency trading system operates.

✓ Enroll in a reputable forex trading system course online and familiarize yourself with the forex currency market with a simulated trading account.

✓ Learn forex investment strategies, including the buy signals that forex charts give traders.

✓ Choose the amount you want to make on every forex trade before you begin trading; this is usually more than or equal to the earnings that you can afford to lose in the forex trade.

✓ Select your forex suppliers and counterparts.

✓ Negotiate forex transactions at more favorable price points.

Approaches to Enterprise Risk Management

DOS AND DON'TS

DO
- Watch charts and indicators.
- Work out how much you are willing to risk per trade.
- Review existing general ledger activity in the foreign currency accounts (gain/loss account and other comprehensive income (OCI) accounts).
- Take a sample historical review or monitor current activity to compare forex rates and forex hedge costs.

DON'T
- Don't ignore factors such as government budget deficits or surpluses, inflation levels and trends, economic growth and health, political conditions, long-term trends, technical trading considerations, and domestic, regional, and international political conditions and events.
- Don't be too greedy—don't expect too much too soon.

MORE INFO

Books:
Cheng, Grace. *7 Winning Strategies for Trading Forex: Real and Actionable Techniques for Profiting from the Currency Markets*. Petersfield, UK: Harriman House, 2007.
Ponsi, Ed. *Forex Patterns & Probabilities: Trading Strategies for Trending & Range-bound Markets*. Hoboken, NJ: Wiley, 2007.

Websites:
A forex guide for beginners: www.forex-guide.net/beginner-investing.html
Insider's Guide to Forex Trading: forextradingonlinehelp.com
International Financial Services London (IFSL) research report, "Foreign exchange 2007": www.ifsl.org.uk/upload/CBS_Foreign_Exchange_2007.pdf

Calculating Your Total Economic Capital

DEFINITION
Economic capital is the amount of risk capital that a company must have to cover any risks it is facing, such as operational risk, credit risk, or market risk. The amount held is that needed to ensure the business could overcome a worst-case scenario and still survive. Economic capital must be realistically estimated to manage the risks and to budget the costs of regulatory capital that needs to be maintained across the different divisions of the company. It is not the same as regulatory capital, which is a mandatory sum that a company must hold. The sum is determined by the regulators. Financial services should aspire to ensure the amount of risk capital they hold is at least equal to their economic capital.

Economic capital is calculated by determining the amount of capital that a company must have at its disposal to ensure it remains solvent over a defined period of time, taking into account the probability of any risks actually occurring. Thus, economic capital is usually calculated as the value-at-risk (VaR), where VaR is defined as the tipping point for the probability of a mark-to-market loss on the business within the predetermined time-frame, assuming the markets are stable and no trading has occurred. There is no universally accepted method for calculating economic capital.

The full economic scenario (FES) method is an approach that takes into account all possible risks for a company, and is useful where the main goal is to determine the economic capital for all the combined risks. However, the FES approach does not allocate any explicit amount of economic capital to any particular risk. It is calculated by applying a set of economic scenarios to all divisions of the company, then applying assumptions for each scenario. These assumptions usually include interest, equity returns, inflation, defaults, and actual versus expected claims for various products.

ADVANTAGES
- A one year mark-to-market, stress-testing approach to calculating economic capital is probably the easiest and fastest way to quantify a company's risk exposure and achieve quantifiable business benefits.

DISADVANTAGES
- Combining results that have been derived over different time horizons, even where they have been calculated consistently, can present difficulties as it allows risks in one time-frame period to be hedged against other risks in a different time-frame, which may be unjustifiable.

ACTION CHECKLIST
✓ First calculate the potential losses for each risk category. The more detailed the calculation, the better, but you may find that you do not have sufficient data to do more than a simple assessment.

✓ Next determine the probability and severity of such losses. Use a VaR model for market price risks, and self-assessment for operational and strategic risk, to generate the possible losses and their distribution across the business. Allow for worst-case scenarios when determining how severe losses could theoretically be.

✓ Consider using scenario analysis to determine the risk probabilities of infrequent but severe events, as these are hard to calculate within economic capital.

DOS AND DON'TS
DO
- Remember that the use of economic capital as an internal model for capital adequacy has been driven by regulatory requirements, particularly the Solvency II proposals, which introduce a comprehensive risk management framework for defining required capital levels, and implementing procedures to identify, measure, and manage risk levels.

DON'T
- Don't forget that strategic risks are not usually calculated when determining economic capital, as it makes no sense to calculate a capital charge for this unless a suitable modeling method is used that considers the benefits of the strategic options.

Approaches to Enterprise Risk Management

MORE INFO
Books:
Porteous, Bruce T., and Tapadar Pradip. *Economic Capital and Financial Risk Management for Financial Services Firms and Conglomerates*. Basingstoke, UK: Palgrave Macmillan, 2005.
van Lelyveld, Iman (ed). *Economic Capital Modelling: Concepts, Measurement and Implementation*. London: Risk Books, 2006.

Captive Insurance Companies: How to Reduce Your Costs

DEFINITION

Captive insurance companies are insurance companies that have the specific objective of financing risks from a parent group or its customers. The process is a risk management technique—a company forms its own insurance company subsidiary to finance its retained losses. Captives are of interest to companies when they find that their insurance premiums have risen significantly as they can reduce costs. In addition, companies can gain greater control by owning an insurance company.

Creating a captive offers a self-financing option for buying insurance. The captive either holds onto the risk of providing insurance or can pay reinsurers to take the risk. Captives are usually based in a country that has a favorable tax regime with more relaxed controls. When a company uses captive insurance, the money buys a service and is invested with a good possibility of a return. Cost savings can be realized through reduced overheads, allowing a larger percentage of the premium to be used for claims payments.

Captives also give access to the reinsurance market, which operates on a lower cost structure than other direct insurers, and there is the potential to earn investment income on unpaid loss reserves.

There are several types of insurance captive:
- Single-parent captive: An insurance or reinsurance company formed primarily to insure the risks of its parent or affiliate.
- Association captive: Owned by a trade, industry, or service group for the benefit of its members.
- Group captive: Jointly owned by a number of companies to provide a vehicle to meet a common insurance need.
- Agency captive: Owned by an insurance agency or brokerage firm for the purpose of reinsuring a portion of their clients' risks.
- Rent-a-captive: Providing captive facilities, for a fee, to others—often companies that are too small to establish their own captive.
- Special purpose vehicle/company: Mostly used for catastrophe bonds and reinsurance "sidecars." They may be formed as a rent-a-captive facility to enable companies that do not have a sufficient volume of insurance premiums to access many of the benefits associated with an offshore captive.

Offshore captive insurers are often more attractive because they enjoy lower tax rates on investment and underwriting income, resulting in reduced expected tax payments. Captives give noninsurers access to reinsurance markets that were previously only accessible to commercial insurance companies. The reasons for creating a captive insurance company are varied, but it may be that the external insurers are charging too much, or that the required coverage is unavailable.

ADVANTAGES

- Premiums paid to a captive insurance company are tax-deductible.
- Insurance can be obtained through the international reinsurance market at a more favorable premium.
- Investment returns can be obtained directly on the invested capital.
- The types of risk that a captive can underwrite include damage to property, public and product liability, professional indemnity, employee benefits, employer's liability, and motor and medical aid expenses. Risks that may be uninsurable or cost-prohibitive can be included.
- Additionally, the parent company's entire family can benefit from group funding of a captive through consolidation of coverage, centralized administrative support, and a significant reduction in insurance expenses.

DISADVANTAGES

- A substantial amount of capital is initially required to ensure that the captive remains financially healthy.
- Third-party dependency on service providers.
- Inadequate loss reserves where actual losses exceed initially expected levels and additional funds need to be allocated. Such a situation could disguise risks to the parent company.
- Reduced availability of other insurance facilities.

Approaches to Enterprise Risk Management

ACTION CHECKLIST
- ✓ Create an insurance program based on the needs of your company.
- ✓ Exercise greater control over your cover because you do not have to choose a standard offer from the commercial market.
- ✓ Keep a clean loss record so that premiums do not increase.

DOS AND DON'TS
DO
- Stabilize the cost of insurance and determine your premiums by your company's own loss experience, not by an industry-wide standard.
- Obtain more competitive wholesale quotes from primary insurers.
- Maximize the yield on the portfolio.
- Structure the maturities to meet your cash flow requirements.

DON'T
- Don't cut corners to save costs.
- Don't assume that your company is too small for captive insurance.
- Don't forget to look at renting rather than buying a captive insurance facility.

MORE INFO
Books:
Bawcutt, Paul A. *Captive Insurance Companies: Establishment, Operation, and Management.* 4th ed. London: Witherby, 1997.

Klingenschmid, Florian. *Captive Insurance Companies in Risk Management.* Saarbrücken, Germany: VDM Verlag, 2008.

Catastrophe Bonds: What They Are and How They Function

DEFINITION
Catastrophe bonds (sometimes abbreviated to cat bonds) are fixed income securities, typically issued by insurance companies, which pay an attractive yield to investors, but with the proviso that should a specific predetermined event, such as a natural or human-inspired disaster occur, bondholders suffer the loss of their income and potentially also their capital. From the perspective of the issuer, catastrophe bonds spread at least some—but not necessarily all—of a particular risk to the buyers of the bonds, in turn helping to protect their balance sheets from some of the impact of massive payouts related to a specific risk. From the bond investors' perspective, catastrophe bonds need to pay a sufficient yield premium, or be priced at a sufficient discount, relative to conventional bonds to compensate for the risk of losing their money entirely.

Catastrophe bonds are generally issued via a special purpose vehicle (SPV) or special purpose entities (SPE), both of which are companies created purely for transactions related to the bond issue. These bonds usually achieve ratings of below investment grade, though the rating agencies will consider a range of factors including regulatory considerations and structural issues, as well as the specific risks for which the bond is intended to provide cover for the issuer.

Though insurance companies are the most common issuers of catastrophe bonds, other bodies seeking protection from pre-identified risks can also make use of catastrophe bonds. For example, in 1999 Tokyo Disneyland issued cat bonds to protect itself against the risk of an earthquake (after finding cat bonds more attractive than using conventional insurance). More recently, FIFA (the Fédération Internationale de Football Association) made use of catastrophe bonds to insure itself effectively against the risk that terrorism could force the cancellation of the 2006 World Cup.

ADVANTAGES
- Cat bonds are a kind of insurance securitization which transfer risk from issuers to investors, in return for a premium yield.
- By presenting an alternative to traditional reinsurance, the development of cat bonds has forced re-insurers to become more competitive with pricing.
- These bonds can present opportunities for fixed income managers to gain a yield pickup, in return for a theoretically low risk of income and capital loss.
- Cat bonds can provide excellent diversification opportunities for bond portfolios, given that cat bonds insurance risk categorization shows little or no correlation with either equities or conventional bonds.

DISADVANTAGES
- Catastrophe bonds are available only to institutional investors.
- The market in cat bonds generally suffers from lower levels of liquidity relative to mainstream bonds.
- The dramatic recent growth in the catastrophe bond market has in turn spurred the launch of some new insurance-related businesses which could potentially undermine the long-term growth prospects of the cat bond market.

ACTION CHECKLIST
✓ Investors in cat bonds need to recognize that the higher returns associated with these securities come with the risk—albeit small—of losing all their money.

✓ Potential issuers of catastrophe bonds should first explore whether conventional insurance services would better meet their requirements.

✓ It is important to understand that the pricing of cat bonds is primarily related to prevailing insurance market prices and the perceived risk of the specified catastrophic loss, rather than to conventional bond pricing considerations such as inflationary or credit-quality risks.

DOS AND DON'TS
DO
- Recognize that the structure of catastrophe bonds may vary considerably between different legal jurisdictions.
- Appreciate that some cat bonds may suffer from liquidity issues.

Approaches to Enterprise Risk Management

DON'T
- Don't ignore the availability of objective, independent research to help assess specific risks related to particular catastrophe bonds. A number of independent organizations exist with specific expertise in peril modeling.
- Don't invest without understanding the product. The catastrophe bond market globally has grown rapidly since the Hurricane Katrina disaster. Given the increasing sophistication of the market, professional asset managers should not invest in catastrophe bonds before seeking expert legal and insurance-related advice as to the suitability of these highly specialized securities for inclusion in their portfolios.

MORE INFO

Books:
Grossi, Patricia, and Howard Kunreuther. *Catastrophe Modeling: A New Approach to Managing Risk.* New York: Springer, 2005.
Thau, Annette. *The Bond Book.* New York: McGraw-Hill, 2000.

Articles:
Moyer, Liz. "Catastrophe bonds." *Forbes* (August 31, 2005). Online at: www.forbes.com/2005/08/31/hurricane-catastrophe-bonds-cx_lm_0831catbonds.html
Wickham, Chris. "New catastrophe bonds on hold pending reinsurance market hardening." *Insurance Journal* (November 24, 2008). Online at: www.insurancejournal.com/news/national/2008/11/24/95752.htm

Websites:
American Insurance Association: www.aiadc.org
Milken Institute: www.milkeninstitute.org (search for "catastrophe bonds").

Directors' and Officers' (D&O) Liability Insurance

DEFINITION
Directors' and Officers' (D&O) insurance provides financial security for the directors and officers of a business in the event that they are sued because of their performance or actions undertaken in the course of their duties as they relate to the company.

This type of insurance is sometimes confused with errors and omissions liability insurance. Errors and omissions liability is concerned with performance failures and negligence with respect to products and services and not the performance or duties of management.

D&O insurance normally incorporates employment practices liability and sometimes fiduciary liability. This includes cover against harassment and discrimination suits, which is where there is the most risk. In the United States, employment practice suits comprise the single largest area of claim activity under D&O policies—more than 50% of D&O claims are related to employment practices.

Businesses should have D&O insurance to protect directors and officers against antitrust or unfair trade practice allegations made by stockholders, employees, clients, regulators, and competitors.

Since a director or officer can be held personally responsible for the acts of the company, most directors and officers will stipulate that they are to be protected. If they were not, their own assets would be at risk.

Banks, investors, and venture capitalists will also demand that businesses have D&O insurance as part of their conditions for funding a company.

A common misconception about D&O insurance is that it allows directors or officers to operate in areas, or be employed in acts, that they know to be incorrect. Intentional actions are not covered by D&O insurance.

Due to recent bank failures (for example, Lehman Brothers), banks and other financial institutions that are facing operational or financial challenges are now finding it difficult to obtain D&O insurance.

ADVANTAGES
- The cost of defending lawsuits might exceed the net worth of most private companies and, therefore, judgments can be financially crippling.
- D&O insurance protects the company's assets, as well as those of the company's directors and officers.
- Conflicts of interest may exist, due to the complexity of responsibilities, and companies may have a difficult time attracting qualified individuals to their boards without D&O coverage.
- Banks, investors, and venture capitalists are more willing to fund businesses that have D&O insurance.

DISADVANTAGES
- Premiums can be high, depending on the industry and the size of the risk.
- It is impossible for insurance to cover all eventualities.

ACTION CHECKLIST
✓ Analyze the risks your business may be facing, their probability, and their likely impact.

✓ Consider how existing D&O policies insure against multiple minor claims as well as more significant/catastrophic single incidents. Examine whether any particular exclusion clauses could leave your business exposed to risks you thought were covered.

✓ Try to quantify in financial terms how falling foul of various risks could affect your business. Only once an actual liability figure is available can you expect an insurance supplier to be able to provide a D&O quotation to cover that risk.

✓ Be prepared to seek the advice of specialist risk consultants. The field of commercial insurance can be far more complex than its consumer equivalent, and risk consultants can help companies to understand and evaluate both risks and potential solutions. Industry-specific experts from specialist risk-management companies can help you to devise customized solutions to protect against potential D&O liabilities.

Approaches to Enterprise Risk Management

DOS AND DON'TS

DO
- Update risk-assessment frameworks regularly, to help keep management informed of the constantly changing business environment and its hazards.

DON'T
- Don't make the mistake of basing a decision purely on price. D&O insurance is a highly complex area and insurance solutions are many and varied.

MORE INFO

Books:
Hoffman, D. G. *Managing Operational Risk: 20 Firmwide Best Practice Strategies*. Hoboken, NJ: Wiley, 2002.
Mathias, J. H., et al. *Directors and Officers Liability: Prevention, Insurance, and Indemnification*. Looseleaf ed. New York: Law Journal Press, 2000.
O'Leary, M., and American Bar Association. *Directors and Officers Liability Insurance Deskbook*. 2nd ed. Chicago, IL: American Bar Association, 2007.

Articles:
Engen, J. R. "Rising cost of liability protection." *Bank Director* (2nd Quarter, 2008). Online at: www.bankdirector.com/issues/articles.pl?article_id=11947.
Read, M. J. "Resting insured." *Community Banker* (August 1, 2008). Online at: www.highbeam.com/doc/1P3-1545226651.html.

Websites:
American Insurance Association (AIA): www.aiadc.org
Association of British Insurers (ABI): www.abi.org.uk

Hedging Credit Risk—Case Study and Strategies

DEFINITION
Credit risk is the uncertainty about the ability of a debtor or the counterparty in an agreement to make a payment. Strategies for managing credit risk use traditional credit analysis techniques to screen counterparties and may also take advantage of hedging via derivatives.

Corporations frequently need to estimate the likelihood of defaults, the exposure, and the severity of loss from a default event. Taking into account these factors and market-based inputs, it is possible to estimate both expected and unexpected losses across a portfolio.

Expected credit losses can be statistically estimated over a period of time. Risk-adjusted credit loss provisions can then be set and factored into pricing as part of the normal cost of doing business. Unexpected losses form the basis for the credit risk capital-allocation process.

INSTRUMENTS
There are three main structures of derivatives that enable an organization to manage credit risks more effectively.

With a credit default swap (CDS), a buyer purchases a contract and makes regular payments to a seller of credit protection. In the event of a default, the buyer receives compensation from the seller. This is commonly seen as an insurance policy for the buyer. It can, however, be used speculatively as there is no requirement for the buyer to hold any asset or have any potentially loss-making relationship with the so-called "reference entity."

Total return swaps are similar to interest rate swaps. One side makes payments based on the total return from an asset. The other makes floating or fixed payments. The notional amount of the underlying asset is the same for both parties.

A credit linked note (CLN) covers a specific credit risk. Investors receive a higher yield in return for accepting risk relating to a specific event. It provides a hedge for borrowers against an explicit risk. A CLN is created through a trust using very low-risk securities as collateral. Investors are paid a floating or fixed rate throughout the period of the note. At its completion they will either receive par or, if the reference entity has defaulted, the recovery rate value of the note.

ADVANTAGES
- Derivatives such as a CDS will reduce or entirely remove the risk of default.

DISADVANTAGES
- The cost of hedging will reduce the return on investment.

CASE STUDY
Credit Default Swap
Although swaps can be used to hedge against any sort of credit risk, they are easiest to explain through a notional case study of an instrument such as a bond. A fund may, for example, hold $8,000,000 of Mega Car Company's five-year bond, and is concerned about the possibility of default due to market conditions arising from rising oil prices, increased government regulation on emissions, or the macroeconomic climate.

The fund decides to buy a credit default swap in a notional amount of $8,000,000 to cover the potential default value. The CDS in this case trades at 150 basis points, so the fund will pay 1.5% of $8,000,000, or $120,000 annually.

If Mega Car Company does not default, the fund will simply receive the full $8,000,000. In this case its return will not be as good as it would have been without the CDS.

On the other hand, if the corporation does default after, say, two years, the fund will receive its $8,000,000 from the seller of the CDS. It could be that the seller will take the bond or pay the difference between the recovery value and the par value of the bond.

Alternatively, Mega Car Company could make a breakthrough in low-emission technology and dramatically improve its credit profile. In that case the fund might decide to reduce its outgoings by selling the remaining period of the CDS.

Approaches to Enterprise Risk Management

MORE INFO
Books:
Chacko, George, Anders Sjöman, Hideto Motohashi, and Vincent Dessain. *Credit Derivatives: A Primer on Credit Risk, Modeling, and Instruments.* Upper Saddle River, NJ: Wharton School Publishing, 2006.
Colquitt, Joetta. *Credit Risk Management: How to Avoid Lending Disasters and Maximize Earnings.* New York: McGraw-Hill, 2007.
de Servigny, Arnaud, and Olivier Renault. *The Standard & Poor's Guide to Measuring and Managing Credit Risk.* New York: McGraw-Hill, 2004.

Hedging Foreign Exchange Risk—Case Studies and Strategies

DEFINITION
A company that imports raw materials, exports finished goods, or has overseas assets or subsidiaries is exposed to fluctuations in exchange rates. Adverse movements can wipe out export profits, while positive changes can increase the price of its products in the foreign market. Equally, the company could benefit from windfall profits as a result of exchange rate fluctuations.

A company trading across national borders therefore has a number of choices. It can take a chance with spot rates, buying currency when required. This leaves it totally at the mercy of exchange rates. The risk can be removed if it books a forward exchange contract that fixes the rate for the date on which it will be needed for a transaction. If the rate improves, however, the company will not be able to take advantage of the improvement.

Using a combination of flexible products allows the company to protect itself against adverse movements while still giving it the ability to profit from improvements. A wide variety of instruments are available that allow companies to pursue this strategy. Which is chosen depends partly on the level of risk and also on the ease of converting the currencies.

OTHER HEDGING PRODUCTS
There are many other ways for companies to hedge against currency variations using derivatives. Currency markets are extremely volatile, and it makes sense for any organization trading across national borders to protect itself from these fluctuations.

CASE STUDIES
The Participating Forward
This product is similar to a forward exchange contract in that it limits risk by offering a worst-case exchange rate for a transaction. If, however, there is a favorable move in exchange rates, the company can take advantage—generally with half its currency. There is usually no premium payable for this product.

Example
A company imports Cava wine from Spain to the United Kingdom. It is April, and a supplier has to be paid €4 million in October in time to catch the Christmas market.

The forward rate is 1.2100, and the company wants the certainty of a worst-case rate but doesn't want to lose out if the rate goes up. The foreign exchange broker offers a rate of 1.1800, with the option to buy half the currency on the spot market two days before completion of the transaction.

Possible Outcomes
Sterling strengthens against the euro and the rate rises to 1.2500. The customer pays £1,694,915 for the first €2,000,000 at the low rate agreed in advance and £1,600,000 for the second €2,000,000 at the spot rate. The average rate is therefore 1.215, slightly better than the forward rate, but not as good as the spot rate.

Alternatively, the euro strengthens against sterling and the spot rate is 1.1600. The company then pays the rate of 1.1800 for the whole transaction.

The advantages of a participating forward are: a guaranteed worst-case rate; total protection against currency falls; a partial benefit from currency gains; and no premium. The disadvantages are: if the currency weakens the rate will not be as good as a forward exchange contract; and the spot rate will be better if there is a positive move in currency.

(*Continued overleaf*)

Approaches to Enterprise Risk Management

The Protection Option
With this service a company pays a premium for an option to exchange currency on a fixed forward date at a predetermined rate. If the spot rate on that date is better than the predetermined rate, the company can decide not to exercise its option to sell at the predetermined rate.

Example
A UK company is selling dresses to a customer in the United States. In six months it will receive $4,000,000. The current forward rate for this date is 2.0000. Fearing that sterling is going to strengthen against the dollar, the company opts to buy a protection option at the forward rate.

Possible Outcomes
Sterling does strengthen against the dollar, taking the rate to 2.1500. The company then exercises its right to sell dollars at 2.0000.

The dollar strengthens against sterling. The rate is now 1.8500. The company takes the better rate on the spot market.

The advantages of the protection option are: a guaranteed worst-case rate; total protection against negative currency fluctuations; and the ability to take full advantage of positive currency movements. The disadvantage is that a premium is payable to the foreign exchange trader.

Hedging Interest Rate Risk—Case Study and Strategies

DEFINITION
Risks arise from the way the value of an investment changes with the level of interest rates. This is most clearly seen in the value of fixed-rate investments such as bonds. If interest rates rise, the opportunity cost from holding the bond falls as it becomes more advantageous to switch to other investments.

Alternatively, a company with a loan at a variable rate of interest may want to adapt its payments to avoid the risk arising from a rise in interest rates. It may also want to aid its financial planning by creating a more even pattern of repayment.

A number of instruments exist to hedge against the risks posed by changing interest rates. For a company that decides to reduce its exposure to rising interest rates associated with variable rate funding, there are two main types of derivative.

A cap will ensure that the company does not have to find more than a maximum agreed level of interest. The company will benefit if interest rate levels stay below that level. A cap is paid for up-front. A variation on this instrument is the cap and collar, whereby the company will pay the seller of the product if interest rates fall below an agreed level.

Swaps allow the company to exchange variable-rate payments for a guaranteed fixed rate. Swaps do not generally require any advance payment to the seller.

There are a huge variety of swap instruments, reflecting the international nature of the debt market. For instance, although there would be no advantage in swapping a fixed rate for another fixed rate within the same currency, as the outcome would be known, it may be desirable to swap fixed rates between two currencies. Every variable of currency, floating, and fixed exchange rate can be swapped.

ADVANTAGES
- A swap is flexible, allowing a company to adjust its maturity, payment frequency, and principal to suit its ongoing financial arrangements.
- Interest rates can be managed independently of financing arrangements.
- There is no requirement for a payment up-front.

DISADVANTAGES
- The arrangement locks the company into a fixed rate that may not be advantageous.
- Early termination may incur a cost.
- There is a slight additional risk of failure from involving an additional financial institution in the swap arrangement.

CASE STUDY
Vanilla Interest Rate Swap
A company enters into a vanilla interest rate swap with a bank to reduce the risk from fluctuations on a $10 million loan it has taken out on a floating rate. The bank agrees to a fixed rate of, for example, 6% over five years, while the floating rates are based on the six-monthly Libor (London Interbank Borrowing Rate) plus 2%. If the Libor is 4% at the start of the agreement, the amount payable is 6% in both cases, although any percentage could be agreed.

If the Libor rises to 6%, the amount payable every six months would be 8% of $10 million divided by two, or $400,000. The company's agreement with the bank is for a rate of 6%, or a payment of $300,000 in this case. The company will receive the difference of $100,000 from the bank.

The amount of the loan does not change hands and the company may continue to make the variable payments. It will receive cash if interest rates rise, and pay the bank if they fall. The net effect on the company is the same as if it had taken out a fixed-rate loan. Although the obvious route would be for a company to take out a fixed-rate loan, initially this may not be available or it may be too expensive.

Moreover, because the amount of the swap is notional, it is not necessary for the company to match the whole amount of the loan or to ensure that its entire life is covered. There may well be occasions when risk managers expect interest rate rises over the short to medium term. Continuing with a swap arrangement after the rises have peaked could wipe out initial gains.

Approaches to Enterprise Risk Management

MORE INFO
Book:
Coyle, Brian. *Interest-Rate Swaps*. London: Financial World Publishing, 2004.

Hedging Liquidity Risk—Case Study and Strategies

DEFINITION
The concept of "liquidity risk" tends to be very loosely defined. It is used most commonly with reference to the banking and finance industry, but it is an important issue for all companies. Broadly, liquidity risk is the danger that it will be difficult or impossible for an organization to sell an asset in order to provide capital to meet short-term financial demands.

A company needs to remain solvent; the liquidity risk is in the secondary market for its assets, which may not be sellable in time to meet short-term financial commitments, or will be sold at a price considerably below the perceived current market value. The problem may arise as the result of a liquidity gap or mismatch. This means that the dates for inflow and outflow of funds do not match up, creating a shortage.

Systemic liquidity risks arise from external factors. National or international recessions and credit crunches have the largest general impact on liquidity. Capital market disruptions, however, are more common. The collapse of the Russian ruble in 1998, for instance, created a global liquidity crisis, with a capital flight to quality away from the highly speculative Russian stock market.

Generally, liquidity is abundant during times when the economy is booming. During a downturn the impact on companies may increase if they continue with strategies based on the assumption that the high liquidity will continue indefinitely.

STRATEGIES
Threats to a company's liquidity seldom happen in isolation but are intertwined with other financial risks. If, for example, a company fails to receive a payment, it may be forced to raise cash elsewhere or default on its payments. In this scenario, credit risk and liquidity risk are linked.

The aim of a liquidity management strategy is to minimize the cost of capital, allowing efficient access to capital and money markets at competitive prices during times of "normal" activity. Concurrently, the strategy should provide high levels of liquidity during periods when the financial markets are impaired.

The latter part of the strategy is often described as "life insurance." At a simple level this can mean organizing lines of credit well in advance of market turmoil, which is the cheapest option. However, the activities of a company and the market it operates in are dynamic. There will be periods when it is cash-rich and others when it is cash-poor. As cash is the ultimate liquid asset, there will be periods when it can "self-insure" and times when it will need to approach an external source for insurance.

CASE STUDY
A company has outgoings of $8,000,000 a month against income from sales of $10,000,000. It faces a number of threats to its liquidity: for example, the price of the commodity it sells has fallen by 25%, leaving its income at $7,500,000 against $8,000,000 outgoings, and it has to find a way to raise the additional $500,000.

Some major customers have axed or cut their orders, leaving the company with a surplus of products to sell on the market. It has lost $4,000,000 in "normal" monthly sales and now has to offload products it is forced to sell, below cost, at 50% of the expected price simply to pay its bills ($6,000,000 in expected sales plus $2,000,000 to meet monthly obligations of $8,000,000).

The company chose to secure its position and iron out liquidity problems in the following ways:
- It held cash to cover some of the shortfall, but it lost the potential income from this capital.
- It set up a line of credit with its bank to help cover the shortfall.
- It sold off some assets in order to meet its financial obligations. This is risky as assets that have to be sold in a hurry may not realize their book price.

All this assumes that the company assessed its liquidity risks accurately and market conditions did not change.

Approaches to Enterprise Risk Management

ACTION CHECKLIST
- ✓ Examine predicted cash flows for the company. Look for any major negatives. Their impact can be stress-tested by analyzing the effect of a default by the major parties.
- ✓ Ensure that inflows and outflows match as far as possible.
- ✓ Assess the risk profile of the company before deciding what measures to put in place. In general liquid assets have a lower rate of return.
- ✓ Start a process of scenario testing. What happens if there is a default within an income stream?
- ✓ Ensure that the impacts of rare events are tested too. They may be unusual in isolation, but the more there are, statistically the higher is the probability that one will occur.

MORE INFO
Book:
Coyle, Brian. *Cash Flow Forecasting & Liquidity*. Risk Management Series: Cash Flow Management. London: Financial World Publishing, 2004.

Identifying and Managing Exposure to Interest and Exchange Rate Risks

DEFINITION
The successful management of a portfolio includes maximizing returns from shifts in exchange and interest rates, which in turn requires an appreciation of the associated exposures. Not knowing the exposure can leave the portfolio open to significant risk.

Exchange rate risk is the risk arising from a change in the price of one currency against another. Companies or institutions that trade internationally are exposed to exchange rate risk if they do not hedge their positions. There are two main risks associated with exposure to exchange rates.
- Transaction risk arises because exchange rates may change unfavorably over time. The best protection is to use forward currency contracts to hedge against such changes.
- Translation risk concerns the accounts, and the level of risk is proportional to the amount of assets held in foreign currencies. Over a period of time, changes in exchange rates will cause the accounts to become inaccurate. To avoid this, assets need to be offset by borrowings in the affected currency.

The significance of the exposure will depend on the portfolio's weightings and operations. Identifying the level of risk in the above exposures should help with selecting a suitable defense strategy.

Interest rate risk relates to changes in the floating rate. Failure to understand exposure to interest rates can lead to substantial risk. The two main areas of concern here should be borrowings and cash investments. The best way of appreciating exposure to changing interest rates is to stress-test various scenarios. How, for example, would a change in rate from 4% to 6% affect your ability to borrow?

MITIGATING THE RISK
Exchange Rate Exposure
Other than the two strategies mentioned above, good strategies for minimizing exchange rate exposure involve employing one or more of the following products.
- **Spot foreign exchange**: An obligation to buy/sell a specified quantity of currency at the current market rate to be settled in two business days.
- **Structured forwards**: Exchange forwards embedded with, generally, more than one currency option. This adaptation allows a more effective hedge and should improve the exchange rate within the client's perception of the market.
- **Currency options**: An option to the right to buy/sell a certain amount of currency at a specific exchange rate on or before a specific future date.

Interest Rate Exposure
Once identified, the risks can be minimized using the following methods:
- **Interest rate swap**: A method for changing the interest rate you earn/pay on an agreed amount for a specified time period.
- **Cross-currency swap**: An exchange of principal and interest payments in separate currencies.
- **Forward rate agreement**: Two parties fix the interest rate that will apply to a loan or deposit.
- **Interest rate caps**: The seller and borrower agree to limit the borrower's floating interest rate to a specified level for a period of time.
- **Structured swap**: An interest rate/cross-currency swap embedded with one or more derivatives. This allows the client to minimize exposure on their perception of the market.

ADVANTAGES
- The one key advantage to identifying exposure to interest and exchange rate fluctuations is the ability to minimize possible losses in the event that your view of the market is wrong. This approach will also minimize the chance of unexpected events disrupting the investment strategy.

DISADVANTAGES
- As with any hedge strategy, minimizing possible losses also reduces potential gains. Only those who are supremely confident in their forecasts and with a cushion to absorb losses should consider taking any extra risk to maximize returns.

Approaches to Enterprise Risk Management

ACTION CHECKLIST
✓ Plan your approach. Establish what your aims are when dealing with exchange rates/foreign currencies. Decide on your strategies for dealing with interest rate exposure. Create risk registers that set out clear procedures for dealing with risks as they arise.

✓ Calculate what losses you can afford, or what profits you need to make, and stick to them.

DOS AND DON'TS
DO
- Set realistic targets.
- Stick to your strategy.
- Research best strategy and implementation.

DON'T
- Don't be overoptimistic.
- Don't alter your strategy midway.
- Don't expose yourself to excessive risk.

MORE INFO
Books:
Fornés, Gastón. *Foreign Exchange Exposure in Emerging Markets: How Companies Can Minimize It.* Basingstoke, UK: Palgrave Macmillan, 2009.
Friberg, Richard. *Exchange Rates and the Firm: Strategies to Manage Exposure and the Impact of EMU.* Basingstoke, UK: Macmillan, 1999.

Identifying Weak Points in Your Liquidity

DEFINITION
The liquidity of an asset is the degree to which it, or a security, can be traded on the market without affecting its price, and how quickly this can be done. Another way of looking at liquidity is to determine how quickly an asset can be converted into cash.

Liquidity became a much-discussed topic during the so-called credit crunch in 2007–08. Following the subprime crisis that started in the United States in 2007, banks all over the world suddenly found themselves unable to borrow money from each other as trust ran out and questions were raised over banks' creditworthiness. This meant that banks had to rely on their own sources of funding, and those with a lack of liquidity suffered. Those that were unable to turn their assets into cash had problems trading.

As a result of the credit crunch, banks had to put new measures in place to identify the weak points in their liquidity. There are companies specializing in liquidity risk management that can help firms to understand and manage their liquidity. A liquidity health check generally involves undertaking a review of processes, systems, and financial reports throughout the company.

When markets are in good health, liquidity is not generally a problem. Liquidity issues tend to become exposed during an economic downturn or recession, even though the origins of these problems can often be traced back to more favorable economic times. In a report entitled "Liquidity management and supervisory challenges" published in 2008, the Basel Committee on Banking Supervision concluded that many banks had previously overlooked some of the basic principles of liquidity management during periods of high liquidity. The report highlighted that many banks' failure to adequately consider the liquidity they could need to meet contingent liabilities during periods of market stress had contributed to the subsequent banking industry crisis.

Having liquidity means having the ability to meet obligations as they become due. Liquidity is crucial to the viability, and credibility, of any bank. Given that practically every financial transaction or commitment has some impact on a company's liquidity, either at the present or at some stage in the future, sound liquidity is vital. Effective liquidity management should ensure that companies are able to satisfy their cash flow obligations. In the case of financial institutions, this is of paramount importance given the increasing globalization of the banking system, as a liquidity failing in even one institution—or even the perception of a shortfall among market participants—can have serious consequences for the entire global banking system. Even a whiff of a rumor of illiquidity can be enough to trigger a run on a bank—for example, the run on Northern Rock in the United Kingdom in 2007. A liquidity shortfall at a single organization can have systemic repercussions, as the credit crunch of 2007–08 showed. That is why managing liquidity is one of the most important activities for banks to perform well.

ADVANTAGES
Identifying weak points in your liquidity is important because:
- it will enable you to manage your assets better during difficult financial periods as well as during good ones;
- it will ensure that you (as an individual or an organization) have a diverse portfolio of assets and investments that will cover more risk scenarios.

DISADVANTAGES
- The effort involved in identifying weak points in your liquidity may seem superfluous in good times.
- It requires expenditure to create and set up the necessary processes for liquidity management.

ACTION CHECKLIST
✓ Analyze your cash flow-based liquidity gap.

✓ Carry out scenario-based analyses.

✓ Perform liability modeling and stress-testing.

✓ Implement a liquidity policy that will identify methods, processes, and responsibilities.

DOS AND DON'TS
DO
- Analyze your liquidity provision.
- Diversify your funds.
- Implement regular liquidity status reporting.
- Consider planning for a contingency fund.
- Make sure your reporting system is accurate, informative, regular, comprehensive, and realistic.
- Conduct stress-testing to help to uncover potential liquidity shortfalls in "worst case" scenarios.

Approaches to Enterprise Risk Management

DON'T
- Don't ignore liquidity when times are good.
- Don't maintain a large number of illiquid assets.
- Don't go too far the other way and turn all your prime assets into cash.

MORE INFO

Books:
Coyle, Brian. *Cash Flow Forecasting & Liquidity*. Risk Management Series: Cash Flow Management. London: Financial World Publishing, 2004.
Matz, Leonard, and Peter Neu (eds). *Liquidity Risk Measurement and Management: A Practitioner's Guide to Global Best Practices*. Singapore: Wiley, 2006.

Reports:
Working Group on Liquidity, Basel Committee on Banking Supervision. "Liquidity risk: Management and supervisory challenges." February 2008. Online at: www.bis.org/publ/bcbs136.htm
Working Group on Liquidity, Basel Committee on Banking Supervision. "Principles for sound liquidity risk management and supervision." September 2008. Online at: www.bis.org/publ/bcbs144.htm

Website:
Cash and liquidity management articles from the Association of Corporate Treasurers: www.treasurers.org/Cash+and+Liquidity+Management

Insuring Against Financial Loss

DEFINITION
Every business faces a unique combination of exposures. The overall impact of an incident can reach far beyond the immediate damage to property and be far more expensive and harmful to the company than the original loss.

Policies covering these areas are often grouped together as "miscellaneous financial loss" or "contingency" insurance. A combination of policies may be required to cover these consequential losses in tandem with a business continuity plan. It will be necessary for the company to weigh up the risks from self-insuring (i.e. having an emergency fund for such contingencies) or buying cover from an insurer.

CHECKLIST OF FINANCIAL RISKS THAT CAN BE COVERED

Weather
Some types of business, particularly in the construction, leisure, and agricultural sectors, may be adversely affected by unfavorable weather conditions.

Business Interruption
Interruption insurance can fill the gaps in existing policies. It can cover both the continuing and emergency costs faced by the business along with loss of income arising from an enforced shutdown.

Breakdown of Machinery
The failure of specialist machinery can lead to losses considerably greater than the cost of repair if it affects the output of the business.

Credit Insurance
Domestic and export credit risks can be covered through a commercial risks policy. This provides protection against events such as a customer becoming insolvent or defaulting on payment for a prolonged period, or a political event delaying or preventing payment.

Crime
A company can be covered against third party theft, employee dishonesty, forgery, copyright theft, and so on. Particular attention should be paid to ensuring that it is not only forced entry that is included in the policy as a larger proportion of crime is committed by insiders than by third parties.

Theft and Personal Injury
Robbery, attempted robbery, and injuries resulting from these crimes can be covered whether they occur on a company's premises, in or out of working hours, or when cash is being transported from a bank safe or from a company strong room.

Key Man Insurance
Many businesses are reliant on particular individuals. Key man cover protects against losses arising from their death or long-term illness. The types of loss that may be included are profits, the cost of hiring a replacement, and the delay before the replacement starts to make a contribution to profits.

Kidnap, Ransom, and Extortion
This type of cover is particularly relevant to companies operating in certain high-risk territories. Companies are often less than transparent about policies that include ransom insurance for fear that it will be seen to encourage kidnapping and extortion.

License Loss
Establishments such as bars, restaurants, hotels, clubs, and casinos are vulnerable to loss of license. Cover may be available against this eventuality.

Cyber Insurance
In recent years there has been an increasing risk arising from so-called "cyber crime." This includes damage from hack attacks, viruses, and defamation. These can all have an effect on profits, as well costing money to resolve and potentially causing damage to third parties.

Single Project Insurance
Sometimes a company faces a specific collection of risks arising from a single major project. A construction company, for example, that wins a government contract may face a combination of public liability, funding, and penalty risks—cover against which may be rolled into a single, limited-time policy for the duration of the project.

ADVANTAGES
- It is possible to insure against almost every eventuality and business risk.

DISADVANTAGES
- The cost of such cover would be prohibitive. A risk profile should be drawn up to analyze which areas of the balance sheet it is cost-effective and appropriate to insure.

Approaches to Enterprise Risk Management

MORE INFO
Books:
Gaughan, Patrick A. *Measuring Business Interruption Losses and Other Commercial Damages*. Hoboken, NJ: Wiley, 2003.
Hoffman, Philip T., Gilles Postel-Vinay, and Jean-Laurent Rosenthal. *Surviving Large Losses: Financial Crises, the Middle Class, and the Development of Capital Markets*. Cambridge, MA: Belknap Press, 2007.

Methods for Dealing with Inflation Risk

DEFINITION
Inflation risk can be defined as the risk that the value of physical or financial assets will be eroded by inflation. To protect against that loss, investment managers need to employ one or more of several tried and tested methods.

Investors generally choose investments that offer "insurance" against inflation risk. However, it is important to remember that the overall risk of an investment comes from all risk sources, not just the risk of inflation.

Inflation hedging, which takes into account the co-movements of inflation rates and asset returns from period to period, is one of the most commonly used methods for managing inflation risk. The less influence the rate of inflation has on the real return of an investment, the more effective the inflation hedge will be for the investment. Popular hedges against inflation include property, equities, or commodities that generally have a rising value. Studies of periods of high inflation in the 1970s and 1980s show that, in the midterm, earnings and the dividend growth rates of equities at least kept pace with inflation.

A popular method for managing inflation risk is the use of inflation protection, which examines the inflation risk of an asset and assesses whether that asset's real return will be lower than a specific target return (such as zero) at the end of a determined investment period. One downside to using this risk metric is that it only takes into consideration the probability of negative deviations from the target return, but not the amount of them.

The third main method is the inflation swap. Here, the swap involves the use of inflation derivatives (or inflation-indexed derivatives) to transfer inflation risk from one party to another and protect against future liabilities. The derivatives used may be over-the-counter or exchange-traded derivatives.

ADVANTAGES
- Taking practical steps to deal with inflation risk minimizes both the possibility of real losses and of losses themselves should they occur.

DISADVANTAGES
- There is no guarantee that any methods used will protect completely against inflation, and there will always be a degree of risk. The real return of an investment is always uncertain, even for safe assets such as default-free zero-coupon bonds that have a maturity equal to the length of the investment period, even though the nominal cash flow is guaranteed.

ACTION CHECKLIST
✓ Check that the dividend yields and payout ratios of your chosen method are suitably high and at least in line with inflation.

✓ Assess each method thoroughly to determine which is likely to give your assets the best protection against inflation.

✓ Run full risk management scenarios that take into account all risks, not just inflation.

DOS AND DON'TS
DO
- Take into account all risk factors, not just the risk of inflation.
- Calculate the probability and amount of any shortfall when making inflation-proof investment decisions.
- Review your decisions if the global economy starts shifting unexpectedly, as you may need to adjust your portfolio for the best protection.

DON'T
- Don't assume that traditionally inflation-proof investments such as property are a safe haven. For example, during the credit crunch of 2007–08, the real value of both property and equities fell steeply while inflation rose sharply.

Approaches to Enterprise Risk Management

MORE INFO

Books:

Baumol, William J., and Alan S. Blinder. *Macroeconomics: Principles and Policy*. 11th ed. Cincinnati, OH: South-Western College Publishing, 2008.

Brice, Benaben (ed). *Inflation-linked Products: A Guide for Investors and Asset & Liability Managers*. London: Risk Books, 2005.

Brigo, Damiano, and Fabio Mercurio. *Interest Rate Models—Theory and Practice, with Smile, Inflation and Credit*. 2nd ed. Berlin: Springer-Verlag, 2007.

Deacon, Mark, Andrew Derry, and Dariush Mirfendereski. *Inflation-indexed Securities: Bonds, Swaps & Other Derivatives*. 2nd ed. Chichester, UK: Wiley, 2004.

Mishkin, Frederic S. *The Economics of Money, Banking, and Financial Markets*. 8th ed. Boston, MA: Addison-Wesley, 2006.

Walmsley, Julian. *The Foreign Exchange and Money Markets Guide*. 2nd ed. New York: Wiley, 2000.

Article:

Federal Reserve Bank of Boston. "Understanding inflation and the implications for monetary policy: A Phillips curve retrospective." 53rd Economic Conference, June 9–11, 2008, Chatham, MA. Presentations online at: www.bos.frb.org/phillips2008

Stress-Testing to Evaluate Insurance Cover

DEFINITION
Stress-testing aims to determine how well systems and procedures perform when subjected to a wide range of operational conditions. It is frequently employed to help assess performance during extreme or unexpected conditions. During stress-testing, a system is subjected either to sudden extreme demands or to gradually higher loads until the point is reached when at least one element of the system stops delivering the desired level of performance. This evaluation helps companies to understand the kind of market conditions under which key elements of their businesses become vulnerable.

Although retail-focused insurance products have become more standardized in recent years, and are increasingly sold via the internet and call centers as consumers focus on price, the commercial insurance industry has retained a high level of complexity. This is largely driven by a broadening of the spectrum of risks faced by businesses in areas such as environmental protection, human resources, product safety, counterparty agreements, and technology. Given the wider range of risks that businesses face, partly as a result of tighter legislation and regulation, ensuring that the appropriate insurance is in place to provide robust protection against unexpected events has never been more important.

ADVANTAGES
- A better understanding of the risks—both systemic and non-systemic—facing a business can help in contingency planning.
- Regular stress-testing can help to keep management vigilant in an environment of constantly changing business risks.
- This type of evaluation can identify multiple, seemingly minor chinks in the armor of a business that cumulatively could have a serious impact.
- What if? analysis can be useful in highlighting event risks that may not otherwise be immediately apparent.
- Robust financial protection can insulate businesses from the risk of a catastrophic event that could otherwise threaten the viability of the entity.

DISADVANTAGES
- Protracted evaluation over extended periods of time could divert key resources away from core business activities, potentially resulting in the business overlooking valuable opportunities.
- Extended periods of evaluation run the risk of "paralysis through analysis." Understanding the shortcomings of available options can be beneficial, but, taken to an extreme, it could be counterproductive.
- Under some circumstances, stress-testing may even run the risk of effectively encouraging risky practices by creating a false sense of control.

ACTION CHECKLIST
✓ Encourage an environment of openness about the kinds of risk facing the business. Some risks are obvious, but more covert risks are sometimes known only to the managers of individual business units.

✓ Involve key business stakeholders in the evaluation of risks and alternative ways to protect against them.

✓ Consider how existing policies insure against multiple minor claims as well as more significant/catastrophic single incidents. Examine whether particular exclusion clauses could leave your business exposed to risks that you thought were covered.

✓ Do try to quantify in financial terms how falling foul of various risks could affect your business. Only once an actual liability figure is available can you expect an insurance provider to be able to provide a quotation to cover that risk.

✓ Be prepared to seek the advice of specialist insurance providers. The field of commercial insurance can be immensely more complex than its consumer equivalent, and risk consultants can help companies to understand and evaluate both risks and potential solutions. Industry-specific experts from specialist risk-management companies can help to devise customized solutions to protect against potential liabilities.

Approaches to Enterprise Risk Management

DOS AND DON'TS

DO
- Remember that emerging risks necessitate regular reviews of the way you protect your business.
- Involve key stakeholders in the evaluation of both risks and potential solutions.
- Consider seeking the help of specialist consultants.

DON'T
- Don't make the mistake of basing a decision purely on price. Commercial insurance is a highly complex field and insurance solutions are many and varied.
- Don't fall into the trap of thinking that insurance can cover absolutely every conceivable risk your business could face.
- Don't see the right insurance for your company as simply another expense. Securing the appropriate protection for your business can help you concentrate on doing what you do best.

MORE INFO

Book:
Overbeck, Ludger, and Gerrit Jan van den Brink. *Integrated Stress Testing for Financial Institutions*. London: Palgrave Macmillan, 2009.

Article:
Hilbers, Paul, and Matthew T. Jones. "What If...?" *Finance & Development* 41:4 (December 2004).

Websites:
Risk consultancy and management companies: Willis: www.willis.com; Watson Wyatt: www.watsonwyatt.com
Society of Actuaries (includes downloadable pdf on "Effective stress testing" from presentation by Mark Chaplin, SOA Annual Meeting, Oct 2007): www.soa.org

Understanding and Calculating the Total Cost of Risk

DEFINITION
Risk exists virtually everywhere in business—from the obvious, easily insurable risks such as cover for property assets to more obscure, yet not insignificant, risks such as the loss of key employees to illness. However, in an effort to cover as many bases as possible, some companies channel resources into their risk management operations, potentially raising questions over whether these units are delivering good value for stakeholders in the company.

The total cost of risk (TCOR) is a tool for measuring the overall costs associated with the running of the corporate risk management operation, including all insurance premiums, risk control and financing costs, administrative costs, and any self-retained losses incurred, relative to other key measures such as overall company revenues, total headcount, and its asset base. Over time, TCOR therefore provides a yardstick to assess how a company's risk-related costs are changing relative to the overall growth rate of the business. In turn, management can then explore potential ways to assess how the company's TCOR is changing relative to industry benchmarks, typically with the use of data derived from research—e.g., "physical" risk research conducted by trade groups and industry organizations. Given that the cost considerations are uppermost in the oil distribution business, yet food producers may focus more on liability insurance risks, working with these industry bodies can be the best way to obtain relevant and comparable risk-related cost data.

ADVANTAGES
- Calculating the total cost of risk can help companies to highlight inconsistencies in their approach to risk management.
- The process can also identify areas where the cost of managing a particular risk may be excessive relative to risks elsewhere, potentially leading to reallocation of some elements of the risk management budget.
- By highlighting inefficiencies in the risk management process, TCOR can also generate direct cost savings.

DISADVANTAGES
- Truly comparable TCOR data can be difficult to access, though trade bodies can help. However, prized data on direct competitors—such as a key rival also pushing into a new, high-growth market segment—are plainly sensitive and therefore not generally available.
- TCOR analysis can be mistakenly seen purely as a cost-cutting exercise.

ACTION CHECKLIST
✓ Use a basic framework to break down costs into component categories such as risk financing, risk administration, risk compliance costs, and self-insured losses.

✓ Identify existing costs for each category, expressed as a percentage of overall company revenues.

✓ Use any available data from industry bodies for comparison with your existing TCOR figures in each category.

✓ Consider possible reasons for differences between your company's numbers and industry-wide figures.

✓ Establish targets for each category for future years.

DOS AND DON'TS
DO
- Remember that industry benchmarks may not always be truly comparable with your company in every aspect.
- Consider whether some minor risks could be covered in-house.
- Make use of specialist software to help you arrive at decisions on issues such as risk retention, as risk management budgeting is by nature complex.

DON'T
- Don't ignore the value added by the risk management function when making budgeting decisions. This is a mistake. Risk management should not be seen purely as a cost.
- Don't expect that TCOR analysis will lead to immediate cost savings. This could lead to disappointment. Be prepared to invest in risk management tools which will deliver financial benefits over time.

(Continued overleaf)

Approaches to Enterprise Risk Management

DON'T (cont.)
- Don't see the management of risk-related costs as an issue for which all possible solutions lie within the company. Explaining your objectives and priorities to external risk management specialists and insurance brokers could be very productive.

MORE INFO

Books:
Frenkel, Michael, Ulrich Hommel, Gunter Dufey, and Markus Rudolf. *Risk Management: Challenge and Opportunity*. 2nd ed. Berlin: Springer, 2005.
Merna, Tony, and Thaisal F. Al-Fani. *Corporate Risk Management: An Organisational Perspective*. Chichester, UK: Wiley, 2008.

Articles:
McDonald, Caroline. "Cost of risk hits 10-year low." *National Underwriter Property & Casualty—Risk & Benefits Management* (January 2001).
Tilley, Keith. "Cost versus risk." *Strategic RISK* (November 2004).

Website:
Risk and Insurance Management Society (RIMS): www.rims.org

Understanding and Using Leverage Ratios

DEFINITION
Leveraging is a way to use funds whereby most of the money is raised by borrowing rather than by stock issue (for a company) or use of capital (by an individual). At its most basic, leveraging means taking out a loan so that you can invest the money and hoping your investment makes more money than you will have to pay in interest on the loan.

The leverage ratio is used to calculate the financial leverage of a company. This information gives an insight into the company's financing methods, or it can be used to measure the company's ability to meet its financial obligations. There are a number of different ratios, but the main factors involved are debt, equity, assets, operating income, and interest expenses.

The most commonly used ratio is debt to equity (D/E, or financial leverage), which indicates how much the business relies on debt financing. In normal circumstances the typical D/E ratio is 2:1, with only one-third of the debt in the long term. A high D/E ratio might show up possible difficulty in paying interest and capital while obtaining extra funding. As an example, if a company has $10 million of debt and $20 million of equity, it has a D/E ratio of 0.5 ($10 million/$20 million).

Another leveraging ratio can be used to measure the operating cost mix. This helps to indicate how any change in output may affect operating income. There are two types of operating costs: fixed and variable. The mix of these will differ depending on the company and the industry. A high operating leverage can lead to forecasting risk. For example, a tiny error made in a sales forecast could trigger far bigger errors when it comes to projecting cash flows based on those sales.

There is also interest coverage, which measures a company's margin of safety and indicates how many times the company can make its interest payments. This figure is calculated by dividing earnings prior to interest and taxes by the interest expense.

ADVANTAGES
Leveraging means borrowing money to invest. Anyone who takes out a mortgage is effectively leveraging. By paying a deposit to obtain a loan, you can buy a home that otherwise you would not be able to afford. Although property prices can and do fall periodically, over the long term property usually increases in value. If it does, you can sell the property and make a profit on your original mortgage loan.

Leveraging enables an individual or a company to gain access to larger capital sums to make investments, with the aim of making a profit by doing so.

Strategies in leveraging run from basic to highly sophisticated, and the degree of risk varies in the same way. The benefits of leveraging will depend on your financial situation, your objectives, and your attitude to risk.

DISADVANTAGES
Anything that has the potential to make money involves some risk. Gains can be better than normal; losses can be worse. A change in interest rates can have an effect on your profit too. There is a risk that your investment will not make enough profit to pay off the interest on your loan.

You can mitigate the risks by diversifying your portfolio, thereby guarding against high losses, although this will probably limit opportunities to make spectacular gains. A fixed-rate loan can protect against a rise in interest rates.

ACTION CHECKLIST
✓ Are you comfortable borrowing money that you might struggle to pay back?

✓ Are you comfortable with high risk in your finances?

✓ Are you confident that interest rates will not rise to add further risk to your borrowings?

✓ Are you confident your investment will make more than the interest you have to pay back on your loan?

DOS AND DON'TS
DO
- Look at leveraging as a way of using other people's money (by way of a loan) to make your own investments.
- Understand how your loan works and what and when you will have to pay back.
- As much research as you can. And then more research.

DON'T
- Don't get involved with leveraging if you are uncomfortable with financial risk.
- Don't choose an investment without a full understanding of what you are investing in.

Approaches to Enterprise Risk Management

MORE INFO
Books:
Marr, Bernard. *Strategic Performance Management: Leveraging and Measuring Your Intangible Value Drivers*. Oxford: Butterworth-Heinemann 2006.
Matthäus-Maier, Ingrid, and J. D. von Pischke (eds). *Microfinance Investment Funds: Leveraging Private Capital for Economic Growth and Poverty Reduction*. Berlin: Springer-Verlag, 2006.
Militello, Frederick C., and Michael D. Schwalberg. *Leverage Competencies: What Financial Executives Need to Lead*. Upper Saddle River, NJ: FT Prentice Hall, 2002.

Index

A
A. M. Best ratings *see* Best's ratings
Abkowitz, Mark   **81**
acquisitions *see* mergers and acquisitions (M&A)
asset liability management (ALM)
    total balance sheet approach to financial risk   **95**
auditing
    forensic auditing   **181**
auditing profession
    Sarbanes–Oxley Act 2002 (SOX)   **39**
auditing standards
    Institute of Internal Auditors (IIA)   **27**

B
BCM *see* business continuity management
Beretz, Paul   **139**
Best's ratings
    enterprise risk management (ERM)   **71**
Bowen, R. Brayton   **51**
Bremmer, Ian   **149**
Buncefield Oil Storage Terminal
    case study on business continuity management (BCM)   **85**
business combinations *see* mergers and acquisitions (M&A)
business continuity management (BCM)   **55, 175**
    preparation for disaster   **85**
    stress-testing   **185**
business interruption *see* business continuity management (BCM)

C
CAE *see* chief audit executive
calculations
    total cost of risk (TCOR)   **219**
    total economic capital   **193**
caps
    hedging interest rate risk   **205, 209**
captive insurance companies
    advantages and disadvantages   **195**
Carroll, Terry   **9, 95**
cash flows
    bank lending requirements   **189**
catastrophe bonds   **197**
catastrophic risk
    all-hazards approach to operational risk management (ORM)   **81**
    strategic framework   **55**
CEN insurance *see* confiscation, expropriation, and nationalization insurance
Chambers, Andrew   **33**

chief audit executive (CAE)
    role and responsibilities   **167**
confiscation, expropriation, and nationalization (CEN) insurance   **143**
contingency management *see* disaster planning
continuity management *see* business continuity management (BCM)
corporate culture
    strategy for cultural alignment   **51**
corporate governance
    Sarbanes–Oxley Act 2002 (SOX)   **39**
corporate image *see* image
corporate risk register *see* risk register
counterparty credit risk
    management   **121**
country risk
    countering   **149**
    export markets   **139**
    measurement   **125**
    measuring company exposure   **129**
    political risk insurance (PRI)   **143**
credit crunch
    financial risk case study   **9**
    see also financial crisis
credit derivatives   **111**
credit risk
    counterparty credit risk   **121**
    hedging strategies   **201**
    management   **111, 177**
culture risk
    export markets   **139**
    strategy for cultural alignment   **51**
currency markets *see* foreign exchange markets
currency risk
    exporting   **139**
    hedging strategies   **105, 203**
    management   **209**

D
Damodaran, Aswath   **125, 129**
Davies, Andy   **45**
debt/equity (D/E) ratio   **221**
derivatives
    FAS 133 hedge accounting   **165**
    hedging credit risk   **201**
    hedging currency risk   **105, 203, 209**
    hedging interest rate risk   **205, 209**
    total balance sheet approach to financial risk   **95**
    see also financial instruments
directors' and officers' liability (D&O) insurance   **199**

Index

disaster planning
  business interruption management   175
  preparation for business continuity   85
  risk management   55, 185
diversification
  political risk   149
D&O insurance *see* directors' and officers' liability insurance
Doney, David A.   39
due diligence
  mergers and acquisitions (M&A)   153, 157

E
economic capital
  calculating total economic capital   193
emerging markets
  measuring company exposure to risk   129
  political risk insurance (PRI)   143
  risk measurement   125
employees
  risk management   75
enterprise risk management (ERM)   171
  Best's ratings   71
  internal auditor's role   23
  Solvency II, implications of   45
European Union (EU)
  Solvency II   45
exchange rate risk *see* currency risk
exporting
  risks and relationships evaluation   139
expropriation insurance   143

F
Fabozzi, Frank J.   111
FASB *see* Financial Accounting Standards Board
Federal-Mogul
  M&A case study   153
Financial Accounting Standards Board (FASB) FAS 133 on hedge accounting   165
financial crisis
  enterprise risk management (ERM) on insurance companies   71
financial instruments
  credit derivatives   111
  see also derivatives
financial modeling
  corporate financial risk   99
financial ratios
  debt/equity (D/E)   221
  leverage   221
financial risk
  businesses   9
  insurance against   213
  integrated corporate financial risk policy   19
  liquidity   207, 211
  quantifying corporate risk   99
  total balance sheet approach   95

financial risk (*cont.*)
  see also risk assessment; risk management
financial services regulation
  Solvency II   45
forecasting
  corporate financial risk   99
foreign exchange markets
  hedging risk   105, 203
  risk management   209
  trading strategies   191
  see also currency risk
forensic auditing
  definition   181
Fraser, Ian   23
fraud
  forensic auditing   181
  managing human risk   75

G
gearing
  ratios   221
geopolitical risk *see* country risk; political risk
Groth, John C.   13

H
hedge accounting
  FAS 133   165
Hiles, Andrew   85
Howson, Peter   153
human risk
  management   75

I
IIA *see* Institute of Internal Auditors
image
  reputation risk   65
inflation risk
  management   215
Institute of Internal Auditors (IIA)
  on enterprise risk management (ERM)   23
  standards   27
insurance
  confiscation, expropriation, and nationalization (CEN)   143
  directors' and officers' liability (D&O)   199
  financial loss   213
  political risk insurance (PRI)   143
  stress-testing to evaluate cover   217
insurance companies
  captive   195
  ERM and Solvency II   45
  ERM, Best's ratings, and financial crisis   71
intangible assets
  reputation   65
interest rate risk
  hedging strategies   205
  management   115, 209

Index

interest rate swaps	205, 209	political risk (*cont.*)	
internal audit		exporting	139
enterprise risk management (ERM)	23	*see also* country risk	
international standards	27	political risk insurance (PRI)	
risk-based	27	emerging markets	143
risk management	23	profession	
see also chief audit executive (CAE); internal control		auditing	39
internal control		R	
chief audit executive (CAE)'s role	167	rating agencies	
effective implementation	33	insurance companies	71
Sarbanes–Oxley Act 2002 (SOX)	33, 39	Rayner, Jenny	65
see also internal audit		real options	
investigative auditing	181	definition	61
		reputation risk	65
K		risk assessment	
key risk indicators (KRI)	179	framework for	171
		internal auditing	27
L		risk registers	169, 173
Lai, Gene C.	71	total cost of risk (TCOR)	219
Lall, Vinod	91	*see also* financial risk; risk management	
leverage ratios	221	risk management	
liability		all-hazards approach to operational risk management (ORM)	81
directors' and officers' liability (D&O) insurance	199	Best's ratings and ERM	71
liquidity management		business continuity management (BCM)	175, 185
hedging liquidity risk	207	business risk	9
identifying weak points in liquidity	211	captive insurance companies	195
liquidity risk		catastrophe management	55, 85
hedging	207	common sense rules	13
identifying weak points in liquidity	211	counterparty credit risk	121
		credit risk	111, 177, 201
M		enterprise risk management (ERM)	45, 171
M&A *see* mergers and acquisitions		exporting	139
management audit *see* internal audit		foreign exchange	105, 203, 209
Martin, Duncan	55	hazard-driven vs opportunity-driven	3
McKaig, Thomas	75	human risk	75
mergers and acquisitions (M&A)		insurance against financial loss	213
due diligence	157	integrated corporate financial risk policy	19
strategic risk management	153	interest rates	115, 205, 209
Moeller, Scott	157	internal audit role	23
Morris, Rod	143	key risk indicators (KRI)	179
		liquidity	207, 211
O		mergers and acquisitions (M&A)	153, 157
operational risk exposure		opportunity-driven vs hazard-driven	3
stress-testing	187	political risk	149
operational risk management (ORM)		political risk insurance (PRI)	143
all-hazards approach	81	reputation risk	65
organizational culture *see* corporate culture		risk registers	169, 173
ORM *see* operational risk management		Sarbanes–Oxley Act 2002 (SOX)	39
		stress-testing to evaluate insurance cover	217
P		supply chain	91
pension funds		*see also* financial risk; risk assessment	
risks on the balance sheet	133	risk register	
political risk		creation	169
countering	149	key components	173

Approaches to Enterprise Risk Management

Index

Robinson, Steve	105
rogue employees	
risk management	75

S
Sarbanes–Oxley Act 2002 (SOX)	
implications	39
securitization	
credit risk	111
Sempra Energy	
political risk insurance (PRI) case study	143
Sharon, Bill	3
Shimko, David C.	**19, 61, 99, 121**
Solvency II	
enterprise risk management (ERM), implications for	45
SOX *see* Sarbanes–Oxley Act 2002	
Spinney, Will	115
strategic options *see* real options	
stress-testing	
business continuity management (BCM)	185
evaluating insurance cover by	217
operational risk exposure	187
supply chain	
risk management	91

swaps	
hedging credit risk	201
interest rate	**205, 209**
Swarup, Amarendra	133

T
takeovers *see* mergers and acquisitions (M&A)	
TCOR *see* total cost of risk	
terrorism	
political risk insurance (PRI)	143
Tonko	
risk management case study	23
total cost of risk (TCOR)	
calculating	219
treasury management	
credit risk	111
see also liquidity management	

U
United States	
Sarbanes–Oxley Act 2002 (SOX)	39

V
Vacca, Sheryl	27